A city in the republic

A city in the republic

Antebellum New York and the origins of machine politics

AMY BRIDGES
HARVARD UNIVERSITY

CORNELL UNIVERSITY PRESS

ITHACA AND LONDON

First published, Cornell Paperbacks, 1987, with a new preface, by Cornell University Press.

Library of Congress Cataloging-in-Publication Data

Bridges, Amy.
  A city in the republic.

  (Cornell paperbacks)
  Bibliography: p.
  Includes index.
  1. New York (N.Y.)—Politics and government—To 1898. 2. Elections—New York (N.Y.)—History—19th century. I. Title.
[JS1227.B74   1987]   324.2747'009034   86-47994
ISBN 0-8014-9392-7 (pbk. : alk. paper)

Printed in the United States of America

In memory of my parents
WARREN AND DOROTHY BRIDGES
whose faith empowered me
and for
HERBERT F. MARPLES
who made everything possible

Preface to the paperback edition

THE PUBLICATION of a paperback edition of *A City in the Republic* provides an opportunity for me to clarify my intent and express some afterthoughts.

I began thinking about issues central to this book in the summer of 1974, when I taught a course on immigrant life in New York City at Queens College of the City University of New York. I hoped in that course to compare the political experience of antebellum immigrants, particularly the Irish, with that of the later wave of nineteenth-century immigrants from southern and eastern Europe. Among the many obstacles I encountered was the absence of any satisfactory account of local politics in the antebellum era. I could hardly determine the role of the Irish in urban political life when so little was known about antebellum city politics in general. Later, as I researched New York City's history in the 1830s, 40s, and 50s, it became clear that although machine politics and reform opposition had conventionally been associated with the late nineteenth century, the beginnings of these arrangements were present well before the Civil War. The result of my research, then, is this account of the origins of machine politics.

The argument offered here differs from other explanations of machine politics and previous accounts of antebellum partisanship. The text and footnotes explain why I found other accounts problematic. In retrospect, my criticisms of other authors who had tried to come to terms with antebellum partisanship, and with the popular bases of machine politics, seem to me too harsh. In general, these authors—Sam Bass Warner, Jr., Lee Benson, Daniel P. Moynihan, James Q. Wilson, and Edward Banfield—focused their arguments on ethnicity and ethnic subcultures. They wrote, however, without that now extensive body of social history research that provides the first real evidence about popular political culture. Like the social historians, I have explored the ways in which "class" was meaningful to antebellum citizens and so wrote an account of machine politics that is about class as well as about immigrants and ethnicity.

By contrast with earlier authors who have tried to explain machine politics, I have had the luxury of heavy reliance on the work of social historians. But for that reason, and because I fail to do so in the text, I should here clarify two important differences between social historians' work and my own. First, because I am a political scientist, and because my question was about the creation of political institutions, party politics is at the center of this story. Social historians have for the most part avoided studying party politics, a neglect that from my disciplinary perspective is wholly regrettable. The Whigs and Democrats, after all, brought unprecedented (and for decades unequaled) popular participation in politics. I try to show how the major parties both echoed and reorganized popular sentiment. I am persuaded that these questions need continued attention, for New York City and other places, for the antebellum and other eras. Second, this work differs from most social histories of the antebellum years in that it ends with 1860 rather than 1850. Here too the difference is both disciplinary and substantive. Political scientists think about American history in periods that coincide with the existence of party systems. From this perspective, the antebellum era is not over until a new party system makes its appearance. The substantive issues are not trivial: studies ending in 1850 tend to emphasize the "collapse" of working-class politics and the disorganization of popular political efforts. From a political scientist's perspective, it seems altogether natural that the relationship between popular groups and politics is tenuous, and citizen views uncertain, at a time when one party system is in disarray and its successor not yet in place. For us to understand what became of the Jacksonian labor movement, the relationship between antebellum unions and parties, the role of popular and ethnic organizations in politics, and the fate of the nativists, we must follow their stories through to the reestablishment of political order.

The central puzzle of this book is that machine politics came to be the common form of urban governance in the United States even though it was not what anyone wanted. I hope the way I solve that puzzle not only provides an alternative to other accounts of the origins of machine politics but also influences how political scientists think about the relationship between citizens and politics more generally. I emphasize how political institutions—parties, electoral arrangements, and the like—influence popular sentiment, encourage or discourage alliances, and make some strategies sensible and others utopian. Machine politics and other political arrangements are not the institutionalization of some political subculture but the result of groups' trying to get what they want by playing according to a given set of rules (although citizens also argue about the rules). This approach should be intuitively appealing to students of social choice, because their premise is that how preferences are aggregated determines political outcomes. Similarly, the argument offered here may be understood as an elaboration of the ways republicanism falls short of democracy.

Preface to the paperback edition

In the acknowledgments to the first edition of this book I committed a sin of omission. Let it stand corrected by my insistence here that I take full responsibility for errors of interpretation, inadequacies of grammar, style, and tact, and any other flaws that may be discovered in this book.

Sincere thanks to Peter Agree for his appreciation of my work and for bringing about the paperback edition from Cornell University Press.

Rick Kronick and I have welcomed two daughters since I thanked him in the acknowledgments three years ago. How little we knew then of campaigning for love and work! The campaign continues, and I thank him again.

Amy Bridges

Cambridge, Massachusetts

Contents

Contents

Figures and tables

Acknowledgments

I HAVE LEARNED a great deal from friends, colleagues, and teachers who read this essay or talked with me about related issues. I hope the text reveals to them how seriously I took advice and criticism that were not, alas, always graciously received. My sincere thanks to Joshua Brown, Walter Dean Burnham, Maarten de Kadt, Jorge Dominguez, Andrew Dunham, Stanley Engerman, Richard E. Foglesong, Sherry Gorelick, John Kurt Jacobsen, Ira Katznelson, Joel Krieger, Bruce Laurie, James Morone, Benjamin I. Page, Paul E. Peterson, H. Douglas Price, Harvey Rishikof, Lloyd I. Rudolph, Martin Shefter, Susan Shirk, Stephan Thernstrom, Sidney Verba, James Q. Wilson, and Aristide Zolberg.

The American Association of University Women awarded me a dissertation grant that offered generous financial assistance. Philip Hart provided the art work. Kevin Gleason and Kenneth Finegold served as able research assistants. Kathy Anderson and Maureen Nute typed the manuscript in its various incarnations.

Susan Allen-Mills at Cambridge University Press was helpful and supportive.

I have also been the beneficiary of the exceptional friendships of Gordon M. Adams, Bernard and Cornelia Baker, Beverly Elkan, Miriam Elson, Carol Foglesong, the Katznelson family, Robert and Joyce Melville, Mary Page, Doris and Richard Taub, and the women of MF1.

Richard Kronick helped me make sense of nineteenth-century censuses and voting returns and provided the data analysis for the text. Well before that, he sustained me through great personal losses and won my heart by tirelessly campaigning that I might have both love and work.

Amy Bridges

West Ossipee
New Hampshire

xiv

I   A city in the republic

A CITY IN THE REPUBLIC provides an account of politics in New York City between the election of Andrew Jackson and the outbreak of the Civil War. Parts of this story are familiar: the Workingmen's Parties and the "Jacksonian revolution," the "ferment of reform" of the 1840s, mass immigration and the Know-Nothing movement, the collapse of the second American party system and the birth of the Republican Party. As in cities and states across the union, local politics in New York bore the imprint of national events. At the same time, New York and other antebellum cities witnessed a distinctively urban political reordering that involved changes in party, government, and ideology.

It was in the antebellum years that city politics came to have an independent existence, turning on its own issues rather than on national events. During the 1830s city politics was merely a reflection of national debates between Whigs and Democrats; by the end of the period reformers battled "rings" and "machines." The local counterpart of the Jacksonian revolution was, on the one hand, the retirement of wealthy men from officeholding and, on the other, the emergence of the career politician in the person of the boss. This change in dramatis personae was associated with changes in the relationship between politics and social life. Political leadership, once based on a more general social deference, came to be based on party organization and mass partisan loyalty.

The functions of city government changed as well. In 1828, fire fighting, policing, charity, and education were civic obligations; these tasks were performed on a volunteer basis or by private or semipublic groups. By the outbreak of the Civil War, these had become the tasks of a professionalized municipal work force. In the same period, city government pulled back from certain functions. City government gave up the eighteenth-century task of economic regulation, because New York's increasing integration into the world economic system made that task impossible. There was also an effort to curtail government's provision of relief, because relief was inconsistent with emerging laissez-faire doctrine.

The change in dramatis personae and government functions marked a

I

redrawing of the line between public and private. In 1828, New York's citizens believed in the interdependence of economic pursuits, that there was a concrete and identifiable common good, and that government's proper concerns included facilitating prosperity by assisting economic development. By the election of Lincoln, few in the city dared claim that the interests of capital and labor were the same, and few citizens believed that *any* set of government policies could ensure prosperity and comfort. All these changes involved controversy. Argument about government's relation to society was joined with argument about a broad range of issues: ethnicity and religion, temperance and government reform, the virtues and evils of party. Whereas the thinking of Jacksonian New Yorkers relied heavily on eighteenth-century republicanism, by the Civil War argument about class, status, and party had produced a more modern and familiar public discourse. Antebellum New Yorkers had begun to forge a set of American values about government in an industrial, ethnically heterogeneous society.

In so doing, New York's citizens were trying to come to terms with the enormous social changes they experienced. The growth of the city alone – from 203,000 in 1830 to 813,700 in 1860 – imposed immense difficulties of communication, sanitation, housing, and transportation. Industrialization recast the social structure and reorganized the social relationships of producing, getting, and spending. Immigration and the creation of an ethnically stratified population provided a setting in which the new and old working classes became, at least sporadically, divided from one another.

In the face of this immense social change, it is not surprising that New York's political reordering was a complex, even chaotic, process. Belying the orderly facade of the second American party system, in the 1830s and 1840s there was a profusion of factions and parties: old, new, and American Republicans; Whigs; and the Temperance Party. In the 1850s, when the second American party system gave way, Hunkers, Barnburners, Soft Shells, and Hard Shells appeared among the Democrats; Silver Grey and Wooly Headed factions divided the Whigs; Know-Nothings, Tammany Hall, Mozart Hall, and City Reform fought for control of the city.

Some order may be imposed on the complex and chaotic process of political reordering by saying that in the antebellum period New York was transformed from an eighteenth-century city into a nineteenth-century city. The same was true of Boston, Newark, Philadelphia, Baltimore, and Pittsburgh. At the election of Jackson, urban life bore strong resemblances to life in the city two or even three generations earlier. By the election of Lincoln, society and politics had taken on the nineteenth-century characteristics that lasted well into the New Deal era.

At the election of Jackson, urban society and politics looked, in significant ways, much as they had in the eighteenth century. The great immigrations still lay ahead. The city's characteristic citizens were the merchant and the artisan. Local political life was dominated by wealthy merchants, and the lines dividing their social, economic, and political leadership were only lightly sketched. Although the idea of party was more widespread and more acceptable than earlier, party organization was practically nonexistent. Fire fighting, policing, charity, and education were tasks performed by private groups, volunteer organizations, or as civic obligations, much as they had been at the time of the War for Independence.

In the antebellum period, cities lost these last resemblances to colonial times. The social order was transformed by industrialization and immigration. The artisan and merchant gave way to the worker, industrialist, and financier. The immigrant displaced the Liberty Boy. Small, paternalist, elite-dominated city government was replaced by career politicians and mass political parties. Fire fighting, policing, charity, and education became paid municipal employments. More profoundly, the consensus and community of the eighteenth-century city were shattered and in their place was a diverse and rather contentious aggregation of interests whose main common concern was the election of city government. To say this is to concretize a commonplace in the study of political development: As authors as different as Antonio Gramsci and Samuel Huntington have argued, in a complex society community does not come naturally, but is a product of politics.[1]

By 1860, that political product exhibited central elements of machine politics. City politics had a life of its own, relatively sheltered from national events and quite distinctively urban. Party competition was a fairly lopsided affair, with one party claiming the loyalty of a clear majority of the electorate. In Pittsburgh, Baltimore, New York, Boston, Providence, and Newark the competition of the second American party system gave way to this lopsided urban competition in the 1850s. The dramatis personae of American city politics had appeared as well. "Bosses" appeared in Boston, Pittsburgh, Baltimore, Philadelphia, and New York. Municipal reformers campaigned in Milwaukee, Springfield, Baltimore, Philadelphia, New York, and Boston.

This too is a commonplace: The cities of the republic created machine politics and municipal reformers. Machine politics was not wholly institutionalized anywhere in 1860. In New York, discipline had yet to be imposed on Democratic bosses. They were, as Martin Shefter put it, entering an era of "rapacious individualism," and it remained for Tweed to begin to tame them. Nor had the respectable element and the bosses learned to live with one another; that awaited Tweed's fall. Nevertheless, in New York and elsewhere the clubs, the patronage, the overwhelming majority, the boss and his reform antagonist were all there. An account of the antebellum city, then, is also a study of the origins of machine politics.

This book is concerned with the reordering of the antebellum city, the relationship between the city's social and political transformations, and the creation of machine politics as the American way of city government. How were the institutional arrangements of machine politics created? How did the urban party system that pitted boss against reformer come into being? How did it happen that the machine served to constitute "community" out of a complex urban society? Asking those questions raises another one: Why was the machine the characteristic form of city government in the nineteenth-century United States? What is it, in other words, about American political development that meant that the form of city politics was machine government and reform opposition?

Machine politics was the characteristic form of city government in the nineteenth-century United States, and so students of American city politics have sought the origins of the machine in the outstanding peculiarities of American culture and politics. In particular, massive immigration and the close association of the machine and ethnic politics suggested that the machine was created by immigrants, a product of immigrant culture and ethnic conflict. The best known of these arguments appears in *City Politics*. There, Edward Banfield and James Q. Wilson, following Hofstadter, argued that nineteenth-century city politics was grounded in an immigrant political ethos at variance with middle-class white Anglo-Saxon Protestant values. The private-regarding values of immigrant voters led them to accept patronage, corruption, and "friendship" rather than insisting on honesty and attention to the public weal.[2] Similarly, Daniel Patrick Moynihan argued that social norms of deference and personal dependence were Irish peasant values of lasting vigor that were essential to machine building and facilitated Irish political success.[3] More recently, Sam Bass Warner, Jr., argued in *The Private City* that the antebellum era saw a shift from class to ethnic politics. This ethnic politics was based in homogeneous communities and their neighborhood associations and paved the way to boss rule.[4]

Two general historical objections may be raised to these accounts. First, in the antebellum city ethnicity was not the whole story, or even the dominant theme, of political life. The Workingmen's Party claimed to oppose "all means of oppressing the producing classes" and defended mechanics as "respectable as any other class."[5] Whigs defended the "commercial class," claiming that America owed its prosperity to the economic leadership of the "mercantile classes."[6] Even in 1844, when nativism was at its height, New York's Tammany Hall opposed nativists by claiming to be the "true home of the working classes." The largest demonstrations in the 1850s in Philadelphia, New York, Newark, Baltimore, and Boston were by working men and women demanding "work or bread" from municipal administrations. In New York, rare indeed was the Tammany politician who did not insist that he was "emphatically the friend of the working man."[7] To these as-

4

sertions of class and its importance were added arguments about national political economy, the virtues and vices of parties, and a long list of other concerns. Although ethnic and cultural affinities played a role in the creation of partisan coalitions, they are far short of the story of antebellum city politics, and they do not account for the emergence of the boss or the institutional arrangements associated with machine politics.

Second, the hallmarks of machine politics and the character of the boss long predate a strong immigrant presence. The partisan abuse of public employment was not new to the Tweed era. The worst partisan abuses of employment controlled by city government were probably committed by Federalists in the 1790s (see Chapter 7). Similarly, personal loyalty and personal deference were the hallmarks of patrician leadership, hardly inventions of the boss. To understand the institutional arrangements we associate with machine politics, we must look further back in American urban history than the arrival of the immigrants or the ascent of the Irish to political power (see Chapter 4).

To these criticisms may be added a third. Machine politics cannot be understood as the institutionalization of a particular set of values. The simple reason for this is that the machine was not what anyone – with the possible exception of the bosses – wanted. Rather, like most other political and governmental arrangements, machine politics was the result of inheritance and transformation, compromise, inadvertence, and conflict. How machine politics constituted community in New York City (and elsewhere) can be understood by looking at the contending social forces there and the political arrangements through which they created a new political order.

The origins of machine politics are found in the antebellum years, when the cities of the United States lost their last resemblance to the eighteenth-century municipality of merchant and artisan and acquired the central elements of the nineteenth-century political order. Despite the fact that machine politics was widespread – indeed, was the characteristic form of city government in the United States – machine politics cannot be explained as the institutionalization of a particular set of values, for machine politics was not what anyone wanted. Nevertheless, the institutional arrangements of that politics created community in the nineteenth-century city, linking social force and dominant group, political faction and government. Because machine politics became the American way of city government, satisfying explanations for the appearance of the machine are bound to be connected to the larger patterns of American political development.

One way to connect the political reordering of the antebellum city to these larger patterns is to recognize it as the local counterpart of transformations in American politics and government that were taking place in the same period nationally, in the state capitals, and in the courts. In those years, two momentous developments changed the shape of American life. First, producing, getting, and spending were reorganized by the beginnings of industrialization. The first generation of a modern working class was created; entrepreneur and financier took their places beside the merchant. In addition, the economy became more integrated across regions and more intricately bound to the world economy. Second, the last property restrictions on white manhood suffrage were abolished, expanding the scope of the political universe.[8] These changes raised important challenges. Economic development provoked controversy about the role of government and the nature of an equitable law.[9] The expansion of the political universe posed the challenge of organizing the many. It was in this setting that politics created community, organized "new linkages between the particular interests of individuals and groups," and "gave new meaning to the common purpose."[10]

The political economy of state government, for example, changed substantially in the antebellum years.[11] Like local government, state government at the beginning of the antebellum period retained eighteenth-century practices and precepts. Economic regulation to promote trade and prosperity was high on the agenda of government obligations, for government was intended to pursue – and to encourage diverse interests to pursue – a common good. In the antebellum period, the "pervasive acceptance" of governmental activism eroded. For artisans, laborers, and farmers, government activism seemed to grant special privileges, "a violation of the first principles of their democratic faith."[12] For their social betters, governmental activism seemed a risky business when their hold on political life was becoming less exclusive. By 1860, a long list of state activities – regulation and franchise, licensing and road building, mixed enterprises – had disappeared, changed function, or changed in meaning. A more powerful market system made government activity appear as "unnecessary, useless, and embarrassing restrictions" of economic laws whose operations were "inherently beneficent."[13] If in 1820 government was the only force that might ensure the common good, by 1860 mismanagement was "necessarily incident" to government intervention. In the new political economy, as Hartz summarized it, "businessmen were heroes and politicians were villains."[14]

The same conflicts of principle and arguments about political economy informed the operation – and the transformation – of local government. The effects of industrialization (and immigration) on social structure and social relations were most radical in cities. The organizational challenges of an expanding suffrage were inevitably posed in every locality. In the cities, the transformations of the antebellum years involved popular policy issues as well as issues of principle parallel to controversies in state government and in the courts. The political reordering of local government involved controversies about religion, temperance, education, class relations, and charity. In local politics, popular access to government and popular assessment of government direction and policy were greater than in the statehouse or in the courts. For those reasons, the reordering of local government was more chaotic, more complex, and more conflictual – the "street-fighting pluralism" of city politics.[15] The resolution of these conflicts produced a distinctly urban political economy. The reordering of urban government produced results that were considerably more ambiguous than the transformations of state government or law. The boss was both rapacious individualist and a paternalist of the most old-fashioned sort, both villain and hero of local political life.

A complementary argument suggests why machine politics became the characteristic form of city government in the nineteenth-century United States. Any explanation of machine politics should connect its appearance to the special characteristics of American political development (and so will be, at least implicitly, comparative). I have already argued that explanations relating machine politics to immigration are not persuasive. Here it may be added that the themes of political life in the antebellum years – charity and intervention, contract, corporation, and character – were not themselves peculiarly American (this point is elaborated below). For example, in England as in the United States there were those who championed the market against activist government, those who strove to educate the working classes to frugal and temperate ways, and those who abandoned the obligations of rich to poor. French and English working classes, like the American, denounced the "industrial system" as immoral and learned political economy from Tom Paine. The themes of political life in the antebellum city were the themes of social and political conflict in other industrializing communities in the late eighteenth and early nineteenth centuries.

By contrast, the political ground on which these conflicts were fought and resolved in the United States was special. American development was distinguished by the fact that industrialization and the abolition of property barriers to suffrage happened simultaneously. The importance of this timing has been argued from a variety of perspectives.[16] For my purposes it is the structural difference this timing made that bears emphasis. Borrowing from theoretical frameworks offered by Louis Althusser and Nicos Poulantzas,[17] it can be said that economic and political arrangements or "structures" coexist as differently organized arenas within which individuals and social forces (interest groups, trade unions, and so on) act. Briefly, economic structures describe the organization of getting, spending, producing, and growth. The process of growth creates social places that might be designated "worker" or "capitalist," "artisan" or "merchant," and also shapes the relationships among these social places. By contrast, the political structure of liberal democracy creates places labeled "voters." If in the economic sphere resources are skill, capital, or the strike, and these resources greatly differentiate some actors from others, in the political arena all voters are equal (although of course there are other political resources, like money and organization).

Among other things, this set of propositions might be understood as a re-posing of familiar questions about how it is that capitalism and democracy live with one another. Here, however, the relevant suggestion is Poulantzas's proposition[18] that patterns of social development may be understood by the differential timing of the appearance of political, economic, and ideological structures in different places. Schematically, the appearance of machine politics in the cities of the United States may be understood as the consequence of placing social conflicts attendant on industrialization in the context of widespread suffrage. That context changed the ways in which social differences were resolved and, as a result, changed the resolution. The very first generation of the industrial working class had the vote in the United States; this meant that conflicts that elsewhere were social were here political. To the strike was added the ballot; to the riot, the nominating convention; to protest, partisan insurgency; to class, party. The social transformations characteristic of early industrialization found expression not only in the factory and the neighborhood but also in electoral politics.

The political reordering of antebellum cities and the appearance of machine politics are best understood as a product of social conflicts that were not particularly special to the United States in a political setting that *was* distinctively American. The machine became the characteristic form of nineteenth-century city government in the United States because here the first generation of industrial workers, and their artisan forebears before them, had the vote. The comparatively broad suffrage of the eighteenth century allowed the popular values of preindustrial society to shape the institutions of city politics inherited by Jacksonian New Yorkers. The even broader suffrage of the nineteenth century meant that the social transformations characteristic of early industrialization were expressed, constrained, disciplined, and empowered by the dynamics of electoral politics. In America's cities, the logical as well as the historical product of this situation was machine politics.

Whether the political reordering of antebellum cities is understood as the local counterpart of a set of national adjustments or as a part of the American resolution of common developmental crises, the same elements of the story require special attention. The first element is the social transformation attendant on industrialization, which provided themes of conflict and undermined the old order. The second element is the shape of the newly created political arena within which social conflicts were resolved. The rules of political life lent their own dynamics to social dissensus. The third element is the special nature of the urban polity, for this influenced the resources and strategies of competing social forces.

8

THE SOCIAL REVOLUTION

Although the United States as a whole did not industrialize until after the Civil War, in the antebellum years the artisan lost ground to the modern wage worker and in some sectors the crafts organization of work gave way to the factory. The early stages of industrialization have been associated with a broad range of social events: the proletarianization of the work force; the degradation of skill and a sharper separation of leisure and work; a changing role for merchants; and a new character for employers. Among the variety of politically active groups in New York, each of these elements was recognized, along with the broad dynamic of the process as a whole. Those recognitions and the political tactics and strategies associated with them formed a good part of the stuff of politics in the antebellum era.

More comprehensively, industrialization is associated with the creation of a different kind of society. As Eric Hobsbawm has written, if the industrial revolution was not a social revolution then the word has no commonsense meaning.[19] Long-standing habits were forsaken and new social relations took their place; old ties were broken and new solidarities forged. These long-standing habits and old ties had been institutionalized in the political life of the colonial city of merchants and artisans. As I discuss more fully in Chapter 4, the colonial city may be described (particularly in contrast to what came later) as a society of mutually dependent interests, regulated by government and led by merchants whose public and private obligations were not much differentiated. The duties and obligations of those in different classes to one another formed the normative basis of social life; the necessity of government oversight of getting and spending was taken for granted. As late as the 1840s, Whig politicians could be found discoursing on "what the rich owe the poor."[20]

After 1800, however, these notions came under increasing attack. Elites more and more rejected the idea that they had obligations to the poor. Charity was a Christian duty, but individual conscience needed to ponder whether it was not the case that "poverty and wretchedness have increased in exact proportion to the efforts . . . made for the subsistence of the poor."[21] In place of the leaders of a "well-regulated society" were advocates of a society of individuals, protected by government, whose relations were regulated by the market. The *Journal of Commerce* described what was wanted: "Let us have fewer laws, and we shall have less trouble. The Creator, when he made the system, gave it laws, the tendency of which is always good."[22]

Advocates of this smaller role for government and of individualism rather than social familism were aggressive in teaching the justice of the contract and promoting a long list of virtues – industriousness, frugality, sobriety, cleanliness, Protestantism, timeliness, manners, obedience, and above all "self-dependence" to create good workers and good citizens. In England and the United States alike the temperance and Sunday School movements, the tract societies and societies for improving the condition of the poor were linked to one another and to a struggle against intractable employees, unions, and workers' political assertiveness. No phrase appears more often in the records of these organizations than "an economical form of police."

The change in social relations, the shift in dominant ideology, and the efforts at persuasion were all challenged. The working classes insisted that the industrial system and the values promoted by its creators were immoral. The industrial system, they argued, renounced the idea of mutual dependence, was un-Christian, fostered selfishness, a lust for quick riches, individualism, gambling, and usury. It was not simply exploitative, but *wrong* that labor, which produced all wealth, was deprived of its profits. It was worse that government promoted these evils. Alongside these protests was an insistence that men "regain their social sympathies once again," respect society as a commonwealth, and return to the justice and reciprocity of a more familistic community.

Whereas individualist and laissez-faire views won converts among their social betters, values of long standing persisted among the working classes. E. P. Thompson summarized those values by characterizing them as the "moral economy" of the poor. Popular grievances, Thompson explained,

> operated within a popular consensus as to what were legitimate and what were illegitimate practices in marketing, milling, baking, etc. This in its turn was grounded upon a consistent traditional view of social norms and obligations, of the proper economic functions of several parties within the community which, taken together, can be said to constitute the moral economy of the poor.

The food riot is the classic expression of moral-economic values because it expresses outrage at the hoarding of food and because it punishes those who fail to perform the social obligations of haves to have-nots. Government was expected to enforce these obligations, an expectation Thompson refers to as "the paternalist tradition of the authorities."[23] That similar values were popular here is suggested by responses to the depression of 1837: There was not only a food riot, but also a demand that government restore the assize on bread in New York.

In the context of changing values among socially dominant groups and the middle classes, such collective actions were, as the Tillys termed them, "reactive." Like machine smashing, they were efforts to maintain a social order that was rapidly falling apart. As the "industrial system" became more formidable – as it became clear that it would not fade away – new forms of association and collective action appeared. Termed by the Tillys "pro-active,"[24] these were efforts to secure a better existence within the system – the union, the strike, and the political campaign.

These new forms were symptomatic not only of an acceptance of certain defeats, but also of a mutual recognition embodied in the consciousness of class. In nineteenth-century Europe, "the 'poor' no longer faced the 'rich.' A specific *class*, the labouring class, ... faced another, the employer or capitalists."[25] "In the United States," argued Democratic politician Michael Walsh, "the affection of the capitalists for labor is no less [hypocritical] than it is in Britain ... we thrive by your neglect."[26] As moral-economic views persisted past the eighteenth century, so too the consciousness of class was informed by eighteenth-century political thought. Republican ideology, the insistence on political equality and "rights," objection to "privilege" and rejection of deference were the political standards of the labor movement.[27] If their social betters read Malthus and Adam Smith, the working classes in England, the United States, and France read Tom Paine. In conjunction with the view that it was government that supported the industrial system, it was a reading that made the labor movement everywhere political. As the working classes recognized that they "thrived by neglect," claims on their social betters were given up (and Paine's political economy along with them) but not their claims on government. Thus, in the depression of 1857, New York's unemployed demanded not the charity of the wealthy, but "work or bread" from City Hall.

A change in relations between classes, the forsaking of old ties, the emergence of new solidarities, and increased ideological diversity all mark New York's social life in the antebellum years. Because so many had access to the political arena, they marked its political life as well. Conflict about economic development, conflict between moral-economic values and laissez-faire precepts, and a change from the "industrious mechanic" to the "working classes" provide the themes of New York's political reordering. These conflicts did not determine the shape of the new political order, but they did effectively undermine the old one. New York's political reordering was a product not only of these and other differences but also of the shape of its political arrangements.

THE POLITICAL RESOLUTION OF SOCIAL CONFLICT

If capitalism was rapidly aggrandizing the few in the first half of the nineteenth century, an expanding franchise was increasing the social power of the many. Political conflict changed the dynamics of social disagreements by subjecting them to the logic and discipline of electoral politics. Politicizing conflict affected the shape of dissensus by reorganizing social forces in contention, creating new solidarities. Political conflict raised the stakes of social disagreement by awarding to those who created majorities the power and authority of government. Social disagreements were resolved and community forged by the complex rules of the political order.

The simplest of these rules is that winning elections requires (in a two-party contest) one-half plus one of the votes cast. Individuals and groups seeking political power need to form alliances; candidates need to organize coalitions. The lines along which these alliances will be formed and coalitions organized are not obvious. It is tempting to think that these coalitions are formed "naturally," along the lines of deepest cleavage within the electorate. Yet social structure does not always have a clear and direct relation to electoral combat. The lack of an obvious relationship between immigration and nativism provides a good example of this. If political nativism were simply the expression of a social response to immigration (if ethnic antagonism were "natural"), then the nativist parties should rise and fall with waves of immigration. Yet in the antebellum period political nativism appeared before the great emigration induced by the famine in Ireland, lost ground just as the effects of the famine immigration were being felt, and disappeared after 1857. In fact, between 1840 and 1930 political nativism appears not in response to waves of immigration, but when the national party system is in crisis: in the 1840s and 1850s, in the 1880s and 1890s, and in the period surrounding and following the First World War.

Social antagonisms are sometimes organized into politics and sometimes fought in the street; social differences are sometimes the source of antagonism and sometimes accommodated easily enough. This means that

> social cleavages are not a datum. Social distinctions become lived as cleavages because they become organized as such. Collective political behavior is not a summation of independent decisions made by autonomous individuals each spontaneously expressing his or her rationality. It is an effect ... of long years of struggle, of organization, disorganization, and reorganization, of successes and failures, of advances and retreats. The political behavior of individuals reflects the long history of struggles among organized groups of men and women to impose a course upon the development of society.[28]

Although the political scientist may want to understand politics as related to "deeply rooted values deriving from the total range of [voters'] ... experiences,"[29] politics may or may not be organized in a way that resonates with those experiences. Social characteristics "have political salience ... only in the context of specific political alternatives,"[30] and it is political parties that provide the alternatives.

Political parties, like unions, organized ethnic groups, or chambers of commerce, argue to "increase or decrease the salience of particular visions of society," and in the process they organize, disorganize, and reorganize social forces. In other words, parties work to promote some solidarities and undermine others.[31] If, on the one hand, politicians are attentive to the frame of mind of their constituents, on the other hand partisanship is also "an effect of the behavior of political parties and of the consequences of this behavior for the visions of society with which men and women go about living their daily lives."[32] This is not to say, with Key, that "the voice of the people is but an echo."[33] Party leaders may shout anything they like at potential constituents, but voters will only sometimes respond (in the antebellum period there were always nativists about, but sometimes they had followings and sometimes they were ignored). It is to insist, rather, that partisan divisions are not simply the epiphenomena of "natural" divisions, and to point out that in ideological combat parties speak with especially loud voices. Like other political institutions, moreover, parties have an existence that is relatively autonomous from the social forces they organize. Thus parties and the visions they promote represent something different from either a simple summing of "deeply rooted values" or the world view of a dominant social force. For all these reasons, in the long run politics produces its own, *partisan* identities and solidarities.

Among other things, this suggests that it is a complex matter to attribute a social meaning to an individual's vote. If votes are not simple "echoes" and parties not straightforward epiphenomena of social cleavages, then the relationship between partisanship and popular culture is a highly contingent one. The political scientist who wishes to understand the relation of politics to "deeply rooted values" among popular groups needs to gauge the relationships between the appeals of politicians and *independent* evidence of popular political culture. Like politicians, social scientists should be attentive to popular hopes, visions, and values, while recognizing that partisanship is also "an effect of the behavior of political parties ..." The "same social characteristic can produce different partisan affiliations,"[34] depending upon the choices offered to the voter. It may be that a voter need not choose between (say) ethnic, occupational, religious, and gender solidarities – a voter might vote Republican because he is white, a professional, Protestant, and a man, and Republicans may try to get his vote on all those counts. It may be that the choices offered force voters to choose among their different identities – as in the case where there is a "religious" party and a "class" party. What is inevitable is only that the voter must choose a party. Since parties try to organize coalitions along multiple lines, since politicians are attentive to popular hopes, visions, and values, and since parties are relatively autonomous of the social forces they organize, partisanship itself provides some identity and solidarities – as when one says "he is a lunchpail Democrat," "she is an old-line Republican," "she is a party regular," or, even, "he is in the party."

Weber wrote that classes live in the economic order, status groups live in the social order, but parties live in a house of power.[35] In addition to organizing coalitions and shaping partisan solidarities, parties link political faction and social forces, participation and government.[36] Like democratic institutions generally, they "render the dominance of one social force compatible with the community of many."[37] Politicizing a conflict changes its dynamics because the activities of parties and governments mean a "socie-talization" of the goals of the social forces they organize. Political conflict raises the stakes of social dissension by putting to the service of the victor the power and authority of government.[38] So to the stakes of ideology, economic development, charity, temperance, and schooling were added the stakes of patronage, party leadership, public office, power, and authority; to the contest for honor and resources was added a contest for control of government. Parties are at the center of this story not only because of their general political roles, but also because in the lopsided urban political systems created in the nineteenth-century United States, machine politics was very nearly one-party politics, and partisan solidarity was the heart and soul of the machine.

THE URBAN POLITY

New York's political transformations, and the emergence of the boss and the reformer more generally, were marked in four major ways by the special characteristics of city politics. First, city politics was distinguished by the simple fact that the characteristic citizens of the city were different than those of the state or the countryside. This difference was especially marked in the antebellum years, when the impacts of immigration and industrialization were felt most radically in the city. It is not surprising that the initial political accommodation of industrialization and immigration was a largely urban process.

Second, city government is more accessible than other levels of government. Because poor people in particular are confined in the scope of their political activities – they demonstrate, riot, strike, and mount party insurgencies rather than disinvest, lobby, and launch presidential campaigns – it is in the city that their impact on political life is greatest. This reinforces the demographics of urban politics: In the rapidly expanding and largely agricultural United States, then, workers and immigrants exercised their greatest political power in cities.

Third, city government is charged with housekeeping functions that determine everything from the value of real estate to the use of police as strikebreakers to the availability of charity or the likelihood of arrest. This means that city politics involves immediate and large stakes for a broad range of people. It is for that reason that Douglas Yates characterized city politics as "street-fighting pluralism."

Fourth, politics in cities is special because cities are not self-contained arenas of political activity. City governments are dependent on the state governments of which they are the creatures, and the boundaries of the urban polity are highly permeable. The dependence and permeability of the urban polity mean that things happen not only *in* cities, but also *to* cities.

The limited capacity of city government and the potential interventions of state (and national) government force political actors in the city to go outside the city itself to achieve their goals, and this changes the configuration of political forces in the city. Working for local goals at the state or national level requires urban political actors to seek allies from outside the city. That requirement enhances the political capacity of some groups and constrains the capacity of others. For example, although the Workingmen's Party in New York State forged an urban–rural alliance opposed to imprisonment for debt, wage laborers found few allies to support ten-hours legislation. If labor was weaker for its inability to recruit rural allies, others were stronger. Temperance advocates, not popular in New York City at all – no one would accept the Temperance nomination for mayor in 1852 – imposed their will on the city by having a temperance law passed by the state legislature. Control of city government, then, may not be an accurate index of the ability of a group or party to achieve its political aims; the analysis of politics requires "following" groups out of the city to understand what happens back home.

The other side of this coin is that city politics is not always the expression of impulses originating locally. The city's school system and its police force were creations of the state legislature, and the pace of legislative interference in city politics quickened as the antebellum period drew to a close. By 1857, many in the city would have agreed with George Templeton Strong when he recorded in his diary, "Heaven be praised for all its mercies. The legislature of the state of New York has adjourned."[39]

In our own time, we are aware of the impact on city politics of impulses originating elsewhere as cities suffer the vagaries of federal programs or the cycles of federal activism and quiescence. In the antebellum city, the central vehicle of urban dependence and permeability was the political party. It was through parties that urban groups formed alliances with groups elsewhere. It was also largely through parties that the republic had an impact on city politics. The urban party system maintained its stability only as long as the second American party system functioned and collapsed with its collapse. Lacking either the promise of state or national representation, or the resources for the maintenance of party organization that the national parties offered, none of the locally based parties that appeared between 1828 and 1863 lasted even five years. While over the antebellum period city politics became more independent of the national party system, even the conflict of the boss and the reformer in succeeding decades was shaped by national partisan conflict. The study of politics in antebellum New York, then, is filled with reminders that there were outside the city a hinterland and higher governments and that these affected the course of local political life.

The institutions of the eighteenth-century city were the inheritance of antebellum New Yorkers. Machine politics and municipal reform were their legacy. The appearance of boss, reformer, club, and a reliable majority were not peculiar to New York City; machine politics was the characteristic form of city government in the nineteenth-century United States. How machine politics came to constitute "community" of nineteenth-century urban society is a complex story. I have argued here that it may be unraveled by being attentive, on the one hand, to what was at stake at the historical moment these institutions were created and, on the other, to the setting in which social forces resolved their differences. By being attentive in particular to the dynamics unleashed by the broad embrace of the franchise, the appearance of machine politics may be linked to the distinguishing characteristics of American political development.

Antebellum New Yorkers themselves recognized the distinctiveness of the United States less in its ideological universe or the immigrant presence than in its republican constitution. Advocates of mass education advised citizens that "popular intelligence and popular virtue are indispensable to the existence and continuance of such a government as ours ..."[40] Nativists worried lest those raised in undemocratic environments would be unable to bear the responsibilities of liberty.[41] Democrats reminded voters that in America democratic principle guarded "the civil and religious rights of the poor man, ... as well as the rich."[42] Labor leaders argued that workingmen had "one weapon ... more powerful than the gun or the chain behind the barricades of Paris. It was the ballot."[43] The organizer of the City Reform Party argued that the political health of the city was an index to the political health of the nation and urged citizens "to remember the WORLD-WIDE importance of the novel experiment of our Federal Government, on which we believe our own and the happiness of the world to be much dependent."[44]

A City in the Republic provides an account of the political reordering of New York, of the reconstitution of community among political faction, social force, dominant group, and government. By the time Abraham Lincoln was elected, the central elements of machine politics were in place and the municipal-reform movement had appeared. Some parts of this account simply retell the story told by others; other parts offer reinterpretations of familiar stories; still others present new data and information to reconstruct the story of the antebellum years. Each chapter shows how one element of the new political order came into being.

Chapter 2 traces the city's party systems over the antebellum decades, beginning with the Workingmen's Parties and the debate between Whigs and Democrats and concluding with the city's characteristic antagonists, the boss and the reformer. Partisan debate reveals the ideological transformation produced by argument about class, status, and party. That change and the appearance of the boss and the reformer define the political reordering that New York shared with other antebellum cities.

Chapter 3 offers a description of New York as an economic community, documenting the transformation in social structure brought about by industrialization and immigration. Like New York's political reordering, the city's social transformation was shared by other cities in the antebellum United States.

The central chapters (4, 5, and 6) are concerned with the relationships between political leaders and their constituents. Chapter 4 looks at the second American party system. It was the leaders of the Whig and Democratic parties who were most directly challenged by the changing social order and the expansion of the franchise. Adapting long-standing habits to new social and political circumstances, they organized party coalitions and placed career politicians at the center of local politics.

Chapter 5 offers an analysis of political nativism and of the relationships among ethnocultural affinities, class loyalties, and partisanship. Whereas in other cities majorities of the native-born were a demographic possibility, any politician who aspired to construct a majority in New York City had to be seen as a friend of the immigrant.

Chapter 6 examines the relationship between the changing working classes and the creation of a majority. Over the antebellum years, Democrats' claim to be the "true home of the working classes" was repeatedly put to the test. The concerns of the working classes, their values, demands, and world view, gave rise to the workingman's advocate, made an imprint on the Democracy, and shaped the character of the boss.

Chapter 7 turns to relationships between party leaders and economic elites. In the years of the second American party system, men of wealth and party leaders created an amicable division of labor. By contrast, the creation of a majority in the 1850s was fraught with provocations to men of wealth, who responded by organizing a municipal reform movement. In the same decade, the rapid expansion of patronage resources in the city freed local politicians of national party discipline. So, in the 1850s a distinctive urban politics appeared, and by mid-decade the battle of boss and reformer was on in earnest.

Chapter 8 looks forward to the institutionalization of the Democracy. I argue that the machine represented a compromise among the respectable element, the boss, and the dangerous classes whose conflict was so chaotic in the 1850s.

2 The chronicles of party

BETWEEN THE ELECTION of Jackson and the election of Lincoln, New York's political life underwent several transformations of party competition and political argument. Party conflict was organized, disorganized, and reorganized. Ideological debate and political rhetoric ranged over issues as diverse as alcohol and banks. The stories of party combat and of ideological debate are of course related, for parties are the most vigorous and consistent purveyors of visions of society. This chapter traces party contests at the polls and the visions they presented.

The chronology of party combat is shown in Figure 1. Until 1852, Whigs and Democrats, the parties of the second American party system, dominated local political life. Nativist parties made a brief appearance in the mid-1830s and were a more important presence in the mid-1840s and again in the mid-1850s. After the collapse of the Whigs, New York's politics involved a profusion of factions and parties vying for local control as a means to national ascendancy. More importantly, in the middle of the 1850s the characteristic urban competition of boss and reformer appeared. If the transformations of antebellum political life were complex, their direction was clear: By the time Abraham Lincoln was elected, New York had a distinctively urban and autonomous political system. Local politics, moreover, was more salient than in earlier years. Figure 2 shows that turnout in mayoral elections was much closer to turnout for presidential elections in the last decade of the antebellum era than in the Age of Jackson.

Some violence has been done to the chronology of party competition to present a sensible discussion of party self-presentation. The chapter begins with a discussion of political culture in the Era of Good Feelings and the Workingmen's Parties. The succeeding section is devoted to the Whig and Democratic parties, and the subsequent section describes the nativist parties. Despite the impending national crisis, local concerns dominated local political debate in the 1850s. The final section describes the conflict of bosses and reformers.

Changes in the organization of party competition involved profound ideological shifts. Parties debated not only banks and tariffs, or corruption and

18

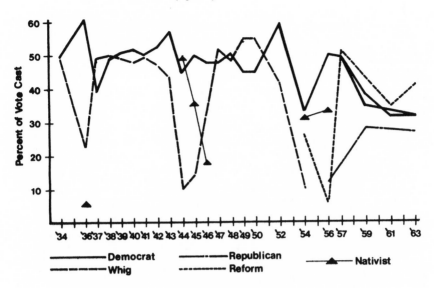

Figure 1. Party voting in New York City: votes for mayor, 1834–63. [*Sources*: James Valentine, *Manual of the City of New York for 1854* (New York: McSpedon and Baker, 1854); *New York Herald*, November 8, 1856; Valentine, *Manual . . . 1862*; Valentine, *Manual . . . 1864*; Horace Greeley and Thomas McElrath, *The Tribune Almanac and Political Register, 1858* (New York: Greeley, 1858); Greeley and McElrath, *Tribune Almanac, 1860* (New York: Greeley, 1860).]

reform, but also drink and immigration, religion and character, and the role of artisans or merchants in building and maintaining the republic. Through arguments about class, status, and party New Yorkers abandoned the axioms of eighteenth-century politics and put in their place elements of a more modern political debate.

The Workingmen's Parties were the last political organization to articulate that earlier set of beliefs. Each party that succeeded them, however, retained elements of eighteenth-century thought articulated by the Workingmen. The language of slavery versus freedom, tyranny versus republicanism was echoed by the nativists; the belief that the state should guide interdependent interests to a prosperous common good became the property of the Whigs; militant workerism and an insistence on equality were taken up by the Democrats. From the election of Jackson through the 1850s, Democrats claimed that because they championed liberty and equality they were the "true home of the working classes." By the mid-1850s, that claim had been so well elaborated that the Democrats had the support of a clear majority of the city's electorate. By then, however, they were no longer the party of Jackson. In addition to the rhetoric of equality, liberty, and workerism, the

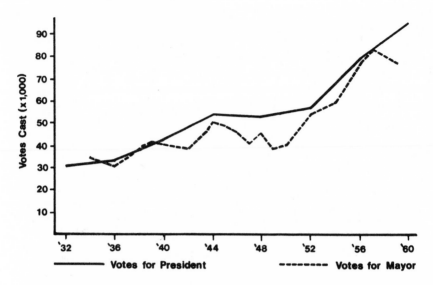

Figure 2. Turnout: votes cast for mayor and president, New York City, 1832–60. [*Sources*: Same sources as Figure 1. Also, O. L. Holley, ed. *The New York State Register for 1845* (New York: Disturnell, 1845); Greeley and MacElrath, *Tribune Almanac, 1861.*]

party represented a kind of primitive social welfare state demanded by the "dangerous classes." By contrast, it was the Reformers who campaigned for small, efficient government; individualism; and laissez-faire. That argument, which would not reach national politics until 1928, was at the heart of local politics for the rest of the nineteenth century and well into the twentieth.

In 1828, politics in New York stood poised between a resolution of eighteenth-century political argument and the creation of the lines of battle of the second American party system. The issues around which the debates of that party system would coalesce had already been raised. In 1825, President Adams outlined a program for an American system, and the 1828 congressional struggle over the tariff was a serious one. Although these issues were prominent, they did not serve to demarcate either stable coalitions of interest or broad ideologies involving political economy, political principle, or political creed.

More prominent than rhetorical precursors to the Whig–Democrat debate were the democratic slogans of the Jeffersonians and the political economy of the Federalists. When Jackson's supporters rallied citizens to his cause in 1828, it was with reminders of the victory of Jefferson: "The revolution of 1800, which saved our Constitution, depended on the elections of this state. It is our peculiar fortune to have this honor again assigned to us."[1]

Workingmen showed their approval of Jackson by calling him a "true Jeffersonian."[2] Nationally, Jefferson's ascendancy had signified the triumph of democracy over elitism, the reassertion of a straightforward republicanism based on sturdy and independent citizens. It meant, at most, a halfhearted and grudging acceptance of the commercial republic, a rejection of the Hamiltonian vision of accumulation and development, and in their place the claim that the best government was the one that governed least. In New York the "revolution of 1800" did not signify all those things, but it did recall the triumph of democracy. Jefferson's election meant an assertion of political liberties exercised by mechanics and tradesmen; recollection of Jefferson's election recalled the triumphs of democratization in the establishment of white manhood suffrage by the 1821 state constitution and the dethronement of King Caucus in 1824. To rally to the revolution of 1800, then, meant to proclaim faith in the political freedoms of common men.

It did not mean – either at the accession of Jefferson or seven presidential administrations later – a call for agrarian democracy. Indeed, it would have been odd if the election of Jefferson had meant, in New York, a rejection of the commercial republic so popularly hailed at the ratification of the Constitution a mere eleven years before. By the election of Jackson, the notion of the commercial republic had been broadened and elaborated. Like other states, New York had fostered the development of manufactures and assisted in the construction of canals and roads; city government continued to supervise and regulate market transactions and to oversee the port. With the opening of the Erie Canal, New York had already taken the appellation "Empire State." The city boasted its status as a commercial emporium, in which the projection of a population of 1 million – if thought to be a century away – was neither unimaginable nor unwelcome. Republicans urged men to support "Jackson, *Commerce*, and Our Country."[3] Side by side, then, with the Jeffersonian defense of the small producer as the guardian of liberty was a commercial vision that argued the partnership of merchant and mechanic working toward an ever increasing prosperity. Government, in New York as elsewhere, was expected to foster this effort. In sum, in 1828 New York's citizens believed in the interdependence of economic pursuits, that there was an identifiable and concrete common good, and that government's proper concern included facilitating prosperity by assisting economic development.[4]

This set of beliefs included themes that were commonly voiced in the eighteenth century. There was a profound suspicion of laissez-faire. Political rhetoric was peppered with the strong terms of tyranny and slavery versus independence, natural rights, equality, and liberty. The slave (that is, the man deprived of all political rights) was opposed to the virtuous yeoman and industrious mechanic who were the surest guardians of liberty. There were tensions among these elements – tensions, for example, between gov ernment regulation and love of liberty – but in the eighteenth century they seemed manageable enough.[5]

In the nineteenth century, these themes formed the heart of the vision of society put forward by the Workingmen's Parties. These parties, formed in a number of states in 1827 and largely gone by 1831, campaigned for the rights and interests of workingmen, broadly defined. In New York, the party was deeply divided, and all three factions together received only a small proportion of the votes cast in the city. They are of interest here because their ideology suggests the persistence of eighteenth-century values in nineteenth-century politics. Moreover, the sentiments voiced by these parties were echoed by labor organizations and by the major parties for some time to come.

Workingmen argued that, contravening the principles of equal rights and equal protection, government had been acting to benefit some citizens at the expense of others. The result was a decline in the material condition of workingmen, in their political status, and even in their moral fiber. Rather than being so one-sided, government should regulate relations between classes so that the weak would be protected and the strong not given legal privilege to reinforce their economic advantage. Workingmen argued, moreover, that if government looked after their interest the well-being of the whole community would naturally follow. To be sure, the definition of "workingmen" was a broad one, including artisans, laborers, farmers, grocers, and merchants, and excluding only those who made their wealth from "speculation." Workingmen were the producers of wealth, the repository of skill, and the manpower of the republic. A decline in their condition, their reduction from independent mechanics to slaves, would endanger the very future of liberty. For more than any other system of government, republican government was dependent on the moral fiber of its people. "Other systems of government," argued Ely Moore,

> are susceptible of renovation – possess, within themselves, certain recuperative powers or principles; and though fallen to-day, may rise again to-morrow – renewed and invigorated. Even the physical world may be smitten by the pestilence, swept by the whirlwind, or convulsed and shattered into atoms by the earthquake; and yet, a *better*, and a *fairer*, may spring from its ruins ... But, when a *moral pestilence* shall have seized upon the vitals of a republic ... then have Despair and Death already marked it for their own.

For the republic, then, as well as for themselves, workingmen needed to unite in a party to regain "a proper standing in the community, and representation in the councils of state."[6]

The central cause of workingmen's precarious position was the domination of politics by the wealthy. "Candidates for public offices," the *New York Sentinel and Workingman's Advocate* explained, "especially for our representatives in the state legislature ... have been taken entirely from that class of citizens denominated or supposed to be rich, or property holders, thereby leaving our own most numerous body without a voice in making those laws which we are compelled to obey."[7] Workingmen were sensitive to those institutional arrangements that functioned as barriers to their participation. They argued, for example, against voter registration and in favor of compensation of jurors, witnesses, and city council members, and for the direct election of the mayor of New York. Once in office, workingmen would be able to eliminate those policies that enabled one class to oppress another and violated the maxim of equal protection.

Of all the inequitable practices grouped under the heading of monopoly and privilege, banking was the most pernicious. The attack on banks contained all the elements of workingmen's world view: the importance of governmental "even-handedness," the evil of failing to produce wealth, and the importance of good character for the future of the republic. Allowed to continue, the paper-money system authorized by the state would create a city of speculators and paupers and a nation of princes and slaves. Banks were pernicious because they did not produce wealth, but only arranged a transfer of the community's wealth to themselves by collecting interest on loans (denounced as unchristian "usury"), discounting paper, and issuing depreciated or even worthless notes. Banks were a threat to republican liberty because through a heavy national debt they might "succeed in making us slaves, by grinding us down with taxes."[8]

As destructive to the republic as banks' power over community and state was their corrosive effect on citizens' character. Since "no individual foresight can prevent failure in business, while the power is in one set of men to increase and decrease the currency at pleasure," the banking system "leads to intemperance and despair."[9] Speculation meant "the creation of a distaste for the steady pursuit of those modes of business by which wealth is gradually acquired," and "the awakening of a desire for enterprises which hold out the dazzling prospect of sudden riches."[10] Clinton Roosevelt saw the same corrosive effects in the doctrines of free trade, which legitimated selfishness:

> The teaching that no other feeling is to be consulted, or can be, in our intercourse in society, tends to contract our sympathies, and man being the creature of habit and education, he will soon become entirely what he is taught to be and has the habit of being ...

The dealer has the habit of operating alone, against his fellows, and his motto is "Laissez-nous faire."

> The sailor, on the contrary, has the habit of operating together with his fellows for their common safety, and his motto is "let us pull together"; and the poor sailor will lend money to a distressed shipmate by handsfull, while the merchant will run in opposition of his fellow, and break

23

him down if he can, and triumph over him when he is down. Thus these principles operate."

Its selfish morality aside, workingmen did not see free trade as the obvious answer to their difficulties. George Henry Evans, for example, though he later became a supporter of Jackson, worked with the Clay Republicans and saw the Bank of the United States as a wholesome, restraining influence on state banks. And Evans argued in relation to a number of monopolies – the New York and Harlem Railroad, the ferries – that their functions *and their revenues* properly belonged to the government. For Evans, then, as for the movement's program as a whole, "equal protection" signified intervention and action as well as elimination of state enabling of private monopolies. It was this active, interventionist government that the Whigs would champion – though their policy prescriptions would be quite different.

The other great journalist of the workingmen, William Leggett, argued in the *Post* for the withdrawal of government generally and for free trade. Banks were but the "venal drippings of unclean legislation"; railroads, ferries, and markets should be left to the activities of individuals. Leggett maintained that

> the true functions of government [are] the making of *general laws* uniform and universal in their operation . . . governments have no right to interfere with the pursuits of individuals . . . by offering encouragements and granting privileges to any particular class of industry, as all men are equally important to the general welfare and equally entitled to protection."

Similarly, the Democratic candidate for governor declared in 1834 that "government goes beyond its proper sphere of action when it undertakes to regulate the business pursuits of our citizens . . ."³ and Democrats would find the cause of inequality in society in bad legislation.

THE SECOND AMERICAN PARTY SYSTEM

The debate between Whigs and Democrats dominated politics in the city from the mid-1830s until 1852. During that time, Whigs and Democrats competed fiercely for the city's vote. Before the appearance of the nativist American Republican Party in 1844, the Democratic Party was generally successful; after 1844, Whigs seem to have had the edge. Of seventeen contests for the mayoralty between 1834 (the first year the mayor was an elected rather than appointed official) and 1852, the Democrats won eleven, the Whigs five (1837, 1838, 1847, 1849, and 1850), and the American Republicans one (1844). Party debate in New York City was largely about political economy, and it was for the most part a straightforward repetition of party debate in Washington: Democrats emphasized politics and Whigs emphasized economics.

24

Democrats insisted they were the party of Jefferson, yet Democratic thinking involved a more complex vision than the simple republic brought to
mind by the name of Jefferson and the slogans of 1800. If one was to
support Jackson, one was for "Jackson, Commerce, and Our Country."[14]
Democrats offered a vision of the city, "the first commercial city in the
union,"[15] in which the preponderance of interests depended on ocean-going
trade, and ocean-going trade depended on free-trade doctrines and a low
tariff:

> Is our reader desirous that the commercial interests of this great city
> should thrive – that our wharves should be crowded with shipping, our
> market with goods, our streets with a busy and bustling multitude –
> that the [call] of the sailor, the clatter of the caulkers' hammers, the
> rattling of the loaded carts, and all the various sounds of commercial
> prosperity should salute his ears in the business part of our metropolis?
> Let him remember that the candidates who, unless his vote is given
> against them, may succeed, are the friends of the hateful tariff system,
> which, if persisted in, will ere long ruin our merchants, drive away our
> ship masters, and desolate our streets.[16]

In this view, the issues raised by the Workingmen were less important than
the national policy decisions that would determine the city's prosperity. For
making distinctions among city residents, Workingmen were denounced by
Tammany's General Committee as "social, political, and economic deviates
whom 'all sober respectable mechanics of New York' ought to shun." On
Tammany's ticket, "the merchant, the seaman, the tradesman, the mechanics, and the professional man, have all their especial representatives."[17]

Tammany did, however, make a distinction between industrious artisans
and mechanics, on the one hand, and the "spinning jenny fanatics" of New
England whom the tariff was meant to serve, on the other.[18] Industrious
artisans and mechanics had prospered with the growth of the nation "and
flourished unpampered with the spoils wrung by the hands of the government from the industry of others."[19] The tariff served merely to restrict
commerce, to confirm the monopolies of the manufacturers, and to tax
farmers, artisans, and merchants for the benefit of the "stockholders in
woolen factories" and other "manufacturers of premature birth."[20] "While
we hear," proclaimed a party resolution of the early 1840s, "of a large
profit already secured by the manufacturing capitalist in the rise of his goods,
and of an advance in the common necessaries of life consumed by the
laborer, we have yet to hear of the first dollar added to his wages."[21]

Like the tariff, the economic program Whigs promoted as the American
System functioned not to advance the general prosperity but to line the
pockets of special interests:

> The "American System" means *High Tariff and Internal Improvements.*
> *High Tariff*, translated into English, is a matter of palpable fraud and

> injustice ... It taxes, *not* the *property* which is *productive*, but articles
> of consumption. It does not tax the *rich man*, but it taxes the *poor man*
> for the benefit of those already wealthy ... [22]

The American System, then, was a species of "class legislation" – legislation
that, like the creation of monopolies, enriched a few at the expense of the
majority. Jackson's veto message was echoed over and over again and its
definition of monopoly echoed in wards throughout the city.[23] The trouble
here was much as the Workingmen had diagnosed it: the influence attendant
upon wealth. Prevention and cure would be found only in a citizenry insistent
(through the party, of course) that government enact laws that would, "as
Heaven does its rains, shower its favor alike on the high and the low, the
rich and the poor ... "[24]

It was the Equal Rights Party – a rebellious Tammany faction that ran
independent slates in the mid-1830s – that elaborated these doctrines. Though
the "Locofoco" Party made a poor showing at the polls, it was their laissez-
faire ideology, combined with their militant defense of labor, that became
party creed. Locofoco reasoning began with a citation of "the revered Jefferson," who held "that ... the true foundation of Republican Government
is the *equal rights* of every citizen."[25] Although the United States declared
itself a republic in 1776, the truth was that it had not yet become one.
"Here, as elsewhere, Man is the slave of Money. 'Law rules the poor and
Money rules the Law.' Lombard street and its precincts in London govern
Wall Street, and Wall Street governs our legislative lobbies."[26] Federal and
state legislatures alike had passed exclusive legislation that exacerbated
material inequalities and, when charters were granted to corporations,
usurped the sovereignty of the people.[27] It was not simply the unfairness of
these laws that made them wrong, but the fact that "whilst laws are unequal
and consequently unjust, the largest portion of the community will be poor
... "[28] Exacerbating inequalities, creating in bankers and other authorized
exploiters a republican variant of aristocracy and thereby undermining the
legal foundations of the republic, unequal legislation undermined as well
that virtue so necessary to the perpetuation of free government. Echoing
the Workingmen, Locofocos declared that

> to the Banking System, and to that alone, can be imputed the present
> demoralizing spirit of gambling speculation, by which vast fortunes are
> accumulated in a short time – extravagance, idleness, dissipation, and
> crime thereby encouraged.[29]

Industriousness was valued by the Locofocos, but the "spirit of traffic"
declared of all others the most incompatible with the spirit of liberty:

> The desire to buy cheap and sell dear, to take much and give little,
> whether it shows itself in the highwayman or the speculator, is equally

hostile to the happiness, and the virtues of society; and from the birth of Carthage down to the present time, the tendency of excessive trade has been to blend the pride of the tyrant with the meanness of the slave in each individual wherever it has been suffered to predominate.[30]

The remedy was twofold. The first part was an abandonment of the speculating system in favor of hard currency and free trade. Free trade was little more than an outgrowth of egalitarian principles, for free trade was the only policy consistent with the doctrine that government treat citizens equally, in deference to their natural rights. Hard currency was a brake to the speculating system and a protection to workingmen. Rather than argue that this Democratic path was the path to prosperity, it was argued that the Whig path was the path to the dread English condition of widespread poverty and "slavery." The Democratic position was, economically, only a promise to minimize citizens' losses, not a promise to maximize their gains.

Second and more important was a thorough reform of political institutions – including the Democratic Party – to fit the doctrine of equality. By the 1840s, Democrats in the city phrased "the old Democratic creed" in this way:

> a perfect equality of political rights; the sovereignty of the State Governments; a strict construction of the Constitution; no privileges to particular sections of the community; no monopolies, trading companies, or corrupt governmental banks; frequent rotation, strict responsibility, and small periods in office; moderate legislation; a revenue meeting the wants of the people and no more; simplicity in the laws; and the least possible restraint upon the mind, person, energy, and industry of every man, consistent with the rights of his fellow men.

Democratic creed involved as well a rejection of the notion of shared interests and it was

> resolved, that the best protectors of the laboring classes are the laborers themselves, and that to the Whig capitalists who volunteer on our behalf we reply ... They grew by your neglect ... the instincts of wealth are the same everywhere – ... the affection of capitalists for the labouring classes is not more [hypocritical] in Great Britain than in the United States – ... in monopolizing the earnings of labour in the former, they march more boldly to their object, while here they work to obtain it by tricks in Tariff, Currency, and Debt.[31]

As a defender of democratic procedures and institutions, as opponents of privilege, the "unterrified Democracy" claimed to be the "true home of the laboring classes."

Like the Democrats, Whigs did not create their views out of whole cloth, but built on an inheritance from the past. They echoed Workingmen's notions that the state's proper object was to guide the variety of interests and groups in the nation on the path to prosperity. These interests were not fundamentally antagonistic; rather, there was a common good that could be embodied in government policy and was embodied in the American System.

The tariff was a crucial element of the American System, both because of its economic function and because the tariff concretized, for the Whigs, the maxim that the classes were mutually dependent. In this view, protection of manufacturers did not mean protection simply for the mill owners at Lowell. Brickmakers, carpenters, tailors, shoemakers, and a long list of others would benefit by protection from competition from degraded European labor. Moreover, protection of the mill owners and the capitalists *was* protection of the workers, for if the tariff were only high enough, wages would be protected:[32] "The employment and thriving of the people depend on the profitable investment of the moneyed capital of the country ... the wages and profits of labor ... depend on the profits accruing from the use of moneyed capital which labor employs." The error of the Democratic policy was that it regarded "moneyed capital" "as a master ... as a hostile power, not as a friendly auxiliary."[33]

Banks were important for trade, and the Bank of the United States, in particular, was defended for its stabilizing effects on the currency. Democratic objections were reduced by Whigs to the motto "perish credit, perish commerce";[34] by contrast, Whig speakers

> lauded the credit system ... [which] had ... given to an infant nation the strength and wisdom of a full grown man ... [and] called upon Heaven to forbid that ever the aristocracy of wealth should supplant the glorious credit system, by which a poor man with industry, integrity, and talent, could compete with and distance the wealthy capitalist.[35]

The possibilities to "distance the wealthy capitalist" were another reason politicians were foolish to advocate class conflict. The availability of opportunity in the United States meant that "there was no room for so nefarious a sentiment as domestic hostility" between rich and poor;[36] "the wheel of fortune is perpetually and steadily turning, and those at the bottom today, will be moving up tomorrow, and ere long be at the top ... "[37] This was the America the Whigs would foster, where "there are few exceptions to the rule that Temperance, and Industry, and Economy, lead to Prosperity."[38] The Whig cause was the "cause of progress," "peculiarly the cause of Young Men of improvement – of Enterprise – of Amelioration – of Ambition."[39] It was an America infused with the spirit of commerce, directed by "the commercial class."[40] Daniel Ullman succinctly summarized the promise of the Whig system by saying that "he would level up not level down."[41]

For government to open the way to prosperity was not simply its choice, but more, its obligation – "the government is not merely a machine for making wars and punishing felons, but is bound to do all that is within its power to promote the welfare of the People – its legitimate scope is not merely negative, representative, defensive, but also affirmative, creative, constructive, beneficent ... "[42] The passivity of the Van Buren administration during the depression of 1837 was peculiarly vulnerable to attack on these grounds: " ... The government which refuses to relieve the people under such circumstances," Thurlow Weed editorialized, "fails to fulfill its highest functions. For what purposes was government instituted, and why are its burthens borne, but to secure for its constituency, protection and relief under all circumstances?"[43]

Local Whig platforms were not altogether consistent with local statement of national party principle. To be sure, the city's status as a commercial emporium (if not *the* leading commercial center of the United States) and New York as the Empire State were proudly boasted about. Yet although a "revenue sufficient for its purposes" was demanded for national government, the local refrain was commonly for a reduction of taxes and city-government expenditure. The Democratic desire at the state level to stop and tax was derided, and the Whigs insistently called for more of "that grand and beneficent system of Internal Policy which has made the name of Clinton immortal and for twenty years constituted the glory and strength of New York." Whigs simultaneously denounced an increase in the city's debt under Democratic administrations as "contrary to the express injunction of Jefferson and the settled maxims of all financiers and statesmen."[44] Although Weed, Greeley, and other Whig spokesmen emphasized that in principle the government was obliged to be constructive and creative, Greeley also editorialized that the "relations of labor and capital present a vast theme ... [and] Government cannot intermeddle with them without doing a great mischief."[45] And one mayoral candidate, arguing that "landlords should be prevented from confining the poor to apartments from which the very light and air ... are almost entirely excluded" advocated that this be accomplished "by public opinion, not through the operations of the law."[46]

The Whigs had a final appeal. What really divided the parties, they claimed, was Whig concern for "the best means to elevate public morals." "No nation – no people – no constitution – no government can stand unless it is founded on the broad and pure principles of religious truth and belief."[47] And the Democratic counterclaim was that the Democracy was the defender of the culture and civil liberties of the working classes. These claims were not a product of the political-economy debate, but a response to the appearance of nativism and its stress on the sources of social honor.

STATUS AND THE SOURCES OF SOCIAL HONOR

Three nativist political parties were formed in New York City: Samuel Morse's Native American Democratic Association in 1836; the American Republican Party in 1844–5; and the Know-Nothings in 1854–6. The party of the thirties received only 6 percent of the total vote (about half as many votes as the Locofoco faction received in the same year). American Republicans, with Whig endorsement, won the charter election of 1844 by campaigning both for municipal reform and against immigrants,[48] but were not again rewarded with victory. Subsequently, nativist groups acted under the wing of the Whig Party. By the mid-1850s (but not before), naturalized voters outnumbered native-born voters, permanently reducing nativist parties to minority status. Know-Nothings did, however, win the allegiance of about 30 percent of the electorate in 1854 and 1856.

Brief as these eruptions of status politics were, they had profound effects on the party system. After the 1844 American Republican victory, the Whig and Democratic parties had more pronounced ethnic followings. In the short run, this helped the Whigs: Whig retention of nativist sentiment made them the stronger party until they fragmented for national reasons after 1850. In the long run, this helped the Democrats, who responded to nativist campaigns by amplifying their claim to be the "true home of the working classes."

Nativism also influenced the course of municipal reform. The alliance of nativist and temperance advocates with reform movements endowed political reform with a narrow and persecuting taint that it did not escape before the Civil War (and, indeed, was not unblemished by afterward). Nativists and reformers alike expressed antiparty sentiment. American Republicans made it clear that they formed an independent party in 1843 because of the inadequacy of existing ones. "We love our institutions too well," they declared, "to see them desecrated by the Mammon of Party ... "[49] Similarly, in his *Defense of the American Policy* (1856), Whitney argued that

> too long we have worshipped "hickory poles" and "hard cider" – too long have the ambitious leaders of party thrown in our eyes the dust of "tariff" and "free trade," "bank" or "no bank," "slavery" or "antislavery," till we have been blinded to the trust which our honest old grandfathers left to us, and our dearest interests have been made the subjects of bargain and sale.[50]

The nativist pamphlet *The Crisis* discussed the evils of party spirit at length. This antiparty sentiment linked the nativist impulse to reform, the second declared aim of the American Republican Party. Their complaints against city government were the familiar ones of extravagance and corruption, coupled with opposition to the common-school system and the hiring of immigrants in city departments. In office, however, American Republicans did little to reform city government save remove immigrants from city jobs. Antiparty feeling infused the Know-Nothing movement of the 1850s as well; reciprocally, the reform movement of the 1850s allied itself with nativists in its effort to win office.

Finally, nativist and temperance emphasis on character forced the issue into political discourse. Nativists related political and social difficulties to the presence of people whose character unsuited them for republican citizenship. This emphasis on character is still more pronounced when the evangelical and temperance movements with which nativism was associated are taken into account. Thomas Whitney's *A Defense of the American Policy* offers a characteristic statement:

> Religion, patriotism, and morality, have been the foundation-stones of our success as a nation, and our happiness and prosperity as a people. These foundation-stones were laid upon the rock of a stern Protestant faith, and their fruits have been all that our institutions promised – civil and religious liberty.[51]

For the American Republican Party it was, similarly, self-evident that "popular intelligence and popular virtue are indispensable to the existence and continuation of a government such as ours."[52] Immigrants posed a threat because they did not exhibit the capacity for independent and responsible thought, for reasoned attachment to principle, or even the "stern Protestant faith" required of a republican citizenry. Coming from the authoritarian countries of Europe, unpracticed in democracy and little schooled in anything else, immigrants could hardly be expected to manage the responsibilities of freedom.[53]

This argument was made with particular urgency about Catholics, and, in fact, nativist argument in New York City was largely anti-Catholic argument. Catholics, it was argued, were trained by the church not to think for themselves, but only to blindly follow authority.[54] The Church of Rome abetted and thrived on superstition; the result was that its devotees were slaves of passion rather than the masters of reason. The very plan of organization of the church, its hierarchical construction, not only demonstrated the behavior for which it trained its adherents, but also suggested that its tenets were incompatible with republicanism.[55] Moreover, as an authoritarian earthly power, the Church of Rome had an interest in the failure of the American experiment in republican government.

The slavish character of immigrants meant their entry into the labor market degraded the social standing of all workers and forced a decline in their wages. And these were the better immigrants. The powers of Europe, knowing a good thing when they saw it, were efficiently dumping their poor onto American shores, filling almshouses and prisons and thereby raising the taxes of American laboring men. "It is well known," the American Republican Party campaigned, "who are the recipients of [almshouse] charity. We are thankful that they are not Americans! No! They are foreign paupers whom American citizens are compelled to support."[56]

Drink was the clearest indication of immigrant vice and the commonest cause of the decline of the formerly virtuous.[57] This was not simply a social but rather a *political* danger, as a look at the countries of Europe revealed. One temperance advocate and prominent nativist explained it this way:

> The cheap wines of France have much to answer for ... They send a genial glow through the veins, and make men at once valiant, voluble, and saucy; they produce a momentary chivalric enthusiasm, bold, daring, uncompromising ... [as a result] we should not be surprised when we witness the effects in ... insubordination and revolution.

In these exuberant moments, the French had overthrown their monarchical oppressors and established republics, but they had not the character to maintain them. "How different the national beverage of ... England. Ale – strong, dreamy, and stupefying ... Give your Englishman after a day's labor, his mug of Ale ... and he will care little who is prime minister or sovereign."[58] It was clear that the only *republican* drink was water. The fact that temperance failed in the United Kingdom showed the movement's republican character – the issue was clearly "Rum or Republic."[59]

These arguments provoked a variety of responses from the Whigs and Democrats. Whigs were staunch in support of temperance but vacillated about nativism. They formed alliances with nativist organizations, sharing candidates with nativist parties. Whigs objected, however, to independent nativist party organization, and as a result their public statements against nativism were strongest when nativists formed parties. Nativists were in any event not the main enemy, and immigration not the main issue. Immigrants were asked to join the Whigs in "leveling up":

> If any adopted citizen be here, let me warn and advise him. The Locofocos have driven thousands out of employment. You have asked for bread, and they have given you a stone. You have come from lands of oppression in search of liberty and happiness, and what have you found? No less than ten thousand foreigners have been obliged to return to their native land ...[60]

After Whig alliance with American Republicans, however, these arguments recruited few foreign-born adherents. The loss was more than made up for by recruits from the native-born.

Democrats flirted with nativism in the 1830s, but by 1844 their position in favor of immigrants was clear. Democrats ridiculed Whig vacillation and traced it to self-interest. Why, they asked, are the Whigs now denouncing nativism?

> Why, the Whig stock jobbers ... are afraid that the hardy foreigners, when they find that they will have no privileges here but those enviable ones of hewing our wood and drawing our water, will seek some more genial shores, and that thus the great works of "internal improvement" will fail.[61]

The Democratic *Post* saw the struggle with nativists as the same old struggle of "political equality warring against the spirit of exclusiveness and proscription."[62] By contrast, the Democratic Party was "based upon the broad principles of universal toleration, and absolute equality [and] ... recognizes no restrictions on the full development and broadest application of these principles ... " The Democrats' resolution on the Know-Nothings was fierce in its attack on

> traitors to the Constitution, and ... bigots and fanatics in religion, those secret and midnight plotters known as "Know-Nothings," who dare not in the day of truth and light advocate their own doctrines or avow their own objects.[63]

Finally, although Whigs supported temperance, Democrats argued that drink was not the root of degradation and crime, but degradation the root of crime and drink. Mike Walsh expressed the view succinctly: "The great and fruitful source of crime and misery on earth is the *inequality of society*, the abject dependence of honest, willing industry upon idle and dishonest capitalists."[64]

By its opposition to temperance and its defense of immigrants, the "unterrified democracy" expanded and reinforced its claims to be the home of the working classes. The Maine Law (restricting the sale of alcoholic beverages) was described by Tammany politicians as "a bill despotic England never dared to place on the statute book ... ," a "sumptuary law" that was the "entering wedge" of a restrictive and coercive system.[65] It was the "hard working democracy," Alexander Ming reminded a party audience, to which "the people will always look for the principles of constitutional liberty."[66] Isaiah Rynders summarized when he asked why a poor man should care for democratic principles. If such a man had no interest in democratic principles, "what better is our country than any other? It is only ... because here the civil and religious rights of the poor man are guarded, as well as the rich, that democratic principles are better than others."[67] With these arguments the Democrats entered the 1850s, to combat not only nativists but also a new antagonist: the municipal-reform movement.

THE APPEARANCE OF AN URBAN PARTY SYSTEM

By the beginning of the last antebellum decade, the effects of the decline of the second American party system were being felt. In the late 1840s, Democrats suffered a revolt of Barnburners and Free Soilers. As a result, they lost the mayoralty to the Whigs in 1849 and 1850. In the fifties, Democrats divided into Hard Shells and Soft Shells, differing in their stance on national issues. Similarly, Whigs divided into the Wooly Headed and Silver Greys over their inability to agree on joining the emerging Republican Party, and by mid-decade the Whigs had all but disappeared. Even the Know-Nothings, though at the height of their power in the middle of the decade, succumbed to the divisive force of the slavery issue.

33

In the midst of national party disarray, the city's own concerns dominated urban campaigning. This does not mean that the national parties and national issues ceased to have an effect on city politics. For one thing, urban elections became three-, four-, five-, and six-way races as a consequence of the collapse of nationally imposed discipline. For another, reform-minded Republicans and Democrats could not join to form a unified city-reform movement because their national goals demanded that they maintain local party organization. Moreover, the emergence of the Republican Party meant shifting allegiances of both leaders and citizens. Finally, with the outbreak of civil war the future shape of the Democratic–Republican struggle began to appear.

Republicans were not to be serious contenders for local power in New York City after the war. Rather, it was Reformers who provided opposition to the Democracy. Early in the last antebellum decade, the city's most prominent businessmen organized a municipal-reform movement to challenge Democratic power. During the 1850s, Reformers waged a series of electoral assaults on Democratic ascendancy. Alone, they could not be successful. Democratic factions collectively claimed the allegiance of 60 percent or more of the city's voters at every election. Thus the Democrats won the mayoralty in 1854, 1856, and 1859. Alliance with a Democratic faction made Reform victories possible in 1857, 1861, and 1863.

It was to this conflict between reform and machine that national issues took second place in the 1850s. Campaign speakers sometimes presented the contest as a matter of "free soil," "union," or "abolitionism,"[68] but they more often made a case for the importance of city government. One editor observed in 1856 that despite the presidential election at hand, "this Mayoralty is overtopping every other political question. One does not hear a whisper among the politicians in relation to Buchanan, Fremont, or Fillmore."[69] A speaker at a Democratic Reform meeting in 1859 argued that "it was nothing to us in our corporate capacity, whether slavery was extended or not."[70] The nominators of Jacob A. Westervelt affirmed in 1852 that there were "in the city of New York ... great and important interests to be promoted by the election of proper persons to be placed at the head of municipal government."[71] The Municipal Reformers of 1854 put the case most forcefully:

> Fellow-Citizens – The Federal government and the state government, in their respective spheres, are of importance in a self-governing country, but the city government reaches your firesides, and becomes your chief safeguard of life and property. Exterior governments may be good or bad without immediately affecting you; but upon this home government, all about you depends, even the healthiness of the air you breathe, the purity of the water you drink, if not the food you eat ... Hence, next

to family government, the city government comes most directly home to your highest earthly interests.[72]

The municipal reformers, of course, were without state or national aspirations as a party. They argued, indeed, against party, presenting their candidates as "untrammelled by party pledges" and therefore able to "enforce the laws ... with fearless impartiality ... owing a common fealty to the whole people ..."[73] And they focused on the ills of city government – the rule of "muscle" in primaries and parties; the corruption of city government and resultant high taxes. The city, reformers argued, "had reached a crisis in political affairs corrupt from the crown of the head to the sole of the foot – with a city debt of $31 million, and an annual tax of $7 million, credit depreciated, and cormorants in every department of the government" – "a city unparalleled for its commerce, it could not sell its bonds." Little was delivered for the enormous sum of $7 million annually. Police protection was inadequate and crime was rife because Tammany was allied with thugs; the streets were dirty. And "who paid this enormous tax? The productive labor of the country ... it was a mistake to suppose that the taxes came out of the pockets of the rich ... They came from the Woman who sews ... and from the laborer ... It therefore behooves all classes of citizens to look to it ..."[74] "Retrenchment," argued the reformers, "is the twin of reform."[75]

Democrats agreed that the city's government was "the most expensive and extravagant of any city in the world" but their analysis of the causes was different.[76] Even if the city council were corrupt, Democrats pointed out, it only controlled a quarter of the city's budget![77] By far the greater part of taxpayers' money was spent by the state-appointed boards that administered municipal operations – the almshouse governors, the commissioners of asylums and police, the Croton Aqueduct Board, and the Central Park Commissioners.[78] What was needed was a reorganization of city government to centralize control in the mayor. Unlike the federal government, New York City's government had no executive to speak of. A simple majority of the city council could override his veto, and state-appointed boards spent freely, hired whom they chose, and were not responsible to him. As a result, the people had no one they could hold responsible.[79] In 1856, Democrats pointed out that whereas the crying need of municipal government was for a stronger executive, reformers' charter amendments of 1854 had, by decentralizing responsibility, simply emasculated city government altogether.[80] This was little more than an attempt on the part of Republicans to punish New York for its Democratic sensibilities, for "the principle of governing by boards is peculiarly black republican."[81] It was, moreover, the state legislature that had sold the railroad franchise for a song, thereby depriving the city of much-needed revenue.[82] The progressive incursion of the state legislature into urban governance meant that municipal liberty itself was at stake. Republicans upstate had "trampled upon the sacredness of municipal independence" while their "vampires feed by means of corrupt legislation upon our city treasury."[83]

At the same time, the alliances of reformers (and later, Republicans) with Americans, Know-Nothings, and temperance advocates allowed Tammany to continue to present itself as the defender of the cultural styles of the working classes. New appeals were added to Democratic claims to be the "true home" of the industrious. As early as 1850, the Democratic candidate for mayor had announced his support for the abolition of the contract system of building public works and initiated proposals for a residential building code.[84] In 1854, the Democratic candidate's supporters pointed out that "he caused the old Almshouse to be taken down, thus giving employment to a large number of workingmen who must otherwise have starved, or been fed by charity."[85] The panics of the mid-1850s made the need of labor for employment more pressing, and its demands (voiced by ad hoc committees formed at mass meetings of the unemployed) more prominent.

The Democratic mayor proposed a relief and public-works program in response to these demands. Just as reformers argued that all Europe watched the fate of the republican experiment in the United States, so Mayor Wood argued that provision for the poor should distinguish the virtues of democracy as compared to aristocracy – "Do not let it be said," he asked the common council, "that labor, which produces every thing, gets nothing, and dies of hunger in our midst, whilst capital, which produces nothing, gets every thing, and pampers in luxury and plenty."[86]

The idea that "it is the business of the State to care for the unemployed" was declared "a grand fallacy" by the *New York Herald*, and the *Post* and *Times* agreed.[87] This was the position the municipal reformers took. Relief was an un-American idea, a request to America's independent workingmen to reduce themselves to dependence and beggary. What citizens witnessed, after all, was simply a depression, of the sort that had happened in 1837. And like that depression, this one too would pass by virtue of the natural workings of a free economy.

Reform, then, became a campaign not only for a retrenchment of municipal expenditures and an end to corruption, but also against rule by "the dangerous classes." William Curtis Noyes argued to a Republican audience,

> your character abroad and at home as a municipal body exercising the
> most important functions of government over a million people, is given
> not by yourselves, not by the best men in the city, not by the best women
> in the city, but by the dangerous classes, who are permitted to dominate,
> because men are so much occupied in their own private affairs and in
> the making of money that they will not attend to governmental affairs.[88]

The "ring" or machine had, in Reform and Republican rhetoric, grown to enormous proportions. One reform politician declared that "nothing can be so true than that modern and monstrous instrument known as the political party machine ... is the source of these evils" of corruption and rising taxes. "That instrument crushes honesty and uprightness as effectually as the wheels of the Juggernaut does its victims ..."[89] From the Republican point of view, there was by the outbreak of the war even more at stake than the city, and the images of war infused the description of the local struggle. Speaking at a "taxpayers' " meeting, Simeon Chittenden argued that

> this infamous government of the city of New York must be put down. If not put down by votes, it will ultimately be put down by bullets. There is no alternative. Free men will not much longer put up with the robbery, the corruption, the infamy which have disgraced city government.[90]

Reformers and Republicans agreed that "we should be ruled by men instead of muscle."[91] "What led," one orator asked his audience after the draft riots, "to the riot which disgraced your city in July?" And the audience answered "The Ring!"[92]

For their part, Democrats argued that they were the real defenders of the Constitution, the Republicans its desecrators. Agreeing, on the one hand, that the "honest masses of this city ... require reform," they went on to demand, on the other, that the city stand firm by Democratic national commitments. Upon the result of the mayoralty "may indeed depend the question whether the city of New York is to become, henceforth, a political spoil of the abolitionists, or preserve the position it has hitherto held of unwavering devotion to the Constitution and the laws."[93] To combat the "black republicans," to preserve the nation, to defend municipal liberty from upstate intervention, to protect the "honest masses," nothing was so necessary as the party. "Without the instrumentality of party," argued a Democratic speaker, "there is no means of opposition ... there can be no combined and uniform effort."[94] "Parties," declared another, "were the great implements of freedom ... [Tammany] has stood a political lighthouse ... amid the darkness and gloom of the political worlds; she still [stands] to warn people from danger and defend them from wrong."[95]

In the antebellum decades, the intense competition of two national parties gave way to a new and distinctly urban competition. The great majority of New York City's electorate was organized in the "unterrified Democracy"; the opposition was a relatively elite minority organized under the banner of municipal reform. The change in party system was the hallmark of urban political development in the years between the election of Jackson and the election of Lincoln. By 1860, Reformers battled bosses in Philadelphia, Baltimore, Milwaukee, Boston, Pittsburgh, and Cincinnati. The creation of new urban antagonists was accompanied by a change in public discourse. The eighteenth-century language of tyranny, slavery, freedom, and character and the political-economy debate of Whigs and Democrats were replaced by the liberty, equality, and workerism of the Democracy and the Reformers' campaign for small, businesslike, nonpartisan government. It remains to be seen to whom these appeals were addressed and what relation they had to the hopes, values, and visions of New York's electorate.

3   Fellow citizens

To WHOM WERE POLITICIANS APPEALING in antebellum New York: Who were the "freemen" and "mechanics," the "hard-working masses" and "dangerous classes," the "best men," "speculators," "stock-jobbers" and "merchants"? What sense can be made of notions like the "commercial emporium," the "industrial interest," the fear of English capital, and the "credit system"? This chapter offers an initial view of New York's fellow citizens, examining the city as a social and more particularly economic community, and describing the transformation in social structure that was simultaneous with the ideological transformation just described.

New York was a contradictory sort of place in the antebellum years. It was, on the one hand, the entry point for European capital and goods to the markets of a capital-scarce and undeveloped country – a country, moreover, that sensed its experiment in republicanism as a threat to the aristocratic and authoritarian world powers. From this perspective, New Yorkers, like Americans elsewhere, expressed a fearful and defensive nationalism. On the other hand, New York was the commercial, financial, and by 1860 the industrial center of the union, extending its tentacles of trade over its continental hinterland and in the process becoming the economic center of a fledgling world power. This role provided New York's dominant and more confident vision, the vision of a thriving republican city that both Democrats and Whigs emphasized in their competing claims about the best path to prosperity. Much as they revered Jefferson, New Yorkers argued that great cities need not be "sores on the body politic," and they summarized their hopes by projecting the city's rapid growth.

The expansion projected, however confidently optimistic it may have seemed at the time, was eclipsed by the growth that actually took place. The population of 203,000 in 1830 quadrupled by 1860, when the city's inhabitants numbered 813,700 (see Table 1). In the same years more than three and a half million immigrants landed in the city, and though the great majority of these continued on to other destinations, by 1855 more than half the city's population was foreign-born (see Table 2). The New York

Table 1. *Population of New York City,*
1825–60

Year	Total number	Percent increase
1825	166,086	
1830	197,112	18.7
1835	270,089	27.0
1840	312,710	15.8
1845	371,223	18.7
1850	515,547	38.9
1855	629,904	22.2
1860	813,669	29.2
1825–60		489.9

Sources: New York State Assembly, *Journal of the Forty-ninth Session* (Albany: E. Crosswell, 1826), part 2, appendix C.; New York State, Secretary of State, *Census of the State of New York, for 1835* (Albany: Crosswell, Van Benthuysen, and Burt, 1836); New York State, Secretary of State, *Census of the State of New York, for 1845* (Albany: Carroll and Cook, 1846); New York State, Secretary of State, *Census of the State of New York, for 1855* (Albany: Van Benthuysen, 1857). U.S Bureau of the Census, *Sixth Census of the United States [1840]* (Washington, D.C.: Thomas Allen, 1841); U.S. Bureau of the Census, *Statistical View of the United States ... Compendium of the Seventh Census [1850]* (Washington, D.C.: Beverly Tucker, Senate Printer, 1854); U.S. Bureau of the Census, *Eighth Census of the United States [1860]* (Washington, D.C.: Government Printing Office, 1865).

State census of 1855 revealed that nearly 30 percent of the city's population had been born in Ireland, and an additional 16 percent in Germany (the next largest immigrant group, the non-Irish Britons, accounted for about 5 percent of the city's population).[1] Eighty percent of the immigrants landed after 1845, and immigrant families found that neither housing nor schools, neither the labor market nor the city's churches, could expand quickly enough to accommodate them. Although the number of public schools, for example, had quadrupled in the same period as the population did – from

Table 2. *Population of New York City by place of birth, 1855*

Place of birth	Number	Percent
United States	303,721	48.2
Ireland	175,735	27.9
Germany and Prussia	95,752	15.2
England, Wales, and Scotland	32,135	5.1
France	6,321	1.0
Other Europe	6,177	1.0
Canada	2,958	0.5
All others	7,105	1.1
Totals	629,904	100.0

Source: New York State, Secretary of State, *Census of the State of New York, for 1855* (Albany: Van Benthuysen, 1857), pp. 117–18.

a dozen in 1830 to fifty in 1857 – they had even at the outset only taught a quarter of the city's children.

With growth came changes in the general configuration of the city (see Figure 3). As early as 1830, Philip Hone recorded in his diary that the city was, in the spring, "undergoing its usual annual metamorphosis; many stores and houses are being pulled down, and others altered, to make every inch of ground productive to its utmost extent."[2] There was pressure on the city government to grade and open streets in ward after ward and to open new markets; newspapers closely followed and proudly reported the value of new construction in the city. The shape of the island meant that extension took place northward, and the wealthy more or less pioneered the movement to the northern parts of the city – that is, the area around Washington Square (some professionals and some of the wealthy moved to, and commuted from, Brooklyn). By the late 1840s, not only were there wealthy families in the first, second, third, and fifth wards, where they had always been, but there were also more wealthy families than there had been in the fifteenth ward, and new settlements in the seventeenth and eighteenth wards. In the southern wards, the abandoned homes of the wealthy were cut up into multiple-dwelling units for the poor and the working classes.

Other homes were torn down as, toward 1860, these wards became less residential and instead housed a concentration of warehouses and industrial establishments. Even as early as 1850, perhaps 15 percent of the whole workforce worked in the second ward. Although there were, in addition to retail establishments and public markets, dozens of small manufacturing establishments in every ward in 1850, the industrial concentration toward the southern tip of the island was unmistakable. Thousands upon thousands

Figure 3. Map of New York City, 1851. Ward 12 is north of 86th Street. During the period 1852–4, wards 20, 21, and 22 were created, successively, north of 26th Street. [Source: *Great Metropolis: or New-York Almanac for 1851* (New York: H. Wilson, 1851).]

of workers in the needle trades, the leather trades, precious metals, and the printing trades found their employment in the second ward. There the ninety small printing establishments and eighty-eight larger ones included the American Bible Society, the American Tract Society, the city's printer, John H. Trow, Barnes, Scribners, and *The Herald* (Greeley's *Tribune* and Harper and Brothers were nearby in the fourth ward). There were other concentrations. Along the East River, the shipbuilding industries – including foundries, ironworks, nautical instrument makers, and other associated trades – made their imprint on the character of the seventh and eleventh wards, while on the West Side of the city trades that retained a smaller-scale, more artisanal character, like woodworking and furniture making, were located in the fifth, eighth, and ninth wards. To the north, in the eighteenth ward, there was room for the stoneyards supplying materials for urban construction, and to house the stables of the city's omnibus companies.

It should be emphasized, however, that at this early date there was industry almost everywhere. If the greatest concentration of shoemakers was in the second ward, for example, there were nevertheless hundreds of shoemakers employed in each of eight other wards; if the first and second wards provided employment for thousands in the needle trades, there was work as well in the sixth and seventh wards for another 4,000 workers and in each of eight other wards for hundreds of others.[3]

One limit to differentiation was that the working classes could not afford to commute to work, but continued to need to live within walking distance. There were similar (and related) limits to the ethnic differentiation of wards. Although there were many Germans in the tenth, eleventh, and seventeenth wards, and although by 1855 the first ward, along with the fourth and sixth wards (these latter being Irish-American communities of long standing), contained a population that was nearly half Irish, and although, finally, the ninth ward remained predominantly native-born in 1855, the most "immigrant" ward in the city was 30 percent native-born, the most native-born ward in the city was 35 percent immigrant, and most wards clustered around the mean of 52 percent foreign-born.[4]

Similar observations may be made about the choices of the wealthy. Although they chose to live on the same blocks as one another and there were notable concentrations of wealth in certain neighborhoods, these were dispersed enough that it could be said of at least half the wards (in 1845, the last year for which there are accurate data)[5] that they partook of a certain gold-coast-and-slum character. Not all wards had fashionable neighborhoods and not all wards had slums but few had neither and probably half had both. The trend of differentiation was clearly the dominant one: After the Civil War, indices of segregation of blacks, of immigrant groups, and of class all rose. Even in the antebellum period contemporary descriptions attributed certain kinds of character to particular wards: One was the seat of Quaker respectability, another the home of temperance, another German, another Irish, and so on. At the same time, the city retained a kind of social wholeness that was both symbolic and real. From the beginning to the end of the period, a mass meeting of merchants was held in the Exchange, a mass meeting of working men when called took place in City Hall Park, a mass meeting of citizens when called took place in Castle Garden. When Germans organized politically, it was not as representatives of the seventeenth ward, but in the citywide German League or German Democracy.

The city had nevertheless lost those underpinnings that enabled, earlier on, its functioning as an economic community bound by the traditions of a moral economy. The colonial city was more isolated from the currents of world trade and its economy – particularly in New York, where a sizable proportion of manufacture was, under imperial contract, to supply the army – could be subjected to various controls. In times of shortage, for example, the export of grain was stopped to keep local prices low. Wholesalers were forbidden to enter the market until the later hours of the day, so that consumers might have first choice of commodities and not be subjected to the price-raising practice of "forestalling." By contrast, the economy of the antebellum city was tied more closely to the development of the nation and the vagaries of world trade. Nothing brings home this relation so well as Peter Temin's rethinking of the panic of 1837. Temin's research demonstrated that the crash was not attributable to the demise of the national bank, to the pressures it brought to bear to perpetuate itself, to the specie circular, or to the practices of smaller state banks in the extension of credit. Rather, "a diminution in the capital flow from England to America was the force that led to the crisis." Similarly, the depression of 1855–7 was precipitated by international rather than local economic events.[6]

The same linkages that caused these crises were of course the basis of the city's economic growth. Through trade, the city's economy was linked to both Europe and the South. New York's merchants imported goods from England and Europe, primarily dry goods, metals, and wine. Of these, textiles were the most important, comprising a third of the imports (measured in value) to the United States, and it was a trade over which New York merchants had a virtual monopoly.[7] Metals in various forms – cutlery and hardware, semifinished bars, sheets, and rods, and heavier iron goods like rails for railroads, were also imported.[8] Some of these goods served as raw materials for New York's own industries; others were marketed, along with the products of New York's industries and the agricultural West, in the South. Southern purchases from New York's merchants were estimated at $76 million in 1849 and $131 million in 1859, as Southerners bought dry goods, boots and shoes, hardware, clothing, liquors, fruit, butter, and cheese from the same men who financed their crops and carried them to England.[9]

New York merchants, finally, also supplied the South with labor: In 1860, the London *Times* awarded New York City "the dubious honor of being the greatest slave-trading depot in the world." New York's merchants amassed tremendous profits conducting the slave trade between Africa and Cuba; the same trade kept up demand in the shipbuilding industries.[10]

The profits of trade, English capital, and the presence of immigrant labor also facilitated the growth of industry, and by 1860 New York was the leading manufacturing city in the nation, its 4,300 manufacturing establishments accounting for 8.1 percent of all U.S. manufacturers.[11] A third of all the nation's publishing happened in the city; New York was first in shipbuilding, sugar refining, and piano making; despite the head start of the New Englanders, by 1860 New York was also first in clothing production; "only the works along the Clyde" could rival the ironworks supplying the East River shipyards.[12]

The expansion of numbers and trade meant more opportunities for longshoremen, cartmen, watchmen, teamsters, laborers, domestic servants, and those in the building trades. In some trades, larger markets meant more opportunities, if credit could be had, to "compete with the wealthy capitalist," and a proliferation of small blacksmithing, metal manufacture, and other shops. Growth also meant, however, a changing organization of production and the appearance of new personages. For example, by 1860 the labor force was 27 percent female, and these women were not engaged in assisting their husbands or fathers but were employed in their own occupations: seamstresses and artificial-flower makers, mantua makers, paperbox makers, bookbinders, and straw workers, in addition to more traditional work in domestic service.[13] For the great majority of bakers, shoemakers, tailors, textile workers, and printers, a changing organization of production meant the end of hopes for master status (with or without credit) and instead a future of "wage-slavery." Growth during the antebellum period was profoundly disorganizing and unsettling, as fraught with anxiety for some as it was pregnant with opportunity for others. Industrialization was transforming the city of artisans and merchants into a city of employers and wage workers.

New York's fellow citizens may be grouped into six classes: capitalists, professionals, small proprietors, artisans, wage workers I, and wage workers II. The size of these classes in 1855 is shown in Table 3. Among *capitalists* are found merchants, bank directors, and self-identified "speculators." *Small proprietors* are owners of commercial and service shops like groceries, clothing stores, and barbers (owners of small manufactories, such as smiths, are included among the artisans). *Professionals* include doctors, lawyers, veterinarians, clergymen, and actors.

Artisans, wage workers I, and *wage workers II* constitute the working

Table 3. *Class structure of New York City, 1855*

Group	Number	Percent
Capitalists[a]	6,398	3.4
Small proprietors[b]	20,030	10.5
Professionals[c]	12,323	6.4
Artisans/mechanics[d]	23,310	12.2
Wage workers I[e]	54,103	28.3
Wage workers II[f]	74,895	39.2
Totals	191,059	100.0

[a]Financiers, manufacturers, merchants.

[b]Clothiers, dry-goods dealers, tobacconists, builders and contractors, hotel and boardinghouse keepers, food stores, restauranteurs, retail shopkeepers, barbers, undertakers, misc.

[c]Engineers, architects, lawyers, doctors, surgeons, teachers, clergy, 20% of clerks, misc.

[d]Blacksmiths, smiths (various), tinsmiths, coach and wagon makers, gunsmiths, musical instrument makers, precision instrument makers, one-third of brewers and distillers, shipbuilding trades, turners, carvers, gilders, half of those in the building trades, half of the cabinetmakers.

[e]Textile workers, weavers, misc. factory, dressmakers, seamstresses, shoemakers, printers, bakers, glassworkers, half of those in the building trades, bookbinders, ironworkers, packers, paperbox makers, straw workers, coopers, stevedores, brassworkers, two-thirds of brewers and distillers, sawyers, stonecutters, hatters, tailors, half of the cabinetmakers.

[f]Domestic servants, housekeepers, janitors, waiters, laundresses, laborers, porters, watchmen, hostelers and grooms, cartmen, draymen, teamsters, drovers, drivers, coachmen, expressmen, policemen, boatmen, railroad employees, 80% of the clerks.

Source: Calculated from Robert Ernst, *Immigrant Life in New York City, 1825–1863* (New York: King's Crown Press of Columbia University Press, 1949), appendix I. Ernst offers a listing, by ethnicity and occupation, of the entire work force reported in the manuscripts of the 1855 census. Table 3 is a total of United States–born, Ireland-born, Germany-born, and England- and Scotland-born workers. My total is somewhat lower than Ernst's, as I was unable to classify certain occupations and left out the smaller ethnic groups. Table 3 includes 89.2% of the total work force (men, women, and children) reported in the 1855 census.

A wide range of sources was used to gain an understanding of the social relations of work in various occupations. Some of the classifications are contentious, but this is in part a result of the fact that the reality was swiftly changing and consequently ambiguous. There are in any event so many occupations here that through a number of classifications and reclassifications the relative proportion of the classes in 1855 remained about the same.

classes. In a general way, it might be said that they differed from one another in income and status. More importantly, however, they differed from one another in the social relations of work, the organization of labor, and the relationship between occupation and the industrialization process. *Artisans* (or *mechanics*) include those journeymen and masters still engaged in traditional forms of production. Using shop size as a guide, perhaps two-thirds or three-quarters of these were journeymen and the rest masters. *Wage workers I* refers to those engaged in occupations that were at one time organized as crafts but had been or were rapidly being reorganized along more modern lines. *Wage workers II* includes many occupations that expanded as a result of population growth, but in which the organization of work was not changed because these occupations were never organized as crafts. Like shopkeepers, more longshoremen, watchmen, domestics, and clerks were needed as the city expanded. Wage workers I and wage workers II, then, are both proletarian classes. Workers in both groups might be expected to form unions, for example, in contrast to the trade or craft associations found among the artisans. Wage workers I and II differ from one another, however, in what might be termed their economic ancestry: Occupations found in the class wage workers I were once organized as crafts, whereas occupations found in the class wage workers II were always performed as wage labor or in conditions of servitude. Each of New York's six classes requires a brief discussion.

Today we refer to the wealthy collectively as "businessmen" or "capitalists"; in the antebellum era men of great wealth were commonly termed "merchants," and in fact overseas trade was the greatest source of fortune before the Civil War. For example, Alexander T. Stewart emigrated to New York from northern Ireland in the 1820s with a stock of lace and became in time New York's "dry goods king," opening a "retail palace" in the city and importing directly from overseas. Like other men of wealth, Stewart diversified his interests. He was a bank director and also invested in street railways.[14] Anson Phelps, a self-made man, was primarily a merchant who imported metals and exported raw cotton and who played an important role by pioneering a regular packet boat to Charleston. Phelps also helped to develop the domestic supply of iron by investing in western Pennsylvania.[15] Moses Taylor, James Boorman, Walter R. Jones, Moses Grinnell, and William H. Aspinwall all made fortunes in trade; like Stewart and Phelps, they also made other investments.[16]

Real estate and finance were prominent among the other sources of wealth. Insurance companies, though they involved severe risks, also delivered great profits.[17] Private bankers like the firm of Prime, Ward, and King and banks more generally were excellent investments. Among those whose names will appear later in discussions of politics were the bankers Preserved Fish, Saul Alley, Stephen Allen, and Moses Grinnell (with the exception of Edward

Prime, none of these men were primarily bankers). Most wealthy men also had investments in real estate. Some, like Henry Brevoort, Evert A. Bancker, the Bleeckers, and the Lawrences, inherited land upstate, on Long Island, or in the city that had been in their families since colonial times. Others invested in city real estate, the Astors being the most famous, and William E. Dodge, Peter Goelet, the Rhinelanders, the Lorillards, the Schermerhorns, and Samuel B. Ruggles among them.[18] Ruggles was in some ways exemplary for the diversity of his interests. In addition to investing in real estate, he was one of the owners of the New York and Harlem Railroad, owned $10,000 worth of stock in the Chemical Bank, and invested in manufacturing.[19]

Some "merchants" did earn fortunes through investment in manufacturing. Most politically prominent was William F. Havemeyer, a sugar refiner who was three times mayor of New York. James P. Allaire, in addition to being a merchant, was also an important manufacturer of marine engines.[20] Peter Cooper began with a glue factory; Effingham Schieffelin[21] was a drug manufacturer; William Colgate was "the soap king";[22] Henry Eckford was a shipbuilder.

Small proprietors – clothiers, grocers, boardinghouse keepers – were in 1855 about 10 percent of the gainfully employed men, the largest group outside the working classes. The growth of the city, particularly in an age when most people could not afford public transportation, meant a proliferation of small shops. This was, moreover, a kind of ownership to which immigrants might reasonably aspire. Of the city's 20,030 small proprietors in 1855, 3,680 (18 percent) were Irish and nearly 6,000 (30 percent) were German.

"Professionals" encompasses a quite diverse group. Schoolteachers and clerks, for example, though they might claim more social status than those who worked with their hands, were not very well paid. Clerks might be employed as accountants or, if they were family members or in mercantile firms, as apprentices en route to becoming partners. Others, however, worked for the government or were what we would term "salespeople." Thus, half the clerks are included here among the professionals, and the remaining half are classed with wage workers II. The lawyers' group was expanding steadily but its quality, at least in the view of George Templeton Strong, declining. Strong's estimation of his fellow lawyers suggests that expanded opportunities to join the ranks of professionals were not altogether welcome:

> About one hundred ornaments of our liberal and enlightened profession
> ... were congregated in the Special Term room this morning. I scru-
> tinized the crowd, to determine how many there were whom I would
> be willing to receive as visitors at this house, or rather whom I would
> not be annoyed and disgusted to receive. There were really not more
> than *three* who were not stamped by appearance, diction, or manner

as belonging to a low social station ... It was manifestly a mob of low-bred, illiterate, tenth-rate attorneys, though it included many successful and conspicuous practitioners. Such is the bar of New York. May our Columbia College law school do something about it.[23]

Three occupations among the professionals had a social and political impact far beyond their numbers. Doctors were the most vocal among those calling for housing codes, "sanitary police," and the like, and they also pressed for professional rather than political staffs at the city's almshouse and hospitals.[24] Though little was done in this regard in the antebellum period, the reports and documents researched by doctors laid the groundwork for such measures.

Second, ministers (among whom there was a variety of wealth and social standing, even as there was for lawyers) organized for – in addition to congregational obligations – education, the temperance movement, and the nativist movement. For many of the city's children, the Sunday School, more of an educational than a religious endeavor, was the only form of education to which they had access. Ministers were prominent in the temperance movement (and the Baptists at a general meeting gave their approval to the Maine liquor law). Organized anti-Catholicism began with efforts of the ministry. Some men, like Hiram Ketchum or Gardiner Spring, were both famous ministers and prominent in politics throughout the antebellum period; many others played roles that, if less eminent, were nevertheless crucial.

Third, the newspaper editors were a powerful political force. It was in the antebellum period that daily papers became mass papers (with the exception of papers like the *Journal of Commerce* – roughly the equivalent of the *Wall Street Journal*) and they were both influential and wholly partisan. In the mid-1830s, the combined circulation of the city's papers was over 30,000; by the mid-1850s the combined circulation of the city's papers, led by the *Herald*, which accounted for about half the papers sold, was probably closer to 100,000. For the modern reader, the partisanship and rhetoric of the antebellum newspaper is quite a shock. A contemporary commentator who nicknamed the city's papers the *Blunder and Bluster, The Jacobin, The Sewer, The Inexpressible,* and the *Episcopal Banner* was not far off the mark. Except for the 1840s, when the *Herald* claimed to be an independent paper (and, I think, was – at least it vacillated in the party it supported) the partisan affiliations of these papers were quite explicit.[25] Their reporting of their own party's affairs, however, is invaluable. And their influence – on collective violence, on party unity, and on men's political fortunes – was great.[26]

In the Jacksonian city, artisans were the largest of the working classes. By artisans, or mechanics, is meant those producers who worked in small shops in which a master craftsman directed journeymen, journeymen might reasonably aspire to master status for themselves, and journeymen trained a small number of apprentices. This system had never operated in the United States with the force it had in Europe, for the opportunities for journeymen to move elsewhere to attain independence (and claim master status) were great. Nevertheless, "master," "journeyman," and "apprentice" were terms that had real meaning not only in the colonial era, but in some trades until well after the Civil War. In the Jacksonian city, they accounted for the largest part of the working classes.[27] Many trades were still being practiced much as they had been a generation before. Leather and saddle making, jewelry production, black- and other smithing, cabinetry, shipbuilding, and many kinds of carpentry, for example, were crafts practiced along traditional lines. The typical workplace of the Jacksonian city was the small shop, craft organization was common, and mechanization barely existed.

In these trades, organizations uniting masters and journeymen persisted as the artisanal organization of work endured. Manufacturing jewelers, coopers, pipemakers, and some cabinetmakers and butchers maintained trade or "protective" organizations. In the building trades, too, there were opportunities for small-scale contracting, and there were also crafts organizations uniting master and journeyman late in the antebellum years. Mechanics' Mutual Protection, for example, was a secret organization mainly of building-trades artisans. Organized in 1841, Mechanics' Mutual Protection chapters were still listed in the city directories in the mid-1850s. Organization leaders made much of MMP's Christian principles, arguing that the interests of masters and journeymen were the same and declaring strikes both unnecessary and pernicious.[28]

Craft sentiment and trade solidarity were not limited to occupations that could be practiced on a small scale. In the shipbuilding trades, workers were very militant and succeeded in winning wage concessions from their employers, maintaining an apprenticeship system and retaining considerable control over production. At the same time, these militant artisans exhibited a sense of the craft that sometimes included even the wealthy shipbuilder. Christian Bergh and Jacob A. Westervelt owned one of the three largest shipbuilding firms in the city, yet at the time of his death Bergh wished it known only that "the oldest ships carpenter in the city" had died.[29] Henry Eckford, owner of another of the big three, worked with his men for the ten-hours movement, organized a volunteer fire company with his workers, and offered the use of his "gang" to his party.[30] For these men and for others in crafts and protective organizations, the brotherhood of craft and trade was stronger than divisions of wealth or status.

Impressive as these solidarities were, by the middle of the 1850s only a few trades maintained either the small shop or the solidarities of the craft. As early as Jackson's first term, contemporary observers were beginning to draw attention to those who "are journeymen, and many of whom will never be anything but journeymen."[31] A strong contingent in the

Workingmen's Party sought to exclude "bosses" from its ranks. After the party's demise, organizations were formed excluding masters, a claim to the "class" interests of journeymen as distinct from the claims of the craft. Tailors, cordwainers, leather dressers, and some building-trades workers organized in journeymen's societies in the 1830s, and in 1833 the General Trades' Union, a union of unions, was organized in New York. For their part, master tailors, employing leather dressers, and manufacturers and retailers of boots and shoes organized to resist the "dangerous" and "subversive" combinations of journeymen.[32] As the creation of these societies suggested, masters (at least the more ambitious, clever, and fortunate ones) were headed in one historical direction, whereas journeymen were headed in another.

Pressure on the artisan's style of production came from various places. Trade with Europe and the American South and Midwest brought the products of New York's artisans into far-flung markets and made producers dependent on merchants. Merchants brought artisans into competition with industrialized producers overseas by importing finished goods.[33] Cabinetmakers were faced with this competition in the middle 1830s, and masters and journeymen struggled together against importing merchants, protesting against and on occasion destroying foreign-made goods. Merchants selling to the Southern market also pressured mechanics to reorganize their work to increase efficiency and make goods cheaper. It was in this way that pressure was put on those tailors, shoemakers, and furniture makers whose products were destined for the Southern market. Although the small shop still predominated in the 1830s, contractors, wholesale manufacturers, and other middlemen contracted work either with masters and journeymen, or directly with journeymen, exerting pressure to lower prices and eroding the autonomy of the trades. Not surprisingly, merchants and contractors became targets for artisan protest. Mechanics voiced the view that the "usurpation" of their rights and "abridgement of their privileges" occurred by

> opposing them in their business with the advantages of a large capital
> ... men who are no mechanics ... are engaged in mechanical concerns
> ... at the expense of the interest of the legitimate mechanics; ... and
> in many cases, preventing the industrious, enterprising, but perhaps
> indigent mechanic, from following his trade to advantage, or from fol-
> lowing it at all.[34]

"It is well known," another artisan wrote, "that innovations upon the rights of journeymen have seldom originated with those who have themselves served a regular apprenticeship, and worked as journeymen. Almost always do they come from speculators, who steal into a business as adventurers."[35]

Such views were more comforting than accurate, for many masters hoped to "compete with the wealthy capitalist."[36] These ex-journeymen had less capital than many of their competitors but they had the advantage of an

intimate knowledge of the craft. That knowledge facilitated the reorganization of production and, in moments of inspiration, led to mechanical
invention as well as complex new divisions of labor that required less skill
among the journeymen. In one of the city's best-known stories of frugal
and intelligent masters-made-good, James Harper and his brothers brought
knowledge of the craft, carefully acquired capital, technical innovation, and
marketing skill to bear on the publication of books. Like other small masters,
they assisted in the transformation of printers' trades into the publishing
industry.

Even more than other craftsmen, printers could look back to the colonial
era for models not only of their skill but also of their importance in the
struggle for liberty. In the eighteenth century, a master printer was in fact
a publisher, on the model made famous by Benjamin Franklin. Printers
wrote and printed newspapers, provided American editions of foreign books,
and published broadsides and political pamphlets. By 1830, "publishers"
had appeared, men who owned newspapers and hired others to produce
them. Commons describes the process in this way:

> The practical printer, in this development, began to lose control of the
> business. When news travelled slowly he could, if he wished to extend
> his general printing business, publish a periodical paper. He could edit
> it, and, with the aid of a journeyman and one or two apprentices, could
> set the type and do the presswork. Under the new order of things a
> knowledge of printing was no longer of first importance; it was rather
> the ability to promote a paper, get funds, win subscribers, and promote
> some special interests. Thus men began to engage in the business not
> primarily for the livelihood, but to propagate an interest such as politics,
> agriculture, industry, or labour.[37]

In the publication of books as well, setting the type and doing the press-
work became divorced from running the business. If James Harper was to
be found from time to time on the shop floor giving advice, his greater
contribution was the development of novel sales strategies aimed at the
Western market. Harper and Brothers pioneered by offering book series for
adults, children, and families. The firm also sold innovative illustrated Bibles.
One volume from the firm's series for older children still serves as the best
description we have of mid-nineteenth-century book printing. *The Harper
Establishment, or How the Story Books are Made* describes the elaborate
and precise division of labor among dozens of men, women, boys, and girls.
The compositor, the author tells us, "has every inducement to learn to work
fast, for he is paid, not by the time, but by the quantity of work which he
accomplishes," more precisely, "the amount of *corrected* work that they
do." Girls rubbing type were "so dextrous and quick, indeed, that you will
have to look very closely to follow." Men and boys smoothing paper also
worked "with a dexterity and rapidity that is surprising." The foreman,

meanwhile, "can survey his whole dominion, and observe the action of all the presses and machinery" from the vantage point of an elevated desk.[38]

The Harper and Brothers' printing establishment represented the most elaborate and advanced industrial organization. It was something of a rarity, for there were not many large factories in the city. Those that did exist were often managed with the kind of paternalism associated with Lowell or Pullman. James Harper was known to be a kind and fatherly employer, often to be seen on the shop floor both superintending and offering personal counsel.[39] Owners of large foundries, James P. Allaire, Henry Worral, and John G. Rohr, seem to have managed their operations similarly. I have found no report of union activities among their employees before 1850. Allaire, moreover, organized a volunteer fire company in the seventh ward, where his foundry was, and Allaire, Worral, and Rohr were all prominent at meetings of Whig "mechanics."[40]

Few ambitious masters, even the successful ones, ended up presiding over neatly organized factory establishments. Rather, the ambitious master was in many ways more like the contractor. A master with expanding trade was likely to find himself increasingly occupied with his suppliers and buyers, with finances, credit, and bookkeeping. At the same time, he was reorganizing production if not engaged in it himself. Apprenticeship was rapidly becoming illusory, a euphemism for child labor. Journeymen too were restricted in their field of operation, performing an ever narrower range of tasks as part of a broadening division of labor. Work was increasingly subdivided, the piece wage used as both carrot and stick in efforts to increase productivity. Some of this reorganization took place in workshops, but more commonly employer and employee were not at the same site; as the size of a master's payroll grew, an increasing proportion of workers were outside his immediate supervision. Employees commonly rented work space in lofts or shacks, or worked at home. These "outworkers" accounted for the majority of employees in the industrializing crafts.[41]

By the middle of the last antebellum decade, these employees were artisans no longer. Most of those engaged in trades producing consumer goods were simply wage workers; 35.5 percent of the working classes were wage workers I. Outworkers in a number of trades tried to organize cooperative workshops and stores but these quickly succumbed to competition. More frequently and more successfully, men and women organized unions. Most journeymen's associations founded in the 1830s had not survived the depression of 1837 and the hard years of the decade that followed. There were some efforts at organization in the 1840s despite hard times. The Laborer's Union Association was organized in 1843 and chartered as a benevolent society by the legislature in 1845. In 1846, the laborers struck, apparently unsuccessfully, for an increase in wages; in 1850, their strike was more successful.[42] In 1845, there was an effort to organize a Female Industry

53

Association, with delegates from the tailoresses, shirtmakers, book folders and stitchers, cap makers, straw workers, dressmakers, crimpers, and fringe and lace makers among those in attendance.[43]

As prosperity returned, organization flowered. In 1850, there was a sudden upsurge in union formation. Hat finishers, white-work weavers, turners, upholsterers, button and fringe makers, quarrymen, marble cutters, stonecutters, boot and shoe workers, saddle and harness makers, boilermakers, iron moulders, journeymen silversmiths, type founders, and tailors organized or reorganized to raise wages or better working conditions.[44] Straw and pamilla sewers organized a union in the same year.[45] Journeymen house carpenters and journeymen painters, who had been organized in the 1830s, formed new organizations after 1850, and laborers in the building trades organized as well.[46]

This burgeoning organizational life was accompanied by a protest against the degradation from independence to "wage slavery." One union broadside, for example, declared that

> competition is an evil only because labor is a marketable commodity, or because labor is dependent upon capital in the hands of other persons than laborers . . . Equally possessed of the means of earning a livelihood, they would be content to do so . . .[47]

Strikes would "prevent the growth of an unwholesome aristocracy, whose only aim is to acquire wealth by robbery of the toiling masses" and enable labor to "take that position which God intended man should fill – truly independent of his fellow, and above the position of mere 'wage-slaves.' "[48] Workers also protested the loss of status that came with the loss of independence. With few exceptions, however, unions announced that it "is useless for us to disguise from ourselves the fact that, under the present arrangement of things, there exists a perpetual antagonism between labor and capital."[49]

Even more numerous than the first group of wage workers was a second, those laborers, clerks, drivers, porters, and domestics whose work had never held the status of the crafts. These workers were 49 percent of the working classes in 1855. Despite their numbers, and perhaps because of their low status, they are the least studied of the working classes. There were many women in this class, for domestic servants, housekeepers, and laundresses were here. It is also the most heavily foreign-born of the classes (see Figure 4). Whereas 73 percent of the artisans and 80 percent of wage workers I were born overseas, 85 percent of wage workers II were immigrants. Perhaps because they had so many sisters, brothers, husbands, and cousins among the wage workers I in the labor movement, the upsurge of unionism in 1850 embraced wage workers II as well. In 1850, not only those in the needle and building trades but also omnibus drivers, public porters, and coachmen

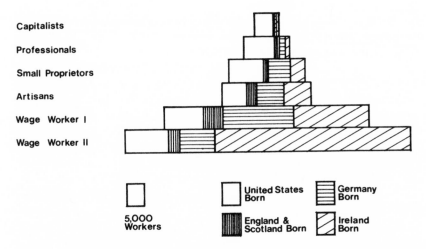

Figure 4. Cultural division of labor in New York City, 1855. [*Source*: Calculated from Robert Ernst, *Immigrant Life in New York City, 1825–1863* (New York: King's Crown Press of Columbia University Press, 1949), appendix I.]

formed unions. Between 1849 and 1852, boot and shoe clerks, dry-goods clerks, grocers' clerks, actors, and barbers also formed employees' organizations.[50]

The foreign-born, who by 1855 constituted half the city's population, accounted for 72 percent of the work force. Only among small proprietors were immigrants represented in proportions approximating their presence in the population as a whole, as the foreign-born contributed only a few to the ranks of capitalists and professionals and filled the great majority of positions among the working classes.

This meant that growth was not only experienced differently by those who occupied different places in the class structure, but also that different ethnic groups experienced growth from divergent vantage points. Unlike those born in the United States, a majority of the foreign-born were found among the wage workers (see Table 4). This was especially true of the Irish, who were found in greatest numbers as laborers and domestics. Their disadvantaged position is revealed not only in the occupations of the men and women, but also in the fact that the Irish had a much higher labor-force participation rate than other groups; their women and children sought work in greater numbers than the family members of other groups. Similarly, though not quite as dramatically, a majority of those born in Germany were found in the working classes. The Germans, however, contributed only a few to the second group of wage workers, as nearly half of all German workers were in the wage workers I category, the most common occupations

Table 4. *Class structure of New York City, 1855, by nation of origin (whole work force)*

| | Ireland-born | | Germany-born | |
	Number	Percent	Number	Percent
Capitalists	306	0.4	663	1.5
Small proprietors	3,680	4.3	5,967	13.9
Professionals	1,627	2.0	1,660	3.9
Mechanics/artisans	7,328	8.6	6,983	16.2
Wage workers I	20,019	23.6	18,727	43.5
Wage workers II	51,740	61.1	9,027	21.0
Totals	84,700	100.0	43,027	100.0

| | U.S.-born | | England- and Scotland-born | |
	Number	Percent	Number	Percent
Capitalists	4,934	9.9	495	3.7
Small proprietors	9,234	18.4	1,149	8.7
Professionals	7,831	15.6	1,205	9.1
Mechanics/artisans	6,190	12.4	2,809	21.2
Wage workers I	10,422	20.8	4,935	37.2
Wage workers II	11,464	22.9	2,664	20.1
Totals	50,075	100.0	13,257	100.0

Source: Calculated from Robert Ernst, *Immigrant Life in New York City, 1825–1863* (New York: King's Crown Press of Columbia University Press, 1949), appendix I.

of German men including tailors, shoemakers, bakers, turners, hatters, and those in the building trades. Another sixth of the German workforce were mechanics, and included in the most common occupations of the Germans are (again) those in the building trades, cabinetmakers, turners, and smiths. The experience of the English and Scottish was similar to that of the Germans. While 20 percent of English and Scottish workers were in the wage workers II class, and an additional 37 percent in the wage workers I class, fully a fifth of these immigrants were found among the mechanics. Like United States–born workers, their most common occupations included clerks, smiths, carpenters, and machinists. Carol Pernicone has shown that, although not as dramatic as in 1855, this cultural division of labor was significant as early as 1820.[51] The picture presented here probably under-represents ethnic layers, for some categories (for example textile, clothing manufacture, and building trades) could not be disaggregated; however, secondary sources suggest that there was an ethnic division of labor within them, in which Germans and American-born workers enjoyed superior positions to the Irish.

It should be clear that it would be incorrect to think of American-born workers as having been "pushed up" by the immigrants: The places opening up at the bottom of the class structure far outnumbered those at the top. If by comparison to the immigrants the United States–born were doing well, by comparison to their situation a generation or two before they had lost a great deal of status and autonomy. The diverse processes that constituted growth reorganized the urban social structure. The artisan and his shop no longer dominated the scene; the proletarian classes formed the great majority of the work force. In place of the artisans' shops were larger manufactures, large-scale outwork, and, in a few trades, factories. In 1840, a firm employing a dozen workers was unusually large. By 1855, more than 90 percent of the manufacturing labor force worked in firms with more than 10 employees, 70 percent worked for employers with more than 25 hands, and 34.5 percent worked for employers whose payrolls exceeded 100 names.[52] Women in particular were employed in factories and by large-scale outwork contractors. Whereas the average number of male workers per establishment was 14.9 in 1855, for women the number was 25.9. In those industries in which women formed the majority of the work force (paper-box making, some sectors of clothing manufacture, artificial flower making, millinery production), the deskilling of the work force and imposition of newer divisions of labor proceeded as rapidly as, if not more rapidly than, in shoemaking and tailoring trades.[53]

Many smaller manufacturing establishments and shops remained. In 1860, there were 2,045 firms that employed ten or fewer persons. Industrialization had affected these as well, however, for the average capital investment in these firms was $3,450. The cost of materials probably equaled this amount.[54] If here can be found those who maintained the small shop and its solidarity, here as well were those who depended on credit to "compete with the wealthy capitalist."

In other cities, as in New York, the social structure was reorganized by industrialization and immigration. Not only in factory towns like Lynn and Lowell, but also in the nation's metropolises, getting, spending, and producing were reordered in the antebellum years. In Baltimore, manufacturers and corporate directors rose to prominence, challenging the city's merchant elite. More than New York, in Baltimore manufacturing was done in factories, but even in the handicraft trades an increased division of labor and the labor of women and children displaced the artisan. Independent, small-shop craftsmen were decimated: Fewer than one in ten of the shops operating in 1850 remained in business in 1860.[55] In Philadelphia, industrialization took many forms. Alongside the artisans' or neighborhood shops the newer forms – outwork, the sweatshop, large-scale manufacturing and factories – employed the preponderance of productive workers by 1850.[56] Philadelphia exhibited an elaborate cultural division of labor by the same date. Nearly half the Irish were employed as day laborers, at carting, or in hand-loom weaving. Nearly 12 percent of the Germans worked as day laborers, whereas two-thirds worked in skilled trades. The United States–born whites were even less engaged in unskilled labor and the industrialized crafts, concentrating instead on "the prestigious building trades and printing and disproportionately represented in commerce and the professions."[57]

In Newark, an increased division of labor and the invention of productive machinery "rendered craftsmen's skills obsolete."[58] At the election of Jackson, the city's major productive pursuits – hatting, leather making, trunk making, jewelry making, saddle making, and shoemaking – were all, save shoemaking, performed in traditional ways. By the election of Lincoln, all had been industrialized to some extent.[59] Here, too, the foreign-born were concentrated in the most industrialized, least skilled, and least secure employments.[60] In Boston, industrial expansion was fueled by massive immigration, with the number employed in major industries doubling between 1845 and 1855 and again between 1855 and 1865. In the needle trades, sugar refining, and furniture making, cheap labor facilitated a more elaborate division of labor and mechanical invention changed the practice of the craft. In the 1850s, new rolling mills, forges, ironworks, and rail factories were also established in the city. With more women employed in the needle trades alone than in the entire male work force, Boston was the site of the archetypal Irish needle woman, and since very nearly half the Ireland-born men worked as day laborers, the Irish took their place here as elsewhere near the bottom of the cultural division of labor.[61] Pittsburgh's iron, glass, and cotton industries all expanded in the antebellum era, the first most spectacularly, and Pittsburgh was the site of considerable industrial combat. Ironworkers struck repeatedly in the 1840s, and women in the cotton mills struck and rioted in the same decade. While "capitalistic aristocrats lolled on sofas and lounged in their princely mansions," their workers were "ground into poverty."[62] There, as in the other cities discussed here, the antebellum years were a time of transformation from an eighteenth- to a nineteenth-century social order.

This sketch of New York City's fellow citizens and social reordering provides important clues in understanding the rhetoric, visions, and appeals of the city's politicians. New York's Workingmen, for example, were hardly mistaken in their claim that the economy of the union was in the hands of English bankers. Early in the period, when the greatest wealth was derived from trade, banking, and real estate, Workingmen had good

Table 5. *New York City electorate, 1825–65*
(number of men legally eligible to vote)

Year	Voters	Percent increase
1825	18,283	
1835	43,091	135.7[a]
1845	63,927	48.4
1855	88,877	39.0
	(46,173 native-born	
	42,704 naturalized)	
1865	128,975	45.1
	(51,500 native-born	
	77,475 naturalized)	
1825–65		605.4

[a]A portion of this increase may be due to eligibility changes enacted in 1827. Leutscher claimed that constitutional changes in 1827 increased the size of the city's electorate by at least 5%. George D. Leutscher, *Early Political Machinery in the United States* (Philadelphia, University of Pennsylvania Press, 1903), p. 16. McCormick, however, found that the constitutional changes of 1821 resulted in "virtually free suffrage" for white men. Richard P. McCormick, "New Perspectives on Jacksonian Politics," in F. A. Bonadio, *Political Parties in American History*, Volume 2, 1828–1890 (New York: Putnam, 1974), p. 52.

Sources: New York State, Secretary of State, *Census of the State of New York, for 1855* (Albany: Van Benthuysen, 1857), pp. xliii, 8. New York State, Secretary of State, *Census of the State of New York, for 1865* (Albany: Van Benthuysen, 1867), p. 9.

reason to locate exploitation in exchange rather than industry. Productive images too, however, were a part of the general imagery, with England as the model both for those who feared the factory system and those who aspired to industrial greatness. The transformation of social structure underlay changes in Democratic rhetoric from appeals to the "independent mechanics" to rallies of the "hard-working masses." Glimpses have been offered here of how those occupying certain social places organized themselves as social forces – unions or Mechanics' Mutual Protection, for example.

These general resonances, however, are not the same as mobilizing the population to vote, nor did they determine the shape of New York's municipal institutions. Social reordering did not prefigure a particular political balance or new political arrangements. The "social revolution" was never-theless central to the city's political reordering. Political economy, class, and status provided themes of political discourse and reason for political argument (though of course there were many other things to argue about). More profoundly, both the stresses and the new solidarities attendant on industrialization were paralleled by changes in social relations in the wards. In conjunction with an expanded electorate, these latter changes made older forms of political organization unworkable. If the reorganization of getting, spending, and producing did not embody a new political life, it did effectively undermine a political order based on elite leadership and the communitarian quality of city and ward. If this were not enough, population growth meant that the electorate was expanding at a very rapid rate (see Table 5). Thus the leaders of the second American party system had an enormous task before them. How they accomplished it is the subject of the next chapter.

4 The second American party system

NEW YORK'S FELLOW CITIZENS in the Jacksonian era were artisan, wage worker, and small proprietor, merchant and employer, immigrant and native-born, Protestant and Catholic. Their social differences were at times the focus of political argument and at times marginal to political debate; their antagonisms were sometimes organized into politics and sometimes fought in the street. The political environment of the antebellum city organized some differences into political life and excluded or reshaped others. That political environment had two elements. The more prominent of these was the establishment of political parties. The second was the persistence of values and habits of long standing in local politics. Cultural inheritance and Jacksonian revolution together provided a tentative political order for New York's social transformation.

In New York, as in cities across the nation, the major contenders for power between 1834 and 1850 were the Whig and Democratic parties. These parties were organized to achieve national rather than local goals. The Tammany organization had existed for decades, but found its partisan banner at the election of Jackson in 1828. Whigs were formally organized in 1834 to oppose Jackson's administration. The debate of the parties in the city was largely a repetition of their congressional argument, and local ascendancy was most valuable as a means to the larger end of national victory.

Each party had nevertheless to recruit constituencies locally. Party-building prospects may have seemed brighter in New York than elsewhere, for New York's upstate politicians had pioneered, a decade earlier, in arguing the legitimacy of party politics. In the view of New York's Albany Regency, not only were parties a boon to the republic, but party loyalty was a virtue and party "usages" were the safeguard of democracy.[1] The thought in some ways outpaced the deed. In 1834, there was little party organization in the city and no ward organization that existed year-round. Rather, as Ronald Formisano has suggested, "early republican politics were rooted far more deeply in pre-party political culture than is conventionally allowed."[2] The organizers of the second American party system faced the task of adapting political habits of long standing to the newer demands of partisanship. Political leadership, for example, had long been the province of wealthy men, an extension of their social leadership in neighborhood and ward, and a tribute (at least in their own view) to their leading role in the economy. At the election of Jackson, most of the city's elective offices were still held by very wealthy men, but over the next decade or so they were replaced by career politicians. These men, though they were the vanguard of a new era of mass politics, also bore a strong stylistic resemblance to the patricians they were replacing. Adapting the patrician style to lesser personal wealth and to the demands of partisanship, the career politician began to create the persona of the boss and the institutions of mass politics. That was the work of the Jacksonian revolution, a revolution that was common to Whig and Democratic parties alike.

WHIGS VERSUS DEMOCRATS

The question, "Who supported the Whigs, and who supported the Democrats?" has been answered in two ways. One view, the "old-fashioned view" of Arthur Schlesinger, Jr.,[3] and later Frank Otto Gatell,[4] is that the Whigs were the party of wealth and the Democrats were the party of the working classes. The second, new-fashioned view of Lee Benson[5] is that partisanship was the product of ethnocultural values and ties. Surely the parties *sounded* like the old-fashioned view was true: Democrats championed the hard-fisted workingmen while Whigs lauded the credit system. In support of the new-fashioned view, the American Republican victory in 1844 argues for the importance of ethnocultural ties. Beyond these indications, there are reasons to be skeptical of both accounts.

The old-fashioned view of Schlesinger and Gatell took Democratic claims to be the "true home of the working classes" at face value, along with Democratic accusations that the Whigs were the "aristocratic" party. Schlesinger saw the Democrats as the natural inheritors of the supporters of the Workingmen's Party; Gatell argued that the great majority of the city's men of wealth supported the Whigs. Neither of these claims is correct.

Both Whigs and Democrats inherited Workingmen leaders and supporters, a fact that is not surprising when it is understood that some factions of the Workingmen's Party, which supported Clay, were probably "proto-Whigs" from the outset. Adoniram Chandler, for example, one of the wealthier Workingmen, successfully ran for state assembly on the Whig ticket in 1837. Simon Clannon, a painter, was a Workingmen's candidate for the State Assembly in 1828, but objected to Tammany's favors to "small fry" banks and joined the Whigs in 1834. He was their (unsuccessful) candidate for alderman of the sixth ward in 1848.[6] Cornelius McLean, a sashmaker, was another prominent Workingman and appeared in 1840 as the Whig candidate for alderman of the fourteenth ward. Isaac Odell was active in the Workingmen's Party in 1829–30. The carpenter's delegate to the General Trades' Union, he was a recognized labor leader and a candidate on the Whig ticket for various offices in the 1830s.[7] Other Workingmen did join Tammany. Nathan Darling, a painter, served on the Workingmen's executive committee in 1830, joined Tammany, and managed to obtain an appointment as an inspector in the Customs House. Stephen Harris, an eighth-ward Workingmen's leader, was twice Democratic candidate for alderman. Shoemaker George W. McPherson joined the Workingmen in 1832 and by 1835 was a member of Tammany's Young Men's General Committee.[8] Like these leaders, the supporters of the Workingmen were found in both parties. Democrats seem to have attracted more support for their mayoral candidates from ex-Workingmen, but the wards that had been strongest in support of the Workingmen sent more Whig than Democratic aldermen to the city council.[9] The Democrats, then, did not inherit the leaders or the supporters of the Workingmen's Party wholesale. As to the city's men of wealth, Chapter 7 will show that they too were divided between the parties. Although the Whigs spoke more loudly about their merchant leaders, Democrats were never at a loss for wealthy supporters.

The new-fashioned, ethnocultural view was a result of an effort to link partisanship to "deeply rooted values deriving from the total range of [voters'] human experiences."[10] Lee Benson examined party images and party platforms and concluded that "Whigs were more likely than Democrats to share puritanical attitudes ... piety, sobriety, thrift, 'steady-habits,' and 'book learning.' " The party received support from "the majority of native Protestants *in every ward*" of the city, and among English, Scots, Welsh, and Protestant Irish immigrants.[11] For their part, Democrats valued "hell-of-a-fellow, individualistic characteristics" like "great personal courage, unusual physical powers," or "the ability to drink a quart of whisky ... without the quiver of a muscle." Insisting that the groups "that voted Democratic also happened to be largely lower class in composition reflects a casual rather than a causal relationship,"[12] Benson found strong Democratic support in the city among Irish Catholics, French, and new German voters.[13]

Several objections may be made to this account. First, Benson did not examine the voting behavior of New York City's electorate. Rather, he inferred the dispositions of the city's ethnic groups from the behavior of similarly defined groups Upstate.[14] Local voting returns collected for this study, however, do not reveal strong partisan dispositions on the part of ethnic groups. Second, Benson greatly overestimated the number of Irish voters in the city in the Jacksonian era; as a result, he underestimated the American-born support for the Democratic Party.[15] If indeed the "majority of native Protestants in every ward" had supported the Whigs, the Whig Party would have been the city's majority party by a considerable margin

Table 6. *Correlations of the Democratic percentage of total vote for mayor, New York, 1838–43*

	38						
38	1	39					
39	.99	1	40				
40	.97	.96	1	41			
41	.95	.96	.96	1	42		
42	.92	.94	.93	.97	1	43	
43	.86	.90	.87	.93	.97	1	

Note: Entries are the correlations of the ward-level Democratic percentage of the total vote. There were 17 wards in 1838–45.

until after 1850. In fact, though the party system in the city was competitive, the Democrats were clearly in the lead until the American Republican Party appeared in 1844. Third, Benson used the election of 1844 to discover partisan preferences for ethnocultural groups. The appearance of the American Republican Party in that year (boasting Whig endorsement), maximized ethnocultural polarization. This had a profound impact on voting patterns in the city's wards, reorganizing partisan coalitions. Thus 1844 is an unfortunate choice as a bench mark for the second American party system.

What can be determined about the second American party system in New York City? First, it was highly competitive. Although the Democrats won seven of the nine mayoral contests from 1834 (the first year the office was elective) to 1843 (the last year before the nativist American Republican Party appeared), they were hardly a confident majority party. In 1834, 1839, and 1841, the Democrats won with less than 51 percent of the two-party vote, and in 1840 and 1842 victory was accomplished with 52 percent of the two-party vote – a more comfortable margin, but hardly firm control. (In 1836 and 1843, the Democrats did win with comfortable margins; in 1835, there was no election; Whigs won in 1837 and 1838. See Figure 1.) Moreover, the Democrats did not control the Common Council as often as they won the mayor's office. In nine elections to select the city's aldermen, Whigs comprised the majority of council members on four occasions (1834, 1837, 1838, and 1842), the Democrats elected the majority an equal number of years (1839, 1840, 1841, and 1843), and in 1836 the council was evenly split.

Second, voting returns from each of the seventeen wards in the city indicate that voting alignments were extremely stable in the second American party system. Table 6 displays the interelection correlations of the Democratic percentage of the two-party vote for the elections from 1838 to 1843. The correlations are quite high, indicating that wards which gave relatively strong support to the Democrats – or the Whigs – in one election maintained this relative level of support in each election during the period. Not only did the wards maintain their relative level of support, the absolute levels also changed very little from 1838–42. For each election pair in this period (1838–9, 1839–40, etc.) the average change across the seventeen wards in the Democratic percentage of the two-party vote was less than 2 percent.

What do these elections reveal about who supported the Democrats and who supported the Whigs? The ward-level voting returns can be used to draw some inferences about who supported each party, but their usefulness is limited by the small number of wards and by the paucity of data available (nineteenth-century census takers were not consistently considerate of twentieth-century psephologists). A limited set of ethnic, religious, and class variables was constructed, and these have been correlated with the average Democratic percentage of the ward vote for mayor from 1838 through 1843. As Table 7 shows, there are positive, though weak, relationships between the Democratic vote and the presence of Germans, mechanics, and Methodists and Baptists. There is a negative but even weaker relationship between the presence of immigrants born in Great Britain (the majority of whom were Irish) and Democratic voting. These relationships disappear, however, when the class composition of the ward is controlled. The Democratic vote is strongly related to the class composition of the ward: In wards where a high proportion of children attended private schools (a good surrogate for class), the Democratic vote was low. Similarly, in wards in which Presbyterian and Episcopalian churches were a large proportion of the churches, the Democratic vote was also low.[16] At first blush, then, Schlesinger seems more right than Benson: The party system had a marked class character.

The absence of strong ethnocultural relationships should not be surprising. In these early years, it would have been difficult for a voter to make a partisan choice on the basis of ethnicity alone. Whigs and Democrats alike solicited the immigrant and particularly the Irish vote. There were German clubs or associations in both parties. What nativist sentiment there was, was similarly found in both parties. Defenders of the Public School Society and leaders of the church militant were more prominent among the Whigs; political nativists in the 1830s were organized in the Native American *Democratic* Association and its leader, Samuel F. B. Morse (inventor of the telegraph) was an ardent Jacksonian.[17]

What can be said of the class character of Whig and Democratic coalitions? Support for the Whigs in wards with many Presbyterians and Episcopalians, and in wards where a relatively high proportion of children attended private schools, suggests that Whigs were strongly preferred by the middle classes. (However, the Whigs did not have a monopoly on support

Table 7. Correlations of selected ward characteristics with Democratic percentage of total vote for mayor, New York, 1838–43

Year	Germans[a]	British[b]	Mechanics[c]	Methodists and Baptists[d]	Presbyterians and Episcopalians[d]	Children in private school[e]
1838	.41	-.35	.43	.49	-.54	-.72
1839	.45	-.38	.46	.55	-.58	-.71
1840	.36	-.15	.25	.47	-.57	-.82
1841	.41	-.21	.29	.43	-.59	-.74
1842	.46	-.15	.34	.43	-.69	-.79
1843	.56	-.17	.32	.51	-.76	-.80
Average 1838–43	.42	-.25	.36	.48	-.60	-.77

[a] "Germans" measures the percentage of ward population born in Germany as counted in the census of 1845.
[b] "British" measures the percentage of ward population born in Great Britain as counted in the census of 1845.
[c] "Mechanics" is the percentage of employees counted in the 1850 census of manufacturers who were classified as mechanics according to the scheme of Table 3.
[d] Religion measures count the percentage of congregations in the ward belonging to the named denominations.
[e] "Children in private school" is percentage of school-age children enrolled in private schools, calculated from the census of 1845.

from wealthy voters, whose preferences are discussed in Chapter 7.) Indeed, Whig rhetoric stressed many of the values that were coming into their own among the middle classes and small master craftsmen in these years: a more pronounced Protestant ethic than the Democrats, a sterner sobriety and more stringent morality than heretofore, and a more distinctive individualism than in earlier times. If the Whig persuasion was anyone's, it was the property of the middle classes.[18]

What about working-class voters? The competitiveness of the party system means that Democrats surely did not have a monopoly of support from the working classes. Both parties organized meetings of "mechanics" and made appeals to working men. Each party offered a political economy purporting to benefit working people and each boasted labor spokesmen. How can Whig and Democratic support from the working classes be characterized? Determining how the parties divided the working classes is difficult because census takers in 1835, 1840, and 1845 did not record occupations. As a result, it is not possible to test directly hypotheses about which groups among the working classes supported each party. Comparative referents and an investigation of labor leaders in politics suggest two hypotheses about Democratic and Whig support from the working classes.

Comparative referents suggest the hypothesis that sectoral alignment influenced the shape of the Jacksonian party system in New York. New York's party system in the Jacksonian era was distinctive for the fact that the Democrats were the majority party. In Boston, Philadelphia, Albany, Pittsburgh, and Newark, the Whigs were the majority party. Whig success in those cities is usually attributed to the power of Whig argument about the tariff.[19] By contrast, Democrats pointed to New York's capacity as a port and the centrality of overseas trade to the city's prosperity. At a time when there was five times as much capital invested in trade as in manufactures, many men might make a connection between their own trades and the thriving of the port – those in shipbuilding and related industries, cartmen and longshoremen, porters and workers in hotels, and makers of clothes, textiles, and shoes, whose goods were destined for the Southern market. (This was surely the case for the city's merchants, large and small. A merchant's tendency to support the Democrats was closely related to the extent of his trade with the South.)[20] Although all those trades cannot be located, the seventh, eleventh, and thirteenth wards can be identified as housing the shipbuilding and related industries, and these were all strong Tammany wards as well. In light of the attachment to manufactures and faith in the tariff that made so many urban voters Whigs in the North, the ability of Democrats in New York to maintain a Democratic majority in the 1830s and early 1840s may have rested on the plausibility – a plausibility that did not exist in Newark, Pittsburgh, Albany, or even Boston – of the arguments that linked prosperity to the thriving of the port.

Parties were not alone in their political-economy debate, for there was also debate in the growing number of labor organizations. It was to the leadership of these organizations that I looked for clues about how the party system divided the working classes. I constructed a list of 651 labor leaders mentioned in newspaper accounts, secondary sources, and labor documents. I compared this list to a list of 2,083 politicians, similarly constructed, and including all candidates for locally elected offices. For the years before 1850, 27 of the labor leaders also appeared in the Whig and Democratic parties. Two of these were men whose connection to the labor movement was brief. Another 4 were men whose occupations were licensed and supervised by city government, 3 cartmen and a butcher. Prudently enough, 2 of these were Whigs and 2 (including the butcher) were Democrats.[21]

Seven of the labor leaders were men who were active in the General Trades' Union. Robert Townsend, David Scott, and Isaac Odell among the Whigs, and Levi Slamm, Ely Moore, and John Commerford among the Democrats functioned as labor spokesmen within the parties. Their commitments and their contributions varied quite a bit. Slamm was editor of a Democratic newspaper aimed at the working classes, *The Plebeian*. Like Townsend and Odell in the Whig Party, Slamm was more politician than laborist. Similarly, Ely Moore, "labor's first congressman," left the labor movement for a career in politics. John Commerford had the longest career of the men considered here. A chairmaker, Commerford succeeded Moore as president of the General Trades' Union. Commerford never held office, but he was active in a broad range of political activities, from the Democratic Party to the National Reform Union and the free-soil movement. Like Commerford, Robert Beatty engaged in a range of political activities as well as being prominent in the General Trades' Union. His ties to the party system were more meager, however, as he supported the Locofoco revolt but not the regular Democrats.[22] These men show that both parties had connections to the labor movement, but their activities do not reveal much about what distinguished the parties.

Another fourteen men – six Whigs and eight Democrats – were leaders in craft or journeymen's organizations and party activists as well. The six Whig labor leaders all represented the building trades. The organizations they belonged to were "benevolent" or "protective" organizations, none of which seems to have excluded masters. George Clark, Joseph Tucker, and William Tucker were all leaders of Mechanics' Mutual Protection chapters, served as Whig candidates for alderman or state assembly, and appeared at Whig meetings.[23] William S. Gregory was active in the Practical Painters' Benevolent Society, appeared at citywide labor meetings, and was three times a Whig candidate for state assembly. Gilbert Cameron represented the stonecutters in the General Trades' Union and also served as a speaker at Whig meetings. Organized to fight competition from prison labor, the

Stonecutters, like MMP, included masters as well as journeymen. Andrew H. White was active in the House Carpenters' Protective Association and also a Whig candidate for state assembly.[24] Whig labor leaders were active, then, in organizations that shared an insistence on the solidarity of the craft.

By contrast, labor leaders with Democratic ties represented a broader group of trades and came from journeymen's organizations. John H. Bowie and James D. Potter, for example, were the representatives of the New York Society of Journeymen Curriers to the General Trades' Union and later, Democratic assembly candidates.[25] John Lodewick was vice-president of the Society of Journeymen House Carpenters, and Felix O'Neill was active in the Journeymen Boot and Shoemakers.[26] The leather trades provided other Democratic activists in Arabel Reede of the Ladies' Cordwainers and Andrew Stewart of the Saddlers. Finally, Alexander Wells, vice-president of the Typographical Association of New York, was also an active Democrat.[27]

Whig and Democratic labor leaders represented not only different trades, but also different responses to the complex political economy of the Jacksonian city. Labor leaders found in Whig ranks were those who represented masters' organizations, craft organizations of journeymen and masters, or those who succeeded at "leveling up." Whig emphasis on mutual dependence among classes was an appeal to those who organized to preserve the craft. Here, too, was the hard-working small master who with piety, patience, industry, and sobriety might "distance the wealthy capitalist." Democratic labor leaders represented men who had forsaken the notion that employer and employee had a common interest and who organized, in Moore's words, "counterpoises against capital" as a "measure of self-defence" for which the natural right was obvious and the legal right demanded.[28] Denouncing "spinning-jenny fanatics" and "manufacturers of premature birth," the party endorsed the labor movement, if only in the symbolic politics of sending Ely Moore to Congress. After the Locofoco revolt of 1837–8, Democrats increased their emphasis on the assertiveness of common men. If Democratic support for unions was symbolic at best, it was significant that *Commonwealth* v. *Hunt* was argued and won by a Democrat, that Van Buren issued a ten-hours order for federal employees, and that, closer to home, the decision that unions were conspiracies under the common law had been made by Whig (later nativist) judge Ogden Edwards. In sum, here were the men who, recognizing that "the affection of capitalists for the laboring classes is not more [hypocritical] in Great Britain than in the United States," used their own political and organizational resources to better their lot.

Whig and Democratic coalitions reflected the effects of "deeply held values," reactions to a changing political economy, and the political choices offered by a national party system to a local electorate. Whig and Democratic constituencies were neither the simply portrayed class antagonists of Arthur Schlesinger, Jr., nor were they the ethnoculturally opposed coalitions sug-

A *city in the republic*

gested by Lee Benson. Rather, if workers voted as labor leaders' participation suggests, we might characterize the partisan coalitions by terming the Whigs "mutualists" and the Democrats "militants." (If the Whigs were pious, frugal, and sober and the Democrats were hard-fisted, then it might be said that Lee Benson had the party images right and their social referents wrong.) Whigs also probably claimed a majority of middle-class voters. Since the class structure exhibited a marked cultural division of labor, it seems likely that there was some ethnocultural coloration to partisanship. On the whole, however, the class character of the party system is more prominent, as might be expected when parties are carrying on a debate that is largely about political economy. In the same years, the parties were carrying out a revolution in politics, an achievement more lasting than the coalitions they constructed in the 1830s.

THE JACKSONIAN REVOLUTION IN TWO PARTIES

The Jacksonian revolution happened in both parties. The emergence of career politicians, the abandonment of the caucus system for nominating national candidates, and the necessity of ward organizations both to get out the vote and to display intraparty democracy were common to Whigs and Democratic Republicans alike. The party system and style of politics they created were not woven of entirely new cloth. Rather, the second American party system was part innovation and part adaptation of political habits of long standing. The political universe of 1830 included substantial remnants of the urban politics of the eighteenth century, and the style of the career politician of the 1830s and 1840s strongly resembled the merchant patrician of a century before.

The social and political arrangements of the eighteenth-century city were the inheritance of Jacksonian New Yorkers. Together artisan and merchant had created a style of political leadership and urban governance that combined an insistence on liberty and republican politics with the precepts of the moral economy and the understanding that only a "well-regulated society" could "rise to a flourishing condition." It was the task of government to determine and pursue the common good, which meant above all prosperity. Government activity was necessary because, unrestrained, "Men of diverse Occupations" might "take the Bread out of their Neighbors Mouths; by which many are wholly impoverish'd, or brought to great straits, notwithstanding their Industry." Thus "where a good Regulation is wanting in Society there must, of necessity, be but little improvement made in Commerce."[29]

These sentiments made for active city government. The city council regulated and owned the markets, ensuring that "housekeepers and farmers [were brought] in direct contact with one another," eliminating the mid-

70

dlemen. Wholesalers were forbidden to enter the market before late in the day; various monopoly practices were illegal. The council set prices on provisions and the assize on bread, regulated the freemanship (not very effectively), and appointed and set the fees of commodity inspectors, cartmen, and other market functionaries. The council was as a result arbitrator of the central economic conflicts of the eighteenth-century city. In 1741, for example, bakers went on strike to force the council to raise the price of bread. The regulation of bakers and butchers was also the arbitration of conflicts between merchants and consumers. Since wheat, flour, and meat were important exports as well as part of the local diet, a high price on bread or meat reflected in part merchants' export of community resources. When the price of bread was particularly high, citizens petitioned the council to curb exports. Farmers objected to selling at prices set by the council; cartmen and farmers competed for the right to transport produce within the city; mechanics of different sorts petitioned the council to stop competition from New Jerseyites, farmers, and blacks. The mayor and city council were expected to resolve all these disputes.[30]

The men who held office and performed these tasks were the city's merchants. It was on occasion claimed that "a poor honest Man [is] preferable to a Rich Knave" or that "there ought to be mechanics, and mechanics only, for our legislature,"[31] but few poor men – honest or otherwise – ran for office, and their fellows were loathe to vote for them. Since there were property qualifications both for voting and for holding office, really poor men did not vote, and even artisans might not qualify to hold office. For all these reasons, and despite the fact that "mechanics ever had it in their power" to elect the city's officials, merchants, and merchants from the most well-established mercantile families, dominated elective office.[32]

The political leadership of the city's merchants followed from their economic and social leadership. Although Hamilton was overconfident in his claim (in the *Federalist*, No. 35) that "mechanics and manufacturers will always be inclined, with few exceptions, to give their votes to merchants," he was correct to argue that they did so in part on the basis of shared interests. In the preindustrial setting, it was merchants who organized growth and prosperity, finding markets for mechanics' products, lending funds for artisan production, and organizing the pursuit of commerce. Mechanics, with merchants, supported the Constitution and its promise of a thriving commercial republic.

Deference (if this is indeed what the election of merchants was) also followed from merchants' social leadership. Politics and the obligations of the rich to the poor worked hand in hand. In the eighteenth century, institutions for the provision of charity and relief involved (to the contemporary eye) such a complex arrangement of formal election and taxes, on the one hand, and voluntary contribution and individual discretion, on the other, that it is impossible to determine where government began and noblesse oblige (and the church) ended.[33] Merchants' tasks as city councilmen were similarly private as well as public. When the city council curtailed the export of grain it was, of course, a group of merchants curtailing their own commercial undertakings. Restrictions against forestalling and the like were restrictions on merchants' own activities. In a variety of ways, then, the lines between public and private pursuits, public and private leadership, and public and private generosity were indistinct ones. However well or ill patricians fulfilled their public trust, rare indeed was the patrician candidate who did not claim to be the "poor man's friend."[34]

At the time of Andrew Jackson's election to the presidency, wealthy men continued to account for the great majority of officeholders. The political leadership of wealthy men was based on the social leadership they exercised, a social leadership that made the ward a cross-class community well into the 1830s. In times of economic distress, for example, ad hoc ward committees were formed to collect funds and then distribute relief. In 1829, these committees distributed aid to 3,500 families, nearly 20 percent of the city's total. In 1831, the committee of the eighth ward fed 1,600 persons each day. The wealthy not only contributed funds for these committees, but also worked from door to door collecting funds and distributing relief. In 1839, nearly 10 percent of the home visitors on relief committees were very wealthy men.[35]

Wealthy men also provided leadership in the volunteer fire department. Whig industrialist James P. Allaire was the foreman of an engine company in the seventh ward, where his foundry also was located. The merchant John S. Giles was also a member and founder of a seventh-ward fire company. Shipbuilders Henry Eckford and William Webb helped their men organize Live Oak Company 55 in the eleventh ward. And other wealthy men – Richard F. Carman, Staats M. Mead, Robert and Peter Goelet, and Peter Rankin – also served as firemen.[36] If the ad hoc ward committees provided an arena in which wealthy men could demonstrate their generosity and concern, the fire company provided an arena in which wealthy men could demonstrate their courage and their capacity for leading other men. As partisans, wealthy men led mobs. Simeon Draper led a Whig mob that stormed the arsenal in the 1834 election riots;[37] Henry Eckford and his partner offered their men for the more hard-fisted aspects of Democratic Party struggle.[38] As officeholders, men of substance could control mobs. The traditional form of riot control, in fact, involved less a show of physical force than the use of "respect."[39]

Like other forms of civic leadership, governance was founded on respect for courage and benevolence. "Even the most prominent citizens," Paul Weinbaum writes, "did not stand apart from the rest of society. Their control of city offices brought them into contact with all classes."[40] In granting licenses, and in their judicial functions, mayor and councilmen appeared as concerned or reproving parents. James Harper offered precisely the same advice as a judge that he offered to his employees on the shop floor.[41] Benevolence was a trait that drew public and private worlds together, as it had three generations before. In February of 1830, for example, a delegation of citizens from the twelfth ward approached the Public School Society, asking that a school be built on Eighth Avenue at Twenty-first Street. The ward's alderman, banker Gideon Lee, sent an accompanying letter supporting the request and offering $500 toward construction costs if the Society decided to build the school. And to be even-handed, Lee offered another $500 toward construction costs if the Society would build a school on the east side of his ward as well.[42]

The civic leadership of the wealthy performed a number of social and political functions. Along with citizens' obligations, like militia or fire company duty, it made of the ward a civic community. Relief committees were uncoordinated with one another; they were communal rather than citywide efforts. At the same time, the civic leadership of wealthy men served to legitimate them as officeholders by allowing them to demonstrate courage, generosity, or the capacity to exercise authority. When social relations in the ward involved cooperation for relief, or fire protection, or when wealthy men as city councillors donated money for schools, the line between public and private was a hazy one, and political leadership followed naturally from social leadership.

By 1845, these forms of social leadership had largely disappeared. This was not the result of geographical shifts: In 1845, there were still enough men of wealth in every ward to form ward committees for charity drives. Yet new forms of organization had appeared to replace the old ward committees. The Association for Improving the Condition of the Poor was a citywide organization, though it was organized by men of wealth and included a ward committee structure. More importantly, it was a private, elite-run, and vaguely professionalized rather than communal organization. Although wealthy men were concerned in numbers great enough to participate in each of the ward committees, they were not among the door-to-door visitors.[43] Charity was no longer, in the association's view, to be a matter of individual good-heartedness. Rather, the purpose of the association was "controlling the evils growing out of almsgiving, which often encouraged idleness and led to crime."[44] More important than generosity was inculcation of "habits of frugality, temperance, industry, and self-dependence" so that the poor might help themselves.

In the fire companies, too, the dozen or so of the city's very wealthiest men who had participated in the volunteer department did so before 1840. By 1845, a wealthy civic leader, industrialist, fireman, and partisan like Whig James Allaire was rare. In politics, wealthy men had been pressed to give way in the wake of the Workingmen's Party. Their social authority was in decline – increasingly, in the 1830s, mobs were neither led nor controllable by men of substance.[45] Both because of popular assertiveness and antagonism, then, and because of their own rejection of a civic role based on a long-standing style of mutuality and face-to-face contacts, the activities that made the ward a communal as well as political space were disappearing – and with them, the close relationship of society and politics with which men of substance were associated.

Their style of political leadership did not disappear with them, however. The less affluent career politicians who were replacing the wealthy in office also boasted of their courage, their generosity, and the benefits they brought to their wards. Like the patrician, the career politician proved his courage and leadership capacity in the fire department. An aldermanic candidate of the eighth ward was described by a supporter in this way:

> Your tried and faithful *brother Fireman*, whose time, since he arrived at manhood, and for nearly twenty years, has been *devoted* to your interests, is before you as a candidate ... [46]

For the career politician, as for the patrician, the ward was the basic unit of political life, and the benefits he brought to the ward served as a claim for reelection. Democrats in the fifth ward were reminded to support the party's city council candidates because of the improvements and

> multiplied conveniences which by their influence and exertions have been secured for the ward – and moreover their benevolent attentions to the poor ... all loudly demand a practical manifestation that you ... are not deficient in gratitude.[47]

The career politician nevertheless lacked the personal resources of the patrician; as a consequence, when the politician provided for his constituents, he did so from the city budget. Municipal construction, the night watch, and an effort to create paying jobs in the fire department supplemented charity as evidence of concern to be put to partisan use. Although the payroll for these was centralized, patronage was dispensed by the ward alderman. Thus the retrospective distinctions made here to differentiate the patrician from the politician – partisan rather than personal victory, municipal funds rather than personal generosity – may well have been unimportant ones to the beneficiary, if indeed the lucky appointee or recipient paid any attention to such things at all. Surely the candidate himself, even if he did serve the higher ends of party triumph, stressed his personal generosity, courage, and benevolence as often as those of his party. In sum, the career politician began where the patrician left off. The friendship for the poor and the workingman that was a hallmark of the persona of the boss was part of the career politician from the very beginning.

74

Career politicians were lacking not only the wealth of earlier political leaders, but also the "machinery" of the later party system. Their initial efforts at organization involved not only the forming of ward or citywide committees, but also an attempt to rely on organizations whose primary purpose was not the delivery of the vote. These organizations – the volunteer fire companies, militia companies, and gangs – were courted with donations, occasional patronage, or freedom (when it was necessary) from arrest. The fire companies continued to provide an arena in which a man who wanted to be a political leader could demonstrate his courage and leadership capability. Yet since none of these organizations was primarily political, they formed a shaky organizational base for the parties. Even when they acquired partisan allegiance, these organizations maintained autonomy and self-direction that made them, from a partisan point of view, unreliable.

The fire department was perhaps the last relic of an age when civic responsibility was thought to be an obligation of every citizen, for it was a volunteer force. The city's legal framework established age requirements, the sizes of companies, and the outlines of hierarchical organization, and provided that men who had served their term would be exempt from jury and militia duty. The city government and the firemen themselves shared responsibility for paying for equipment and its maintenance, for creating uniforms, for the selection of the chief engineer, and for the establishment of new companies.[48]

Company members created each company's distinct identity. Some company names, like Lafayette, Franklin, Washington, Americus, and Forrest, suggested patriotism; some, like Clinton and Jackson, partisan spirit; some, like Merchants, Mechanics, and Live Oak, class or occupation; and some, like Aetna or Mutual, the insurance company that helped fund them. Finally, but only at the very end of the 1850s, companies like Hibernia boasted of national origin.[49] The Mechanics Company in the eleventh ward was formed by men who had taken part in the ten-hour movement. Americus Engine Company No. 6 was formed in a printing-ink factory and was later reorganized by Tweed;[50] like Engine Company No. 15, it was a Tammany company. Live Oak Engine Company No. 44 was organized by shipwrights, and this company,[51] like Engine Company No. 40 in the thirteenth ward and Tompkins Company No. 30 in the eleventh ward, was associated with the nativist movement[52] (interestingly, by the time Company No. 30 was organized in this ward, the Mechanics Company had moved out).

Although fire companies allied with parties, they resisted being used by them. The struggle of the fire department as a whole to maintain autonomy from partisan manipulation and city-council dominance demonstrated a commitment to maintain control of an organization that was, after all, as much a creation of its members as of the city government. In the struggle for autonomy and self-government, the firemen were in many ways successful. The means of selecting the chief engineer was steadily democratized between 1816 and the mid-1830s, as was the selection of assistant engineers. Originally appointed by the common council, these officers were elected, as provisions were changed, by successively wider categories of firemen, until all regular firemen had a voice in their selection. Departmental solidarity was demonstrated when a Tammany Common Council removed the chief engineer. Hundreds of firemen resigned; wooed by the Whigs, the ex-chief ran for city register and won, substantially ahead of his ticket. Later, when a Tammany council tried to create a group of companies of whose support it could be certain, Tammany and Whig firemen alike refused to allow these companies to function. Thus, although individual companies had partisan affiliations, as a whole the department succeeded in maintaining partisan autonomy, and any individual company might change its allegiance.[53]

More than a firm basis of organizational support for parties, fire companies provided an arena in which those who wished to exercise political leadership could win men's loyalty by demonstrating their ability. No doubt the most famous of those whose political careers began in the firehouse was William Tweed. A host of aldermen – Samuel Willis of the seventeenth ward, William Adams of the fifth, Alonzo Alvord of the eighteenth, and many others, were firemen before they became city officials; Mayors Bowne, Allen, Varian, Tiemann, and Gunther had been firemen as well.[54] Taken together, they cover most of the political spectrum (nativist leader Barker had also been a fireman) over the antebellum period. In the company setting, these men had been able to prove loyalty, civic virtue, and courage to the satisfaction of their fellows, thereby proving themselves worthy of support and loyalty in return.

Antebellum militia companies were organizations without a clearly defined status. Generally sponsored by a fire company, the line between a gang, a target company, a secret society, and an official (that is, state-recognized) militia company was rather indistinct. At the very least, unofficial target and militia companies served a social function, that of organizing men for military exercises and more clearly social excursions to the countryside, when girlfriends, friends, and families came along. Like the fire companies, target companies "lent dignity and prestige to their members" and, like the fire companies, they had partisan ties.[55] Guards and fire companies were also associated with gangs. Gang leaders Bill Poole, Tom Hyer, and Moses Humphreys were firemen and target-company members as well. Poole, Hyer, and Humphreys were all nativists; Hyer was later a Republican, rewarded for the hard-fisted contribution he made to the party by being taken along to the 1860 presidential nominating convention (belying thereby the sanctimoniousness of prominent Republican leaders).[56] Yankee Sullivan and his men were equally devoted to the Democrats.[57] Gangs, if they were tough (and they were), were not criminal, nor especially young, nor particularly poor. Gang members were not laborers, but butchers, carpenters, or mechanics of various sorts; one well-known leader was a printer for the *Sun*.[58] Headquartered at a saloon or liquor-grocery, gangs had distinctive dress and names, fashioning clothing styles that became their hallmark. Evan Stark has pointed to these styles as one element in a more general pattern of a defensive culture, asserting its distinct identity to outsiders and enforcing conformity on its members.[59] Names, too, were assertions of identity. The Bowery Boys were named for their turf; Dead Rabbits and Plug Uglies drew on slang; Kerryonians, American Guards, Orangemen, and Wide-Awakes expressed ethnicity or nativism.

Although gangs might move to defend the ballot boxes almost anywhere, gang formation and gang activity were confined to a few wards in the center of the city (the sixth, the fourteenth, the tenth, and the seventh outline the rough part of town, though there were notable toughs associated with the fire departments elsewhere).[60] With two important exceptions (the antitemperance disturbances of 1857 and the draft riots), gangs were absent from the more prominent expressions of collective action in politics and from labor conflicts. In general, gang leaders who had any political role were, like Bill Poole, ward heelers. Whereas the fire companies sought autonomy from politics, gangs sought through politics to promote the political fortunes of those whom they supported. Sometimes for a price, they kept opponents away from the polls, guarded ballot boxes, and attempted to enforce political conformity.

Whatever the political contribution these groups made, they were a poor substitute for ward organization or for a permanent partisan presence in the wards. Collectively, they served to give the parties popular ties and a popular base; individually, most of them were unreliable, more tied to individuals than to parties, capable of changing partisan affiliation (as a number of them did when the nativist parties appeared), and jealous of their autonomy. The efforts of career politicians to establish ties to these organizations were symptomatic of the withdrawal of the wealthy from political leadership and the decline of the ward as a cross-class community, for the gang, the militia company, and even the fire company were largely organizations of the working classes. Unable to build on the dense network of face-to-face contacts that characterized social – and as a result political – life in an earlier period, career politicians could not command the personal followings of the patrician. Neither could they yet command reliable partisan loyalties, and the absence of really partisan organizations was symptomatic of this.

TENSIONS IN THE NEW ORDER

The second American party system had neither as broad nor as deep a hold on politics in the city as its dominance of public debate suggests. There were tensions between the parties and the electorate, manifest in criticisms of both parties in the organized-labor press and in third-party insurgencies in the late 1830s. There also were tensions within the Democratic Party, providing evidence of differences between the groups in the coalition the Democracy represented. These tensions foreshadowed the challenges of the 1840s and 1850s, and they show that if the leaders of the second American party system succeeded in reorganizing New York's political life, the ties among political factions, social forces, dominant groups, and government were tenuous.

The Democracy may fairly be said to have invited its own troubles. Democratic emphasis on the political assertiveness of common men invited assertiveness within the party itself. The party's rhetoric invited the constant measure of party practice against party principle, with the result that there were continuous efforts to democratize party procedures. Hardly a year went by that some ward did not resolve, as the eighth did in 1833, that

> as Republicans, attached to the free and prosperous institutions of our country, and to wholesome rules of order, we will not submit to have a "Hickory Club" in the ward, control our political affairs by secret management, or fix a standard of political principles ... [61]

For their part, the ward committees against which these rebellions were launched demanded respect for "usages," the procedures promoted by the party's governing bodies. Between those bodies, too – the Old Men's General Committee, the Young Men's General Committee, and the Workingmen's General Committee – the same differences reappeared. The Old Men's Committee advocated "the maxims of sensible, efficient democracy" and argued that the "wise, intelligent, and virtuous" should control the party.[62] In this context, "usages" quickly became a code word for elitist and undemocratic intraparty practices. Workingmen's General Committee member Michael Walsh insisted that the working classes were "the only honest, virtuous part of the Democratic Party," and when he was reprimanded for criticizing practices within the party, he responded:

> You exclaim, "this is no place for such remarks." ... But I wish you distinctly to understand me when I tell you that Tammany Hall belongs to us ... and ... we are determined to keep possession of it until you are able to dispossess us ... [63]

Though Walsh's followers did fight to keep possession of the hall (Reformers' campaigns, later, against the rule of "muscle" were not pure fabrication) their determination and assertiveness did not make the Democracy their possession. Even the triumph of Locofoco ideology, with Van Buren's support, did not mean that Tammany was in the hands of radicals or workingmen. The "radical" ideology was the ideology of laissez-faire, and it had its conservative uses. As historian Bray Hammond observed, it was impos-

78

sible "to tell what a tirade against [for example, banks] might mean without looking up the speaker's sleeve."[64] Although bank Democrats like Saul Alley, Dennis McCarthy, and Henry Eckford reaped the profits of their charters, radicals like Leggett denounced the charters as the "unclean drippings of venal legislation." In both policy and party practice, Democrats embraced conflicting views. As the Locofoco revolt and Walsh's gang on one side, or desertions of bank Democrats to the "foul embraces of the Whigs" on the other demonstrated, the Democratic coalition was in constant danger of disaggregation.

To these criticisms from within were added criticisms of both Whigs and Democrats from without. The National Trades' Union denounced the tariff and simultaneously demanded protection for the "mechanic arts."[65] The General Trades' Union in New York attacked the Democrats as hypocrites and objected to the use of government payrolls for partisan purposes (see Chapter 6). The promises of the major parties that their policies would bring prosperity were met with skepticism and critique. The 1830s witnessed a tremendous outpouring of tracts and theories about the workings of the economy. In these the logic of natural science, the justice of natural right, and the ethics of Christianity were mobilized in varying proportions to grasp the operation of economic forces and recommend their management. Many of these tracts were by authors connected with the Workingmen's Party, and their conclusions pointed neither to Whig nor to Democratic economic policies.[66] Free trade was denounced as an inhumane doctrine and protection as a sop to the wealthy. If each party echoed the ideology of the eighteenth century, in the presses and the voices of the spokesmen of organized labor it persisted whole. Moreover, for the retailer, the building trades, and all those dependent on the local market, the operation of protection or the port was a step removed from social relations they could see or experience, whereas the general prosperity promised by the parties were precisely the condition they required. The most articulate criticism of the economic doctrines of the major parties came from the ranks of organized labor, but many other voters might also have felt the alternatives offered by the parties to be either inadequate or abstract.

More important, party policy, government practices, and elite behavior were all moving away from long-standing habits for which there was strong popular support. The hard times of 1837 and subsequent years brought to the fore divisions about governmental and elite responsibility for those in need. In 1838, the committee on charity and the almshouse of New York's common council declared that because the causes of poverty and pauperism had been the object of much "public attention, in England and this country" and that because the "zealous investigations" of "able individuals" concurred in establishing the "tendency of charitable societies to increase pauperism," to "diminish the industry and economy of the poor," "and to promote a lamentable dependency," it was therefore necessary to drastically reduce the city's support of charitable societies – "a departure from a practice . . . long established."[67] In the same year, citizens petitioned the common council for a restoration of the assize on bread, and the *Journal of Commerce* was quick to editorialize:

> We say, let every man look out for himself. If you weigh the loaf, you know what it weighs, but if it is stamped with the weight, you do not know. Let us have fewer laws, and we shall have less trouble. The Creator, when he made the system, gave it laws, the tendency of which is always good. Half the laws which men made, do but aggravate the evils they are intended to cure.[68]

Here were both the call to laissez-faire and the abandonment of claims to mutual dependence.

Not only petitions to the common council but also mass behavior signaled the persistence of old-fashioned views in the populace. When the Locofocos in February of 1837 called a meeting in the park, their handbill read "Bread, Meat, Rent, and Fuel! *Their prices must come down!*" Once a crowd had gathered, Democrat Alexander Ming, Jr., read a long list of resolutions about banks and hard money, and a memorial to the state legislature was adopted, calling for the prohibition of small notes, the abolition of indirect taxes, and an end to interference in trade. When this business had been accomplished, the party dissidents were at the end of their agenda but "a stream of population, which had come down Chatham street, entered the Park, and then a man mounted the platform and addressed the multitude. His speech was directed against flour dealers and he added 'go to the flour stores and offer a fair price, and if refused, take the flour.' "[69] Someone called out "To Hart's flour store!" and, against the protests of the Locofocos, the crowd made its way to Eli Hart's. There, and at Herrick and Son, the crowd dumped and destroyed flour. A "tall athletic fellow in a carman's frock" shouted "No plunder, no plunder; destroy as much as you please." In accord with the precepts of the moral economy, the men punished the wealthy for having abandoned their responsibilities to the poor (though the women gathered flour in their aprons).[70]

The food riot was not the only evidence of the persistence of older concepts of a good and just social order. Nativists hoped to close the "fatal chasm in our social system, [to knit] up those social sympathies again . . . "[71] Every movement that claimed to speak for working people before 1850 expressed grieving and loss for a society remembered, if a bit romantically, as characterized by mutuality, reciprocity, and familial relationships between high and low.

In other matters, too, the parties resisted popular pressures. If for the Democratic Party laissez-faire ideology provided common rhetorical ground for businessmen and prolabor radicals, the same ideology, fortified with

Whiggish faith in accumulation and government by the best men, outlines the common ground of both parties in the administration of city government. Neither party supported legislation regulating tenements and landlords. Democrats and Whigs alike opposed democratization of school management. When ward-level-elected school boards were created, men from both parties formed union tickets to keep education in the hands of a respectable element. Neither party supported compensation for members of the common council or democratized its own internal organization.

For all these reasons, the turnout for local elections was lower than for national elections. The vote for president exceeded the votes for mayor by about 15 percent in the 1830s and 1840s, a gap that was narrowed significantly in the 1850s. Added to apathetic support of the major parties were the insurgencies of Locofocos and nativists. Although neither group received much support citywide, added together the third-party vote was as much as 30 percent in some wards. In these wards was concentrated the disaffection that became powerful with the appearance of the American Republican Party in the 1840s and tested the claim of Tammany to be the "true home of the working classes" in the 1850s. As the impending national crisis challenged the major parties from above, the tensions of class and ethnicity transformed them from below.

The shape of the new and tentative political order was determined in important ways by transformations larger than those New Yorkers accomplished on their own. The most obvious of these was the creation of the Whig and Democratic parties and their dominance of political life in the city. The parties did not represent a summing of individual predispositions, nor did party visions reflect some "natural" underlying cleavage. Rather, since "social cleavages are not a datum," the partisan choices offered in New York's fellow citizens inevitably shaped the party coalitions formed there.

In the same years, the social revolution reordered social relations in the wards, undermining older patterns of elite leadership and popular deference; the expansion of the suffrage presented a momentous task of local party organization. By taking on the style of the patrician, career politicians were conceding to strongly held popular values. These concessions, however, were not enough. There were other tensions between the electorate and politicians and within the Democratic coalition. A less tentative political order would have to accommodate those tensions.

If the ties among political faction, social force, dominant group, and government were tenuous in the 1830s, the men and the relationships of the second American party system were nevertheless tidings of things to come. Although disaffection challenged the parties and nativism briefly loosed their hold on elective offices, neither displaced the major parties as the main combatants in electoral contest. Leaders of the major parties were, if clumsily, attempting to create partisan community in the wards. The most prominent Democratic politicians of the 1850s were already at work in Tammany's Young Men's General Committee by 1840; Horace Greeley, national spokesman for the Whigs and later the Republicans, established his *Tribune* in 1841. Despite the shakiness of party organizations and the grumblings of disaffection, the second American party system established parties at the center of political life and career politicians as their leaders.

5 Status and solidarities

THE WHIG AND DEMOCRATIC PARTIES dominated electoral debate in the Age of Jackson, but the coalitions they assembled were fragile and their hold on the electorate was tenuous. Organized labor, for example, consistently voiced positions critical of both parties. Immigrants were publicly courted by both parties and genuinely welcome in neither. The nativists' situation was the mirror image of this: There was real sympathy for them in both parties, but both parties resisted public endorsement of nativist goals. Small wonder, then, that adamant nativists felt they might have some success with a party of their own.

The first effort, Samuel Morse's foray from anti-Catholic demagoguery into electoral politics in the mid-1830s, was not well rewarded at the polls. A decade later and in the mid-1850s nativist politicians were more successful. In 1844, the American Republican Party won control of city government as 50,345 voters – a turnout 5,430 voters larger than the preceding year, and which would not be matched until 1852 – went to the polls. Whigs had endorsed this effort, and when Whig support was withdrawn in 1845 the American Republicans quickly lost strength. By 1847, the party was gone. The events of the 1850s were similar. When the Know-Nothing Order (as the American Party) fielded its own candidates in 1854, nearly 5,800 more votes were cast than had been cast in the previous mayoral election. In 1854 and 1856, Know-Nothings were supported by about a third of the electorate. Though as a minority party the Americans could not win an election outright, their excellent organization and substantial strength attracted other party factions to alliances with them, particularly the City Reform League.

Nativist politics had dramatic effects on the second American party system. First, it changed patterns of support for the major parties across the wards. As shown in Table 8, ward support for the major parties was disrupted by the election of 1844 and never returned to its former configuration. Second, as this suggests, the coalitions supporting the parties changed. The relationships between measures of Irish and mechanics' presence in the wards and partisanship shifted (see Figure 5). Although the relationship

Table 8. *Correlations of the Democratic percentage of the total vote for mayor, New York, 1842–52*

	42	43	44	45	46	47	48	49	50	52
42	1									
43	.97	1								
44	.64	.62	1							
45	.73	.73	.97	1						
46	.62	.65	.93	.96	1					
47	.77	.80	.92	.97	.96	1				
48	.67	.69	.82	.89	.91	.92	1			
49	.64	.67	.87	.89	.91	.90	.88	1		
50	.57	.61	.90	.92	.90	.89	.93	.89	1	
52	.60	.65	.81	.86	.87	.85	.89	.80	.93	1

Note: Entries are the correlations of the ward-level Democratic percentage of the total vote. There were 17 wards in 1838–45, 18 in 1846–9, 19 in 1850, and 20 in 1852.

between either of these measures and partisanship is weak, the magnitude of the change is worthy of attention. American Republican success in 1844 gained support for the Whigs from United States–born voters, who had previously not voted or had voted Democratic, while making firm Democrats of the Irish. Thus one effect of nativist politics was to lend the party system a stronger ethnic cast. Third, these changes in party support made the Whigs a stronger party than the Democrats for the first time. Whigs maintained that lead until their collapse (of national causes) in the early 1850s.

The politicization of ethnic differences raised the stakes of cultural conflict and influenced the shape of the coalitions that were party to it. Nativist politics was more, however, than cultural antagonism in political guise. Along with cultural differences, class solidarities contributed both to political nativism and to the opposition to it. Moreover, the historical trajectory of political nativism throughout the nineteenth century and into the twentieth – appearing each time the national party system was in crisis – suggests that political grievances played an important role in the rise and fall of antiimmigrant parties.[1]

The first section of this chapter traces the cultural antagonisms that predated the appearance of the American Republican Party. The next section describes patterns of support for the American Republican and Know-Nothing parties, and the subsequent section describes the opposing Democratic coalition. For both nativists and their opponents, the links between cultural affinities, class solidarities, political grievances, and partisan choices are explored.

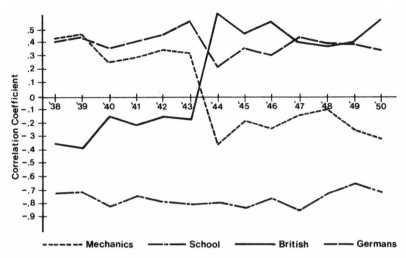

Figure 5. Correlations of selected ward characteristics with the Democratic percentage of the vote cast for mayor, New York City, 1838–50. "Germans" is the percentage of ward population born in Germany as counted in the New York State census of 1845. "Mechanics" is the percentage of employees counted in the U.S. census of manufactures for 1850, who were classified as mechanics rather than wage workers I, using the classification system of Table 3. "School" is the percentage of school-age children enrolled in private schools, as counted in the New York State census of 1845. "British" is the percentage of ward population born in Great Britain, as counted in the New York State census of 1845.

RELIGION, STATUS, AND SOLIDARITIES

The appearance of political nativism in New York City was preceded by the evangelical and temperance activities of militant Protestantism and by a conflict between Protestants and Catholics about public education. The conflict over education demonstrated both how politically weak Catholics were in New York City and how ostensibly cultural conflict had political and class dimensions. Evangelical and temperance activities reveal tensions among Protestants that kept them from forming a united anti-Catholic front. In both the conflict over schooling and the activities of the church militant, the American-born seemed torn between class and ethnic loyalties.

The school controversy began as a Catholic–Protestant conflict. Elsewhere in New York State public schools were administered by elected boards or commissioners of education, but in New York City the schools were administered by the Public School Society. The Society was a closed corporation chartered by the state. Technically the common council had control of the disbursement of common-school funds, and occasionally non-Society Schools were subsidized, but as a practical matter the city's schools were in the hands of the Public School Society.[2]

85

In 1840, a committee of Catholics petitioned for an allocation of school moneys to eight Catholic schools. The Methodists also petitioned for a portion of the funds, as they had on earlier occasions. The Catholics were encouraged in their effort by the support of Governor Seward, whose annual message had endorsed the establishment of schools in which pupils were taught by teachers "professing the same faith."[3] The Catholic petition was opposed by the School Society and by the leading lights of the church militant. Theodore Sedgewick and the Reverend Hiram Ketchum, who later served as the Society's lobbyist in Albany, the Reverend Dr. John Knox of the Dutch Reformed Church, and the Reverend Gardiner Spring of the Brick Presbyterian Church all testified against the Catholics. The Methodists abandoned their petition to create a more united Protestant front, and Methodists David Reese and Nathan Bangs joined in testimony against the Catholic petition. With the lone exception of Alderman Daniel C. Pentz, the common council agreed with the Protestants, and the petition of the Catholics was denied.

Early the next year, the Catholics took their petition to Albany. Things looked brighter there as both Seward and Whig Assemblyman John Spencer (who prepared a report on the Catholic petition for the legislature) supported the Catholic request for funds. The Catholics hoped to strengthen their position in Albany by the election of a sympathetic delegation of state assemblymen from the city. Both Whigs and Democrats, however, supported the Public School Society (though Democrats made a concession to Catholic feeling by including ex-alderman Pentz on their assembly slate). Thus rebuffed, the Catholics gathered in Carroll Hall and endorsed the ten candidates on the Democratic ticket thought to be sympathetic to the Catholic claim and nominated three additional candidates, not endorsed by either major party, to fill out a thirteen-candidate slate. Seven of the Democrats endorsed by the Catholics rejected the Carroll Hall endorsement and announced their support of the Public School Society. Samuel F. B. Morse announced a set of nativist endorsements, six Democrats and seven Whigs. Three Democrats had both nativist and Carroll Hall endorsements. In the confused election that followed, ten Democrats and three Whigs were elected.[4]

The three candidates running only on the Carroll Hall ticket polled about 2,100 votes each. This represented about 7 percent of the vote cast in most general elections, a small but perhaps crucial margin for the Democrats. On the other hand, to alienate American-born voters meant certain disaster. As a result, the Democrats condemned Hughes for attempting to discredit their ticket – not by failing to endorse three Democrats but by actually endorsing ten of them![5] Playing both sides of the street, the Democrats held meetings to denounce nativism but kept the Irish off their tickets and continued to waffle on the school issue.

The governor was determined to establish a common-school system for the city of New York, despite bipartisan support of the School Society. In 1842, the state legislature passed a common-school bill for the city. This legislation both extended the common-school system to New York City and allowed the Public School Society to continue to manage their schools, but under the general direction of commissioners of education elected in each ward. The bill, largely the work of Democrat William B. Maclay, was accompanied by a report that stressed the inappropriateness of the elitist Public School Society in a republican country and the importance of parents and citizens democratically controlling their schools. Despite the fact that this legislation was pioneered by Whigs Seward and Spencer, the Democrats claimed that the passage of the bill "must show to our adopted citizens, in language that cannot be misunderstood, that the Democracy are, in trying times, their friends" (Catholics disagreed and in the charter elections of April 1842 continued to withhold their votes from the Democrats).[6]

The extension of the common-school system to New York City was both a political solution and a political provocation. It was hard for anyone to defend the "aristocratic" Public School Society in the Age of Jackson, particularly against an elected board of education. The Democrats and Sewardite Whigs both claimed credit for broadening the sphere of republican government. At the same time, the Catholics saw clearly that they had few political allies and that the struggle to control the schools, now passed to the ward level, would allow them some influence only in the sixth ward. Anti-Catholics saw the legislation as a Catholic victory, an inflammatory courting of Catholic power on the part of Seward and some of the Democrats.

In June of 1842, elections were held in each ward to select commissioners for the new common-school system. That election served as a referendum on the new system, for candidates did not run on party slates but rather on pro–common-school slates or on pro–Public-School-Society slates. The latter, most of which had bipartisan endorsement, promised to work for repeal of the common-school bill. The PSS tickets won in eight wards, the common-school tickets won in four wards, and five wards split. The Public School Society tickets succeeded in wards where Presbyterian and Episcopalian congregations outnumbered the poorer congregations. In the same wards, many children were sent to private schools, suggesting that affluent voters, in supporting the School Society, were making a statement about how *other* people's children should be educated. The common-school slates were supported where Methodist and Baptist congregations outnumbered the wealthier Protestant sects. The presence of the foreign-born or even Catholics was not as important as this division in the native-born Protestant community.[7]

Support for the School Society or the common-school system did not, moreover, prefigure support for the American Republicans two years later:[8] Of the four wards that favored the common-school system, three became strong nativist wards; of the eight that favored the Public School Society, three would be strong nativist wards. The conflict over education, if it provoked the formation of the American Republican Party as some have thought, did not assemble a popular coalition of Protestant Americans against Catholic immigrants. Nativist political victory, then, would not come "naturally," but would have to transcend divisions among the native-born.

The evangelical and temperance movements experienced the same interdenominational strains revealed by the common-school election. The larger evangelical societies were left to the Episcopalians, Congregationalists, Presbyterians, and Dutch Reformed congregations, whereas Baptists and Methodists went their own way. After its first year, for example, the American Tract Society had no Methodist representation in its publishing committee. Methodist Nathan Bangs worked in the 1820s to build the Methodist Book Concern in New York, and there was also a Methodist Sunday School Union. The Baptists began their own tract society in 1824 and broke entirely from the larger American Tract Society in 1836.[9]

These tensions embodied differences in feeling and constituency as well as differences about Christian doctrine. Charles Foster explains that Baptist and Methodist churches

> were the denominations for poor people. They required their ministers to be earnest and enthusiastic. They could not pay for an educated ministry nor did they, for the most part, really want it. Both the Methodists and the Baptists were aware that the prestige denominations held them in low esteem.[10]

The work of a revivalist like Charles Grandison Finney, or the upsurge of lay preaching among Methodists and Baptists, rejecting theocentric for anthropocentric religion, urged "the priesthood of all believers," and declared "democracy the form of government most approved by God," emphasizing the capacity of all men and women for reason and virtue.[11]

Similarly, there was in the temperance movement tension between older, elite-led, and newer organizations, like the Washingtonians, whose "uneducated" leadership, more emotional and dramatic in style than the leadership of earlier organizations, delivered the temperance message in settings and lectures that "were not always of an elevating character."[12] Gusfield has argued that temperance "became a major social and political force in American life only as it was freed of the symbols of aristocratic dominance and converted into a popular movement to achieve self-perfection among the middle and lower classes ... "[13] The General Trades' Union's paper, *The Union*, repeatedly endorsed the temperance cause (though not temperance or sabbatarian legislation). Paul Faler has argued that among "rebel" shoemakers in Lynn, Massachusetts, drink and poverty were attributed to despair in the face of capitalist exploitation, and that militant shoemakers used the cultural values expressed in the temperance and evangelical movements "in the service of their own class interests."[14]

Within the sphere of religious and temperance reform, these impulses corresponded to the rejection of deference and claim to self-government that we associate with the Age of Jackson. Here the exhibition of Christian sensibility and temperate habits in conjunction with the democratic and humanistic aspects of these movements represented a claim to hope, self-esteem, and social status. These claims were particularly urgent for the working classes at a time when their well-being was increasingly precarious and their honor was under attack. The views that wealth was a testimony to virtue and poverty to a dissolute character, that the tendency to vice was innate, and that the distinction between the worthy and the unworthy poor must be made, were gaining ground. In the face of these views, the exhibition of sober habits and Protestant faith represented a claim to honorable status. Where the great majority of the poor were foreign-born, it was an adaptation requiring that the aspirant to respectability "not risk the possibility that he might be classed with the immigrants."[15]

In the efforts of the wealthier Presbyterian, Congregationalist, Dutch Reformed, and Episcopalian churches, and of the larger religious societies they dominated, there was a clear impulse to social management – a fear of infidelity, licentiousness, skepticism, and their inevitable outcome, mob rule. Often these fears were explicit. Sometimes these fears were signaled by the recurrent use of the phrase "economical police" to refer to the Bible, morality, temperance, or education. According to Gardiner Spring, for example, free government and "the absurd doctrine of liberty and equality" were responsible for "the bold assumption of the power of law by an infuriated mob,"[16] a reference not to any particular incident but to the general course of events.[17]

If the more democratic moments of the temperance and evangelical movements provided opportunities for self-assertion and self-esteem among common people, the more elitist and authority-oriented moments of the church militant offered a promise: the promise to return to the societal familism that was increasingly abandoned in practice. Temperance, it was argued, was "the most effectual means of closing this fatal chasm in our social system, of knitting up those social sympathies again ... "[18] The power of this promise was enormous at a time when every organization, every party – the Workingmen, the General Trades' Union, even the Locofocos – that claimed to speak for working people before 1850 denounced commercial values and expressed grieving and loss for a society remembered, if a bit romantically, as characterized by mutuality, reciprocity, and familial relations between high and low. Like the claim that all believers might aspire to priesthood, the belief that among Christians the acceptance of poverty and subordinate status by some would be met by the faithful stewardship of wealth by others[19] represented an adaptation to difficult circumstances that drew upon political and cultural resources broader than the evangelical movement itself. Like the claim of the sober and the faithful to social status, however, the community founded "on the rock of a stern Protestant faith" excluded the Catholic immigrant.

American Republicanism appeared to transcend the divisions within the Protestant crusade by emphasizing the values common to its various impulses – Protestantism, sobriety, and nativism – and emphasizing that these aspects of character distinguished not only the respectable from the dissolute or the worthy from the unworthy poor, but also the citizen from the slave. This meant that American Republicanism and Know-Nothingism not only linked together various strands of cultural conflict, but also that in so doing they introduced into cultural struggle political stakes, the stakes of "Rum or Republic." Bishop Hughes saw this from the beginning. He led Catholics in their struggle with the Public School Society and introduced the Catholic church into electoral politics in 1841 because the alternative was "civil suicide."

Yet more was at stake in the campaigns of political nativism than rum, Romanism, and republic. American Republicans, by unifying the Protestant crusade politically, brought cultural antagonism to the fore and pushed class differences among Protestants aside. As a result, there was tension between the benevolent empire and labor spokesmen. As early as 1832 the Public School Society was attacked by the *Working Man's Advocate* as "a secret engine of bigotry and aristocracy."[20] The Industrial Congress of 1850 investigated and attacked the labor practices of the American Tract Society. Whitney's *Defense of the American Policy*, reciprocally, attacked the Industrial Congress. Workingman Clinton Roosevelt and Democrat Mike Walsh both opposed the argument that intemperance and vice were the causes of poverty, arguing instead that the causality was the other way around.[21] When we add to this evidence of tension between labor advocates and Protestant crusaders the fact that the Democracy, the main political alternative to both the American Republican and the Know-Nothing parties, styled itself the "true home of the working classes" it seems clear that the political choices available in the elections of 1844 and 1854–6 were ethnic solidarity or class loyalty.

SOLIDARITIES AND VOTES: THE NATIVISTS

When the American Republican Party constructed its slate for the charter election of 1844, James Harper was chosen as its mayoral candidate. Harper was not an active campaigner, but the choice was significant, for Harper embodied the themes that held the nativist movement in politics together. Harper was a self-made man, one of four sons of "sturdy, upright, inflexible," teetotaling Methodist parents. The publishing firm Harper owned jointly with his brothers was just then publishing a handsomely illustrated edition of the Bible. Harper and Brothers had also arranged for the publication – without the firm's imprint – of Maria Monk's *Awful Disclosures*, more or less pornographic entertainment that claimed to be an exposé of life in a convent. Harper was president of the Lady Washington Temperance Society, and in 1843 he had campaigned for the Public School Society and against the extension of the common-school system to New York City. As an employer, Harper had a reputation for fatherly advice, scolding, and concern (Harper and Brothers was not unionized). The choice of James Harper, then, was a choice endorsing paternalism, sobriety, Protestantism, hard work, and Whiggish leveling up.[22]

Who among the American-born supported the Democrats, and who closed ranks with the nativists? This is an important question, because nativist parties recruited only a portion of their potential constituency to their cause. American Republicans were not a viable party without Whig endorsement; Know-Nothings competed well but did not monopolize the votes of the United States–born a decade later. How did nativists differ from other voters in class, religion, or neighborhood? Finding evidence about variation in support of the native-born for nativist parties is difficult for a number of reasons. There is an extremely strong negative relationship, as one might expect, between nativist voting and the presence of British (largely Irish) immigrants (in 1844, -.76; in 1845, -.75; in 1846, -.79). In multiple regression equations controlling for British presence, the effects of other population characteristics on partisanship are uniformly small. This is in part because of the small number of data points (seventeen wards in the mid-1840s). The cultural division of labor reinforces this problem: There is a strong negative relationship between the presence of British voters and plausible class measures. For example, the correlation between the presence of British immigrants in 1845 and the presence of mechanics is -.84.[23] Quite simply, this means that wherever one finds United States–born wage workers one finds immigrants as well – there are no predominantly American-born wards that are also predominantly wards of wage workers. As a result, determining which American-born voters were nativists necessarily relies primarily on anecdotal and qualitative evidence.

Three hypotheses about which American-born voters supported nativist parties seem plausible. First, it may have been that those United States–born voters who most directly competed with immigrants for jobs voted for American Republicans and Know-Nothings. Second, nativist politics might have been the political expression of competition for neighborhoods. Third, it may have been the United States–born who were more socially (and spatially) distant from the immigrants – the mechanics – who voted for American Republican and Know-Nothing candidates. The same wards provided support to nativist parties in both eras: The correlation between American Republican votes in 1845 and Know-Nothing votes in 1854 was

.74; between 1845 and 1856, .78. The discussion that follows, then, uses information from both decades to find nativist voters.

Perhaps those who were more proletarianized had most to fear from immigrant competition for neighborhoods and for jobs. It seems logical to think, for example, that nativism had most appeal for those who felt their neighborhoods threatened by "invasions" of immigrant neighbors, or that the nativist vote represented the protest of American-born citizens who, because of their poverty, were trapped in neighborhoods in which they were the cultural minority.

There is some evidence that this happened. The American Republican Party received strong support in the fourteenth and sixteenth wards, more proletarian wards where there was a small but recently arrived immigrant population. There is also contrary evidence. In the second ward, which was overwhelmingly native-born until the 1840s, nativists found very little support. Those second-ward citizens who did vote for the American Republican Party in 1844 quickly deserted the third-party movement. Similarly, in the third ward, in which there were many more foreign-born residents than there had been in 1835, and in which many of the foreign-born were aliens, Whig voters remained more loyal to their party than elsewhere, and the third-party vote not only represented a relatively smaller proportion of the native-born electorate than elsewhere, but also retired quickly from third-party support. In the fourth and sixth wards, also "invaded," the nativists received little support. If the fourteenth and sixteenth wards, then, were expressing anger at "invasion," the second and third wards did not do so, and the fourth and sixth wards did not display the vote they should have if nativism was an expression of a culturally isolated minority.

Similarly, it could be hypothesized that the gang conflicts in the tough neighborhoods were only one expression of conflict between native- and foreign-born, and that votes cast for the American Republican Party were another expression of the same competition for "turf." When the tough part of town went to the polls, however, ethnic solidarity was not always prominent. For example, the seventh ward, like some of the other strong nativist wards, was part of the fire district in which most gang and fire-company conflicts occurred – the rough part of town. Though the fourteenth ward was also in the "rough" part of town – many Bowery Boys lived here – its support for the nativists was only moderate, and very brief, despite street fighting and the possibilities for native-born political power. Four-teenth-ward voters after 1844 were predominantly Democratic, but continued to have gang fights. Not surprisingly, in the rough part of town, nativists were tough, and in the quieter parts of town (the west side and the sixteenth ward, where there were many nativists), nativists were quiet. Since some neighborhoods in which street fights expressed ethnic antagonism did not give support to the nativist parties, nativist politics cannot be understood as simply the political expression of conflict over "turf."[24]

The wards in which the American-born were most strongly drawn to the American Republican Party were the wards in which the American-born predominated numerically. Moreover, the wards that supported the American Republicans most strongly are distinguished by the high proportions of workers who remained in trades still characterized by artisan relations of production. The wards that had the highest proportions of mechanics were all strong American Republican wards, and most of them supported the Know-Nothings in the 1850s as well. The tenth ward, for example, had hundreds of men employed in about two-dozen woodworking shops, making cabinets, chairs, and the like; the thirteenth ward had more than three-dozen such establishments, employing 350 men, as well as many small metals-manufacturing firms and black- or whitesmith shops. The eighth ward was also a center for the woodworking trades and, in addition, of the building trades; dozens of small shops employed jewelers, instrument makers, machinists, smiths, and the like. The seventeenth and eleventh wards were similar. In addition, the eleventh ward included over a thousand men in the shipbuilding trades. By contrast, in other wards, like the first, third, fourth, and fifth, upward of 70 percent of the manufacturing employees were in the more proletarianized trades of boot and shoemaking, the needle trades, printing, or miscellaneous manufactures like straw or paper makers.

The labor leaders found in the nativist movement were also from mechanics' crafts rather than the more proletarianized trades, and three of these leaders, men who had also been or later were Whigs, were leaders of Mechanics' Mutual Protection, the secret organization among building-trades workers: Joseph Tucker, William Tucker, and George Clark. Another labor leader among the American Republicans, Andrew Thompson, was a ship carpenter from the seventh ward who represented shipwrights and caulkers at the Tailors' Support meeting in 1850. Joseph Hufty, the brushmaker, had been their delegate to the General Trades' Union. Since the least proletarianized workers also were more strongly Whig than Democratic, it should not be surprising that the nativist parties were more closely aligned with the Whigs and found the majority of their supporters in Whig ranks.

The organizational life of the nativist movement suggests the same social basis of support. Between the American Republican Party's decline and the appearance of the Know-Nothings in politics, nativists organized a number of organizations rather like Mechanics' Mutual Protection. Some of these were, like MMP, secret societies that included benefit provisions for unemployment, burial, or old age. The Native Sons of America, the Order of United Americans, the Order of United American Mechanics, and the Order of the Star Spangled Banner (this last the organization that came to be known as the Know-Nothings), the American Protestant Association, and the Benevolent Order of Bereans were all openly nativistic and, unlike Mechanics' Mutual Protection, organized after the appearance of American Republicanism. Little is known of the membership of these organizations but their style, their statements, and their location in the city suggest that they were, like MMP, composed of the elite sector of the working classes.[25]

A mapping of the chapters or lodges of the Order of United Americans, the American Protestant Association, Mechanics' Mutual Protection, and temperance organizations in the mid-1850s reveals that they flourished in the wards that had in the 1840s and would again in the 1850s deliver a substantial nativist vote. The tenth ward, for example, housed not only a chapter of MMP, but also four chapters of the Order of United Americans, a lodge of the Sons of Temperance, and, nearby, three assemblies of the American Protestant Association. The eleventh ward similarly had residents in all four organizations. The ninth, though lacking MMP, was the home of five lodges of the OUA and four assemblies of the American Protestant Association, as well as two temperance organizations, and it was in this ward that fire companies first had pledged themselves to temperance. None of these organizations had much life in the seven lower wards or in the wards far uptown (the twentieth and twenty-second) – though these wards contained nearly 40 percent of the United States–born population in 1855.[26]

In other cities, too, the nativist parties relied heavily on artisan voters for support. Michael Holt found in Pittsburgh that skilled artisans gave unusually strong support to the nativist parties.[27] David Montgomery suggested that in Philadelphia shoemakers, tailors, and laborers were not well represented among American Republican Party activists and factory workers were "conspicuously absent."[28] A closer look at Philadelphia's American Republicans, by Bruce Laurie, revealed that while the Democratic Party in that city was "a classic coalition of the very rich and the poor ... American Republican leadership was the exclusive preserve of artisans and tradesmen ... drawn disproportionately from ... honorable occupations." The party united master and journeyman of the craft in political action.[29]

Why were mechanics so drawn to the nativist parties? For one thing, American Republican rhetoric – even in New York, where party leadership drew on society's elite as well as artisans – appealed to a mechanic's self-conceived character and special qualifications for citizenship. In so doing, American Republicanism seemed to restore the independent, industrious, and knowledgeable mechanic to the central place in politics. American Republican emphasis on character represents a continuity – though a partial one – with Workingmen's Party ideology. The earlier party, it will be recalled, stressed both the importance of character in a republican citizenry and the contribution of the independent and industrious mechanic to the Revolution and to the perpetuation of liberty. The parties that succeeded the Workingmen appealed to mechanics, but in their visions of society the mechanic was being displaced – in the Whig vision, by the "industrial interest" and the "credit system," and in the Democratic vision by a broader notion of the working classes, a notion that grouped the mechanic and his unwelcome future of wage slavery together.

Mechanics' Mutual Protection, the labor organization closely tied to the American Republican Party, voiced both the sense of loss of status and the argument that the mechanics' well-being was crucial to the life of republican government. Their purpose was "the elevation of the mechanic to his true position in society," "to raise the dignity of our callings by honoring labor."[30] Not only was "Honest Industry" the "true wealth of nations," but the "Happiness of our whole people depends upon the remuneration which our Mechanics receive for their labor and skill and our freedom reposes on this anchor ... "[31] Poverty, it was argued, "crushes and enslaves both soul and body," whereas education and fair remuneration "[confer] an honor on the workingman ... which gives him a nobility of soul, and an erect and manly republican independence which cannot but be a blessing to the whole commonwealth ... " Thus the "perpetuation of our Free Institutions" depends upon the continued well-being of the mechanic.[32] The same arguments are found in the nativist labor paper, the *Champion of American Labor*. The *Champion* declared that it sought "to elevate the poor, downtrodden American manual operatives in every branch of industry ... we seek to restore them to that proud position which they once held among men."[33] Mechanics' adherence to American Republicanism, then, was in part a Mugwumpish effort at regaining political status.[34]

There was also an effort to revive the master–journeyman cohesion of the craft. Mechanics' Mutual Protection spokesmen argued that neither the strike nor violence, but mechanics' solidarity and a feeling of Christian brotherhood, would promote the goals of higher pay, an end to prison labor, and the institution of the ten-hours system. Hostility between classes was not inevitable, but followed from a "spirit of competition" that could be rooted out by an emphasis on Christian brotherhood.[35] Similarly, a meeting announced in the *Champion*, to organize for raising the dignity of labor, showed the master–journeyman solidarity that was hoped for: Among those present were J. D. Young, "boss painter"; Luther Stebbins, "boss blacksmith"; and J. H. Hull, "boss mason"; as well as a tinman, a tailor, a shoemaker, a cabinetmaker, and a carpenter.[36] As David Montgomery observed for Philadelphia, American Republican journeymen chose to "align themselves not with each other, but with employers of their respective ethnic groups."[37]

That mechanics chose this "ethnic" rather than "class" solidarity was perhaps because the emerging class strategy for economic self-protection was not a workable one for those in nonindustrialized trades. Whereas tailors, printers, and shoemakers, who had already become wage laborers, could organize together with immigrants to protect themselves through unions, those in nonindustrialized crafts could only protect themselves if they could stave off industrialization. And here was a second political displacement, that the policies of neither Whigs nor Democrats could accomplish this task. The fear of industrialization was a deep and readily articulated one. To those in Mechanics' Mutual Protection, for example, the evil of the factory system was obvious – in England it had "been long rooting out the physical constitution and moral nature of the people."[38] The Workingmen's Party and the National Trades' Union had denounced the "speculating system" and banks and had attempted to remove various state encouragements to them by restricting banks and their activities. Insofar as these efforts had as their goal restricting the "incursions of capital" into the trades, they were not successful. The alternative was to stymie industrialization by restricting the influx of labor.

It is in this sense that nativist-labor complaints about immigrant "competition" need to be understood: not the competition of those who will do one's own job, but the competition of a labor force whose presence allowed a reorganization of work. The craft solidarity of American Republicans, their Whiggish master–journeyman cohesion, in conjunction with their laborism, produced the arguments of the *Champion of American Labor* – on the one hand, the Democrats were denounced for stirring up class feeling, while, on the other hand, it was insisted that there was good reason for class strife, and the wealthy men of the United States could only prove their concern for the well-being of the laboring classes by restricting immigration.[39]

In this light, the formulation of the last section – that political nativism forced a choice between ethnic and class loyalties – if it states a truth, is also only a partial, if not facile, understanding of what happened. For some of its adherents, American Republicanism "conveyed a strong sense of class identity."[40] This class – mechanics – had its place in the merchant-artisan city, but only a smaller and increasingly tenuous one in the industrializing nineteenth-century city. If some of those who saw antagonism between capital and labor as unnecessary were simply trying to legitimate the new order (one thinks here of the Harpers, financier Edward Prime, or temperance leader Myron Clark), for others class simply continued to signify the journeymen and masters of the crafts.

By the time the Know-Nothings appeared in politics, there were additional kinds of political displacement. One of these was the disappearance of the Whig Party. After the decline of the American Republicans, the Whigs were stronger than before and stronger than Tammany. Part of the reason for this shift in relative party strengths was that Tammany suffered from the Barnburner–Free Soil exodus of the late 1840s. Whigs also, however, gained the adherence of former nativists in most wards in which nativists had been strong: In the seventh, eighth, ninth, tenth, thirteenth, sixteenth, and seventeenth wards, Whigs were stronger after 1846 than they had been through 1843, though the eleventh and fourteenth wards returned to Tammany. The disappearance of the Whigs after 1852 was not the end of a gradual decline but rather, in the city, the rather sudden withdrawal of an important political force, leaving its adherents without a banner. In addition, there was disaffection with Tammany on local grounds. Beginning in 1850, there was increased insurgency within the Democratic ranks, ward organizations contesting "tyrannical" intraparty practices. From the point of view of these grievances, the Know-Nothings presented an attractive alternative. The party was organized by councils, with each ward in the city having a council and in addition elaborate subward organizations. Scisco wrote that

> the Know-Nothing council in its best days was, in point of fairness and decency, a vast improvement over the average party caucus of the time. Every voter in the council had free expression, and the ultimate decision was executed by proper officers with energy and system ...

He concluded that "the individual voter in the secret order probably had more real influence upon politics than the average individual in the parties outside the Order."[41]

The broad contours of the history of political nativism in the United States also suggest that its political as well as "cultural" origins deserve attention. Political nativism flourished nationally in the 1850s, in the decade from 1886 to 1896, and from World War I into the 1920s – all eras of crisis in the national party system. Like the Progressives or anti-Masons, who also appeared in periods of realignment, the nativist movement was symptomatic of general political crisis.[42] The trajectory of political nativism in the antebellum era supports the notion that its adherents had specifically *political* grievances. Not only did the American Republicans provoke an enormous increase in turnout, but as the party declined the electorate shrank again, suggesting that many of those who found American Republicanism supportable did not find an alternative they could support in the major parties. In the 1850s, while the Know-Nothings also provoked an increase in turnout, these new voters did not retire when the party disappeared – an argument for the view that those in the movement could support one of the emerging major parties.

Political nativism, then, embraced a complex set of impulses. There was a desire, inherited from the temperance and related movements, to distinguish oneself from the poor and spendthrift immigrant. There was a desire, in the face of complex and disruptive changes both in neighborhoods and in getting and spending, for a return to (an obviously romanticized notion of) a homogeneous society, for "closing this fatal chasm in our social system, ... knitting up those social sympathies again." There was, simply, hatred and fear of Catholics as fellow citizens and of the Church of Rome.

As important as any of these was the fact that the mechanics found so little resonance between their own artisan republicanism and the visions of society put forward by the major parties. For artisans, politics and their place in politics were at the center of their whole understanding of the world. Political nativism was symptomatic not only of the general political crisis we understand as the decline of a party system, but also of the crisis of artisan republicanism provoked by the destruction of Workingmen's ideology by the major parties. The platforms of the major parties not only presented visions that displaced the mechanics rhetorically, but also embraced policies that abandoned them in fact. Political nativism offered remedies for both the symbolic and the objective grievances. Nativism promised not only to restore the independent mechanic to his former role of political centrality, thereby raising his status, but also to restore his social centrality by bringing immigration – and with it, the advance of the industrial system – to a halt. Then men might knit up their social sympathies once again.

SOLIDARITIES AND VOTES: THE DEMOCRATS

Political grievances, craft solidarities, and cultural affinities all contributed to support for American Republicans and Know-Nothings. Democratic partisanship too was a product of political dynamics, class loyalties, and cultural self-defense. Democrats did not at first cater to those immigrants who became in time its supporters. Democrats opposed the claims of nativists by insisting that the Democracy was the "true home of the working classes." The party's rhetorical attacks on "aristocracy" and its insistence on equality provided arguments supporting popular antipathy to the Public School Society even while the party hierarchy opposed the common-school system. The party's militant prolabor rhetoric contributed to labor's alienation from the benevolent empire. For these and other reasons, union leaders and labor radicals as well as many American-born wage workers supported the party in preference to the alternatives. Because the working classes were largely foreign-born, it was perhaps inevitable that the party claiming to protect their political interests was bound, once religion and culture became politicized, to protect their cultural interests as well. As the Democracy's stance in the school controversy demonstrates, it was not in a great hurry to defend immigrants' cultural interests. Yet once the Whigs openly allied themselves with American Republicans, the Democracy became, half despite itself, the party of choice of much of the immigrant electorate.

Like the native-born, immigrant voters were responding to available political choices, cultural ties, and shared class experience. Three immigrant groups were numerous enough to receive political attention in antebellum New York: the British Protestants, the Germans, and the Irish Catholics. Of these, the first group was by far the smallest, and though the nativists worked hard to win their votes (and probably did win more than half of them) the major parties did not pay much attention to them. More than twice as numerous, the Germans by 1855 accounted for perhaps 10,000 votes (or about 15 percent of the electorate). Their political history is one of consistent division between the major parties. In the 1840s, German Whigs and German Democrats were organized factions, demanding a share of patronage and nominations.[43] Like the more strongly Democratic Irish, German voters cared deeply about school and temperance. In the 1850s, German Democrats endorsed those nominees of various Democratic factions they thought supported nonnativist, antitemperance, and sometimes land-reform platforms.[44] Unlike the Irish, however, the Germans were heavily engaged in trades still organized along craft lines. For them, the promise of tariff protection was a strong argument in favor first of Whig and then Republican partisanship. Land reform and hope of tariff protection drew some Germans (like some native-born and radical workingmen) into the Republican party in the late 1850s,[45] though the majority of Germans probably remained within the Democratic party.

The Irish Catholics were the special object of nativist politics and evangelical crusading, they were far and away the city's most numerous immigrant group, and they have been the central figures in the history of machine politics. Their support for Tammany Hall and their rapid ascent to power within it are legendary. Like most legends, those about the fervent partisanship and political power of the Irish are partly mythical. The stance of the Democrats during the school controversy is ample evidence that the party was hardly more anxious than the Whigs to be known as an ally of Irish Catholics. Tammany was slow to give nominations to the Irish and gave them only the lowest of patronage jobs. Irish politicians like Michael Walsh (described in the next chapter) and John Kelley began their careers fighting Tammany Hall. The first hurrah was a long time coming.

Indeed, it did not come until after the Civil War. In the antebellum period, Democrats in power did not stop government from assisting the cultural offensive of the evangelicals. Democratic politicians, like others, funded Protestant proselytizing through charitable agencies, much to the disgust of the *Freeman's Journal*.[46] As late as the 1850s, common-school teachers who refused to read to their classes from the Protestant Bible were fired, over the protests of Catholic parents. The firings were confined to the fourth, sixth and fourteenth wards – all centers of Irish settlement and Democratic votes.[47]

In addition to their cultural grievances, the Irish were prominent in the labor movement and joined in its demands. Nearly all the officers of the New York Tailors' Union were Irish in 1854, and the Irish were important in the organization of longshoremen and laborers.[48] Leaders of Irish descent were found as well in the trade organizations of blacksmiths, cigar makers, boilermakers, porters, shoemakers, printers, and the construction trades[49] and, through these, in the New York City Industrial Congress. There Irish-American Edward Mallon of the tailors was well known as an advocate of political action to remedy the difficulties of the working classes. In 1853, the Irish Societies Convention, a labor organization, pressured candidates to vote for ten-hours legislation.[50] Like other workers, Irish workers objected to the contract system and the requirement of political endorsement to secure employment on public works.[51] The Irish Societies Convention argued that only contractors and politicians gained from the system.[52] And in the 1850s Irishmen like James McGuire were prominent in the demonstrations of the unemployed (see Chapter 6).

Despite these grievances, after the open alliance of the Whigs with the American Republicans, Tammany had become increasingly adamant in its opposition to nativism, and the Irish were solidly Democratic, if somewhat cynically so. The *Irish American* explained Irish support for the Democrats in this way in 1852:

> The Democratic Party may have anti-adopted citizens and anti-Irish views and prejudices (and we believe they are not exempt from them) but [by putting some Irishmen on their tickets] they act as if they loved us. We ask the Whigs to do the same, and then they will have a clear stage, and no favor for the "Irish Vote."[53]

The appearance of loving was built on the skillful combination of cultural and class issues with republican civil liberties. Democratic rhetoric joined the issues of culture, class, and liberty, as when the Maine Law (temperance legislation) was denounced as a "sumptuary law," and as such, "the bane of all republics ... "[54] Democrats were strong in their opposition to temperance legislation, hailing the election of a Democratic governor in 1855 as "a triumph of social, political, and religious rights ... over the malign and dangerous influences of fanaticism, bigotry, and intolerance ... ."[55] Know-Nothings were denounced as "traitors to the Constitution, and ... bigots and fanatics in religion, ... secret and midnight plotters ... who dare not in the day of truth and light advocate their own doctrines or avow their own objects."[56] Democratic opponents were charged with discrimination, as when one was accused of having refused Catholics freedom of worship and forbidden nuns to visit when he was governor of the almshouse.[57] "The Democratic Party alone," it was insisted, "helped the working classes, was in favor of education of the children of the poor man, ... of granting religious tolerance ... [Citizens] were alone indebted to the Democratic Party that they were allowed to worship God according to the dictates of their consciences."[58]

The ties binding civil liberties, social freedoms, and Democratic votes were strengthened in the 1850s. In April 1855, the state legislature passed a Maine Law, an abomination to the city's drinkers and especially to its

German and Irish immigrants. The Democratic mayor, Fernando Wood, gave lip service to the law but was clearly unwilling to enforce it.[59] To follow through, the legislature in 1857 created a metropolitan police force for Kings, Westchester, Richmond, and New York counties and abolished the city's police force. Not only was the legislature protemperance, it was also Republican, as were the new police commissioners and, if the commissioners hired as they were expected to, the policemen as well. The city government contested the legality of these arrangements in the courts and lost.[60] In the meantime, however, the metropolitan police were seen in the immigrant community as temperance thugs, and their presence provoked riots among the Irish and Germans. Opposition to the police in the name of "municipal liberty," combined with the partisan origins and temperance intentions of the police, bound the Irish and a portion of the Germans to the Democratic Party.[61]

In the 1850s, these voters were, more emphatically than they were Democrats, supporters of Mayor Fernando Wood. Wood distinguished himself not only by being the "first true friend of the Irish" among the Democrats but also by being responsive to the demands of the working classes.[62] On both accounts he had the support of the Irish press throughout the 1850s. When he left Tammany Hall to found his own organization, he paid special attention to his immigrant constituency. Wood housed his own organization in Mozart Hall, a meeting place of the Germans. Unlike his predecessors, Wood took special care that Mozart Hall assisted immigrant wards in organizing sympathetic slates to run for the ward school boards.[63] Like Tweed after him, Wood associated himself openly with the "dangerous classes." If in 1842 the support of the foreign-born, and particularly Irish Catholics, had been unimportant, by 1855 foreign-born voters accounted for half the electorate, and the day was past when a man could become mayor who was not seen as their friend.

The era of status politics created some of the enduring features of New York's party system. For the rest of the century, the Democracy was the party of immigrant voters, and its opponents bore the narrow and persecuting taint of nativism. These alignments and the status politics that preceded them were not simply a "natural" outcome of ethnic diversity. Sometimes social differences are not matters of conflict at all; sometimes they are fought out in the street; sometimes they are matters of political controversy. Nativism and political nativism are a case in point. Although there were always nativists about in the nineteenth century and well into the twentieth, the timing of *political* nativism is strongly related to eras of realignment of the national party system, and at other times nativists have for the most part been ignored. This suggests that political nativism succeeds when its prospective adherents are experiencing *political* displacement. Similarly, attention to political grievances and political subcultures helps to explain why some of the United States–born became nativists and others did not.

For New York's artisans, politics and their place in politics were at the center of a common belief system, a vision of society largely unchanged for generations. The major parties, by abandoning that vision, abandoned artisans symbolically[64] (as their policies abandoned them in fact). Later, the disappearance of the Whigs left former Whigs (and American Republicans) without any political banner until the Know-Nothings appeared. American Republicanism and the Know-Nothing Council seemed to restore the hardworking, independent, and thoughtful mechanic to his rightful place in the political system. Moreover, both nativist parties built on craft solidarity and artisan pride. This should not be surprising: The cultural division of labor meant that ethnic and status solidarities also had class referents. The "mutualism" of American Republican, Whig, and Know-Nothing politics embraced status, politics, and craft.

Elsewhere, too, status politics involved both class referents and political grievances, thought these were not always the same from place to place, nor was the style of nativist politics everywhere the same. In Baltimore as in New York, Know-Nothing strength was born of political disorder.[65] There, too, the class dimensions of Know-Nothingism were clear, but they were of a different sort. Know-Nothing success in politics followed hard on the heels of the first industrial strike in Baltimore. In 1853, nearly 4,000 ironworkers across the city went on strike for higher wages. Led by the Organization of United American Mechanics and other nativist groups, militant workers succeeded in securing some wage concessions. For their part, Baltimore Democrats sided with the employers. Moreover, Maryland's Democratic Party claimed many of the state's Catholic landed elite. Thus in Baltimore political nativism had a more proletarian cast, and the Democratic Party was an alliance of wealth and poverty. Baltimore Know-Nothings chose as their symbol the shoemaker's awl, and the party found support among the gangs and "dangerous classes."[66] The party's most popular leader, Henry Winter Davis, was a party boss. Similarly, Philadelphia's Joel Sutherland and Pittsburgh's Joel Barker were nativists not in the "mutualist" style, but in the militant style that in New York was associated with the Democracy.

In New York, some of those who remained artisans were eventually won to the slogan, "free soil, free labor, free men." Others, and the far more numerous wage workers, joined the Democracy. Like those who voted Republican, the wage workers too were inheritors of artisan republicanism. Their task in the antebellum era was to refashion that vision to better accord with the world of nineteenth-century work and politics. That change in world view, and its political importance, is the subject of the next chapter.

6 The voice of industry

THE WORKING CLASSES changed dramatically over the antebellum years. Growth and industrialization created new social places in which the working classes got, spent, and labored, and determined their increasing distinctiveness from other social groups as the wage laborer replaced the artisan. The changing character of the working classes also involved changes in their patterns of collective behavior, their political values, and their political demands. Since the new working classes were largely urban, it was in the city that their political capacity was greatest and that they had a significant impact on political life.

The transformation and the persistence in the political aims and values of the working classes helped to produce the broader ideological changes of the antebellum city, the increasing distinctiveness of city politics, and the persona of the boss. The working classes were empowered by the franchise, disciplined by their need to make political alliances, and constrained by available political choices. Like other social forces, their political will was mediated by the rules and order of politics. This chapter traces the relationships between the changing working classes and the city's political order.

THE AGE OF JACKSON

The mechanics of the Jacksonian era were the proud bearers of the ideology of Paine and the Revolution. They voiced, through the Workingmen's Parties and the General Trades' Union, a distinctive republicanism. Mechanics' demands were justified in the terms of a political understanding founded in natural rights and claiming that the object of government is "the promotion of the happiness and prosperity of the governed." Within this world view, the Workingmen's Parties voiced demands drawing on the needs of upstate mechanics and farmers as well as mechanics, laborers, and small businessmen in the city. The General Trades' Union justified unionization in republican, political terms. These included the notion that the members of society should be bound together as a family; mechanics objected to the "spirit of trade" that encouraged individualism and turned men away from their social obligations. These elements of the political culture of the working classes kept their political views distinct from those of the major parties, but also provided the themes of their attachment to the parties.

At the beginning of the Age of Jackson, the Workingmen's Parties claimed to be the representatives of mechanics, farmers, and laborers. The complex tale of party factions, famous radicals, pro-Clay opportunists, and more genuine representatives of what came to be the labor movement cannot be retold here. For this account of the working classes in city politics, two aspects of the Workingmen's experience are important. First, certain ambiguous qualities of the parties reveal changes that had occurred between the eighteenth-century heyday of the artisan and the appearance of wage labor in the nineteenth century. Second, the programmatic successes and failures, and party division after 1831, foreshadow much of the history of antebellum workingmen.

The Workingmen's Party was not the first of a new set of activities of an emergent wage-labor force, but the last appearance of a form of political action that was traditional among mechanics.[1] This group had long exhibited both craft and class consciousness; their interventions in politics have a long political history. From time to time in New York City, beginning in 1734, the "mechanics" ran tickets for assembly and city council (even under the restricted franchise, workingmen formed a majority of the electorate). The earliest of these were in fact organized by opposition leaders from elite political factions. The same was true of the early years of the Sons of Liberty. Yet during the prerevolutionary disturbances, mechanics in the Sons of Liberty increasingly pushed merchants and lawyers out of positions of leadership. In addition, they formed an organization of their own, the General Society of Mechanics and Tradesmen (GSMT), an organization of journeymen and masters. The GSMT agitated for independence, worked as one of the ad hoc bodies enforcing the decisions of the Continental Congress, and continued political activity after the Revolution. This later political activity involved running separate slates for city and state elections. The GSMT formed an alliance with the Federalists in the struggle for the Constitution in the eighties, and in the nineties, for a variety of reasons that need not be discussed here, their allegiance was split by Federalists and Republicans. These parties ran mechanic candidates on their tickets, and separate GSMT tickets were given up. Once the Federalist Party declined, however, in the absence of an opposition party, mechanics periodically split off from Republicans to nominate their own tickets for state assembly, and the forerunners of the Workingmen's Parties of 1828–31 may be identified in the mechanic factions of the Era of Good Feelings.[2]

Unlike the mechanic factions of earlier times, however, the Workingmen's Party was not the expression of a unified producing or industrial interest. For example, though some masters were active in the Workingmen's Party, there was an effort to keep out any "boss who employed a large number of hands."[3] For their part, masters were likely to be found in the GSMT, which had become largely their own organization, expressing an ideology increasingly divergent from that of the journeymen.[4] Despite some hostility to "bosses" and lack of emphasis on the needs of common laborers, the Workingmen's Party defined the producing classes broadly – including anyone "who followed any *useful* occupation, mental or physical, for a livelihood."[5] Party demands represented widespread needs. Farmers, for example, also suffered from the militia system and from imprisonment for debt; the lien law was a pressing issue "followed up and echoed from almost every chartered village of any magnitude in the state."[6] So Upstate "in most ... places farmers were included" and branches of the party bore names like the "Committee of the Farmers, Mechanics, and other Working Men" in Albany.[7]

In the city, the demands of the Workingmen for democratization – demands for single-member districts for state assemblymen, the direct election of the mayor, a simplification of laws, compensation for city-council members, and an improved public-school system – as well as objection to the auction system affected others besides mechanics and wage laborers. It is not surprising, then, that democratically minded grocers, physicians, and attorneys were activists in the party.[8] The prison-labor issue affected particular crafts (stoneworkers, shoemakers, and locksmiths among them), and representatives of these trades were especially prominent in the party. Finally, the right to unionize and the desire for a legal limit to the working day affected both mechanics and wage laborers and drew their support.

This variety in the party's bases of support was important, for, with few exceptions, its demands required action by the state government. The alliances within the party supporting particular demands had a great deal to do with the party's success. Where broad groups Upstate as well as in the city were affected, the party was successful. A lien law was passed in 1832 (and subsequently more stringent lien laws were passed in 1844, 1851, 1855, and 1861).[9] Imprisonment for debt was abolished in 1831.[10] The militia system, too, though it was not abolished, was not rigorously enforced, and in 1846 was essentially discontinued under the new state constitution. Similarly, democratizing reforms for the city were also largely achieved. The mayor became an elected official in 1834, simplification of the laws was proceeding under additional impetus, voter registration (which Workingmen regarded as a measure that would decrease workingmen's participation) was not seriously attempted until the mid-1840s, and although the common-school system was not extended to New York City until 1842, a real-estate tax for the purpose of funding public schools was levied by the state assembly in 1829 and the rate was raised in 1831.[11]

Those issues directly affecting journeymen mechanics and wage laborers received less attention. Compensation for the common council, jurors, and witnesses was not achieved, nor were ten-hours legislation or the abolition of prison labor.[12] Ten hours was established as the regular workday, in New York and other cities, by economic action.[13]

This pattern of success and failure foreshadows much of the experience of the next generation of the working classes: the opposition of the major parties to independent political action on the part of labor, success where other interests could be allied to their needs, the turn to economic action, and labor's political isolation in the cities. The disintegration of mechanics' political world view at the hands of politicians of the dominant parties helps to explain both the adamantly nonpartisan position of later organizations of the working classes and the division of the Workingmen – leaders and followers alike – between the two parties.

The demise of the party did not mean the disappearance of its views. In 1833, the General Trades' Union, a union of unions, was formed in the city. By the year's end, twenty-one societies from New York, Brooklyn, and Newark had joined the organization, prepared to sustain one another's "combined efforts for the purpose of self-protection." The trades prominent in the GTU, building trades, tailors, shoemakers, cabinetmakers, and bakers, show that although the organization was an organization of journeymen, these were skilled men, and the GTU had little to do with unskilled workers and common laborers.[14]

If the political rhetoric of the Jacksonian era had eighteenth-century leitmotifs, nowhere in the city did those themes sound so clearly as among New York's organized mechanics. The republicanism articulated by journeymen, like that voiced by the Workingmen's Parties, managed the tensions of liberty and equality, particular interest and common good, state interventionism and freedom of action, that the major parties opposed to one another.[15] Moreover, they retained an emphasis on character and morality that, in the party system, found full expression only in the nativist parties. These aspects of artisan republicanism not only distinguished it from the republicanism of the major parties, but were also an expression, as I indicated in Chapter 2, of views that in the eighteenth century and beyond the turn of the century were consensual. The rhetorical oppositions of freeman and slave, aristocracy and republicanism; the denunciation of demagogues and championing of the industrious and virtuous artisan and farmer; the expectation of even-handed regulation by the state of the pursuit of wealth and the emphasis on natural rights, gave eighteenth-century republicanism its power and nineteenth-century journeymen both a weapon for justifying their interests and a radical *political* critique of their opponents. "Our republicanism," the GTU declared, is "founded in the laws of nature, of equality, and reciprocity."[16]

The activity of trade unions seeking to prevent pay cuts, obtain raises, or simply establish their legitimacy were understood in these terms. When employing curriers refused to hire members, the GTU's press praised the journeymen curriers for having "properly resisted their attempted tyrannical coalition like freemen ..."[17] Wage labor, too, was seen in political terms: "We are satisfied," Seth Luther argued to the 1835 National Trades' Union Convention in New York City, "that the present system of manufacturing is a system of mental and physical slavery, to which the sons and daughters of freemen ought never to submit."[18] It was of course as freemen that Americans were distinguished from journeymen elsewhere. "In reviewing the history of nations," the GTU editorialized, "we find that laws have always been found on their records, which were purposely enacted to screen the few from receiving the merited chastisement of the many. The justice of such legislation was not fairly considered, until the period of our revolution – the declaration that 'all men are born free and equal' gave a new aspect to the condition of the species. Under this God-given sentiment oppression must wither, however much it may suit the vicious to sneer, or the tyrant to grumble. The tree will ultimately bear, and the fruit will be reached."[19]

Not only was the language of self-defense political, but the analysis of the degradation of labor also revealed to the mechanics the *political* causes of their distress. Arguing that American mechanics need not fear that immigration would cause an oversupply of labor and consequent reduction of wages, *The Union* declared that

> the low prices which the operatives of England receive is not caused by the scarcity of employment: but their insufficient pay arises from the unequal influence which capital is permitted to sway in that country. The capitalists there are daily adding to their wealth .... The capitalist will not forego his profit – he must be enriched, and consequently the people do not toil alone for the support of the government, but they are forced to create wealth for the trading nabobs of the country.[20]

This marked a perversion of "the object of government," which "should be the happiness and comfort of its citizens." "It is in duty bound," the National Trades' Union declared, "when any of them are oppressed, to remove all just cause of complaint, as far as in its power lies ... "[21]

These views cut across party lines, but they also meant that mechanics' attention to politics was vital. The fear of "incurring the wrath of the parties" meant, however, that labor organizations were careful. On these grounds, the National Trades' Union decided to substitute the word "intellectual" for the word "political" in its resolutions.[22] The National Trades' Union was in any event ambivalent at best toward the policies of the major parties. The NTU's resolution on the tariff, for example, declared that although the union could "repudiate the principle and practices of government in levying high tariff duties on the importation of foreign merchandize, we nevertheless conceive it to be the bounden duty of our government to protect the mechanic arts that have grown up with the country ... "[23] Neither party behaved to the union's satisfaction. John Commerford called the female employees of the cotton mills "the miserable victims of the American system."[24] In the city, the GTU attacked the hypocrisy of those who claimed to protect the working classes, but did not behave accordingly. In October 1835, a bipartisan committee of the common council refused to provide rooms for the National Trades' Union convention, "affording emphatic proof," according to GTU, "that loud-mouth denunciations showered so plentifully [by these men on their political opponents] were but the empty and wicked bellowings of designing political demagogues."[25]

On these grounds, Tammany was especially vulnerable to attack. After Tammany refused space for a union meeting in Tammany Hall (the meeting was to protest judicial decisions in the tailors' conspiracy trial), *The Union* attacked "the bold face hypocrisy of those who are always the most boisterous in their professions of democracy to the people ... the mechanics generally are convinced, that the reputed leaders of this ... party are they who have been the most prominent in getting up the crusade, which is now going on to batten down the rights and privileges of the laboring classes."[26]

The Union was also sensitive to the potential abuse of government payrolls for partisan purposes. At the first efforts to create a paid fire-fighting force, *The Union* commented that "when this takes place, the authorities will have to pay men to perform duties which are now performed out of emulation and independence." It was, *The Union* editorialized, "clearly an effort to create a partisan machine." Moreover, the increased expense would be borne by workingmen. "The Insurance Companies and property holders will not be the losers; consequently, the tenants will be saddled with the whole of the expense. The scheme will create another pretext for raising the rents of our already overburdened citizens."[27]

The GTU, like the Workingmen's Party before it, supported ten-hours legislation, public education, and the abolition of prison labor. Only on the first was real progress made, and this by economic action. So, on their visits to New York or at the National Trades' Union convention, cities and trades reported their progress. In Philadelphia, New York City, and Baltimore, the system was "generally established"; in Newark, among outdoor mechanics; in Albany, Troy, and Schenectady, by some of the building and metal trades and among coach makers. Nowhere successful in achieving ten-hours legislation, workingmen won the ten-hour day craft by craft, city by city, through organization and strikes. The single political victory – and an important one it was – was Van Buren's ten-hour order for federal employees.[28]

The overriding issue for labor was unionization. This was so not only because of the effectiveness of unionization where it occurred, but also because of the resistance of unionization by the courts. In June 1836, culminating a series of such decisions across the union, Judge Ogden Edwards in New York ruled that twenty-five members of the Union Society of Journeymen Tailors were guilty of conspiracy. A meeting was called in City Hall Park. Robert Townsend, Jr. (a Whig), who had been active in the Workingmen's Party, presided, and labor's prominent leaders were there – John H. Bowie, James McBeath, William Masterson, and Isaac Odell of the General Trades' Union. Alexander Ming, Jr., and Levi D. Slamm of the Democratic Workingmen's General Committee were there as well. Edwards's decision was declared "manifestly partial and unjust," part of "a concerted plan of the aristocracy to take from them that Liberty which was bequeathed to them, as a sacred inheritance by their sires – an inheritance purchased by their blood, and consummated by their patriotism and wisdom." And since there was a "close alliance ... between the leaders of the two great political parties of this state, to crush the laboring men," it was resolved that workingmen throughout the state should send delegates to a convention at Utica to found a political party. By the fall elections, the Equal Rights Party was established.[29]

Whatever its role Upstate or elsewhere in the union, the Equal Rights Party – the Locofocos – was not, in the city, a re-forming of the Workingmen's Party.[30] Locofocos were in their constituency, as they were ideologically, radical Democrats. After a brief insurgency, they quickly returned to Tammany Hall. Yet they were important for the political development of the workingmen, and the insurgency had an impact on Tammany Hall. The radicals who became prominent through the Locofocos, especially those who had been leaders in the General Trades' Union as well, John Commerford and Ely Moore, served as political spokesmen for labor throughout the antebellum years. Moore was elected to Congress and, as "labor's first Congressman" and author of a widely reprinted speech defending workingmen politically, was a national champion of their interests.[31] Commerford became committed to land reform and eventually joined the Republicans, but remained a labor spokesman in the Democracy until well into the 1850s. Alexander Ming, Jr., also rose to prominence in the Locofoco revolt. These men became labor's spokesmen in Tammany and often outside it. Not least among their achievements, the radical contingent in Tammany pressed successfully for the democratizing reforms of the new state constitution of 1846.[32]

Tammany rhetoric had a considerably more radical ring to it after the Locofoco revolt. Radical Democrats, with Van Buren in the lead, spoke of conspiracies and the political ascendancy of the rich, and workingmen agreed that this was a pernicious situation. Yet workingmen also had expectations of reciprocity between rich and poor that did not suit the small government, laissez-faire stance of the Democrats. Labor leaders were angry not simply that the rich monopolized governmental offices but that when they did so they turned political power to the ends of personal aggrandizement. This was to be expected, for "when men are bent on enriching themselves, they generally endeavor to destroy the affinity that should subsist between them as members of one common family." Rather than governing "solely for the benefit of the people who compose it as well as for the general good of mankind," rich men in government acted to the end of "individual aggrandizement."[33] These notions were at the center of workingmen's criticism of those devoted to the "spirit of trade," and the "study of accumulation" rather than "the happiness of the people."

In the Age of Jackson, then, the working classes persisted in holding views that distinguished them from the major parties. Their values and demands, expressed in the Workingmen's Party, enabled them to secure rural allies Upstate and allies from the middle classes in the city. As industrialization progressed and the working classes became more proletarian and more foreign-born, they were increasingly isolated in the city. There, their analysis of the causes of their discontent changed from an understanding centered on political inequalities to one that emphasized socioeconomic arrangements. As the industrial system was recognized as a force in its own right, workingmen for the most gave up their hopes for a society united like "members of one family." Yet their notions of justice and of the rights of workingmen persisted. The result was that although the organized working classes expected less from their employers, they demanded more from city government.

INTERIM

After the demise of the General Trades' Union in the panic of 1837, workingmen were without a unified voice. Workers in the 1840s waged a bitter struggle in the workplace for the ten-hour day, but in the same decade labor was relatively silent in politics. The forties are appropriately remembered, then, more as a decade of political reform movements than as a decade of labor politics. There were nevertheless two important political developments for workingmen in the 1840s. The first was the appearance of a new persona in politics, the workingman's advocate. The second development was the radical reform movements themselves. Their relation to the labor movement was both tenuous and complex, yet in the 1840s radicals formed a network among themselves, with labor, and with the parties, that served labor in the 1850s. In the city, this meant the contribution of organizational and leadership skills and the promotion of a platform that enabled workingmen to have an impact on the Democrats. At the same time, the work of land reformers laid the groundwork for Republican adherents from the working class. Taken together, these two developments point both to the political capacity of the working classes and to their fragmentation and dependence on party.

The workingman's advocate was sometimes genuinely committed to and identified with the cause of labor and in other cases an opportunist – I mean the term to describe a political style. Although there had always been labor spokesmen in the parties, the workingman's advocate was different. Flamboyant and tough, he denounced capitalists, speculators, and exploiters, championed the laborer, and associated himself conspicuously with the rougher elements. It was a style suggested by labor's most plentiful resource – muscle – and a stance that was successful both because of the stylistic identification and because the workingman's advocate articulated popular grievances. Not enough of an organization man to be a true boss, and likely to lose his constituency if he seemed to be working too well with the major parties, the workingman's advocate boasted a loyal personal following and potentially a broader popularity.

In New York, the first workingman's advocate was Mike Walsh. His career foreshadows both the demagoguery of Fernando Wood and, beyond him, of the boss. Walsh's popularity in combination with the tensions between him and the radicals, on the one hand, and the regular party, on the other, reveal something of popular sentiment. His truculent self-presentation was necessitated by the resistance of the party to his program, and his program embodied what would be the essentials of workerist reform for two decades to come. Finally, his failures reveal the political isolation of the emerging working class.

Walsh was a Democrat; an opponent of banks and the tariff; an admirer of Calhoun and defender of the rights of slaveholders; and a supporter of hard money, rotation in office, reasonable pay for officeholders, and the like. He was also, however, a workerist who fought prison labor and contract labor; opposed land grants to railroads; worked for an end to child labor, ten-hours legislation, a reform of landlord laws, and land reform; supported Thomas Dorr and the antirenters; and fought sabbatarianism at every opportunity. Although these positions made Walsh popular, they also made for tensions between him and his party.[34]

Walsh's own political base was the Spartan Association, founded in 1840, a gang whose members lived in the sixth and fourteenth wards. In 1842, he was estimated to have 400 followers.[35] Walsh also published a newspaper, the *Subterranean*, which was "uncompromising in its support of the working class and merciless in its exposure of corruption" both in other parties and his own.[36] The Democrats offered Walsh a place on their assembly ticket if he would give up the Spartans. Instead, Walsh literally forced his way into Tammany, the Spartans taking over a nominating meeting to ensure Walsh a place on the ticket. In the race and in the assembly, Walsh remained as outspoken in favor of labor's interests and in criticism of party "hypocrisy" as before.

The party was denounced for presenting nonmechanics to preside at mechanics' meetings, and Walsh argued that the only mechanics who received nominations were "milk and water men." He called on the working classes to purify their party, claiming that if the party only adhered to its principles it "need never apprehend defeat." And the party was greatly in need of purification. Its nominating meetings were "a most ridiculous and insulting farce," in which those who benefited from city or state contracts organized their employees – "poor men whose spirits have been broken and whose frames have been withered and bowed by the worst form of slavery" – to ratify the choices of the party hierarchy, even if the choices were those of "their LABOR'S PLUNDERER." The party itself valued contributions of money, but not the hours of devoted workingmen.

In the assembly, Walsh introduced ten-hours legislation, fought the contract system, and tried to have child labor outlawed, but found very few allies. Even his proposal to amend the General Manufacturing Act to limit the hours of labor of women and children to ten a day and sixty a week was defeated by a vote of 71 to 37.[37] Thus, while Walsh was a force to be reckoned with in the city, he could at most be a gadfly in the assembly, and later in Congress, just as the force he represented had its greatest strength in the urban setting.

Walsh was connected with the labor movement and with land reformers as well. In 1844, he and George Henry Evans traveled to Lowell and to the Working Men's Convention in Boston; in the same year, the *Subterranean* and Evans's *Working Men's Advocate* were briefly merged. Yet Walsh was more concerned with the "purification" of the Democrats to bring immediate relief – say, through ten-hours legislation – than with whatever ultimate relief might be granted through land reform.[38]

Radicals, too, were interested in more immediate measures than land reform. In the 1840s, in addition to a series of political efforts at land reform, Evans and others articulated a program that, like Walsh's, embodied the essentials of what in the 1850s would even more clearly constitute workerist reform. In 1844, for example, Evans outlined a program for reform of the city government that included pay for aldermen, economical administration, and relief of distress as a right, not a charity.[39] And in 1845, even the *Herald* – a paper notorious for its "anti-ism" stance – published Evans's program for political reform, which included not only land limitation and the common list of Democratic reforms, but also a change in the tax system and the construction of public works by the community rather than by contractors.[40] Land reformers did support ten-hours legislation, if not because they believed in its own value, then because they desired the alliance of labor. As a result, the land reform congresses, the New York

State Industrial Legislature, and the New York City Industrial Congress all involved both radical and labor representatives. In the mid-1840s, with labor planks included in their platforms, land reformers organized alternately to run for office or to demand that candidates of the major parties pledge themselves to land-reform platforms. In this they were not generally successful. In 1844, for example, not a single statewide candidate responded to their requests, though in subsequent years they did better.[41]

Whatever the difficulties of enacting land-reform legislation itself, the years of activity in the 1840s represented a fund of experience both with labor and with electoral politics. The lack of viability of their own party combined with some legislative response and marginal achievements for land reform at the New York State Constitutional Convention in 1846 brought radicals into loose association with the Democrats. Some, like John Commerford, John Windt, and Alexander Ming, had long been mediators between the labor movement, radicals, and the Democrats. Others, like William V. Barr, an English émigré who worked in the seventeenth-ward land-reform association, and Ira B. Davis, who ran the Protective Union (an organization encouraging cooperative ventures), formed ties with the Democrats around 1850. In that year, the party was making special overtures to labor in response to the upsurge in union formation and the organization of the New York City Industrial Congress. The revival of the labor movement enabled the working classes to make their mark on the party.

THE WORKING CLASSES AND THE BOSS

The New York City Industrial Congress was formed in June of 1850. It was a diverse organization, including land reformers and other radicals, trade unionists who wanted unionism "pure and simple," leaders of protective organizations that continued to unite master and journeymen of a single craft, and leaders of the Workingmen's Party of a generation before. At a meeting in City Hall Park in August 1850, in support of journeymen tailors who were establishing a cooperative clothing store, all these were represented.[42] Gilbert Vale and George Henry Evans, leaders of the Workingmen's Party twenty years before, were among those appointed secretaries, as was the German socialist Wilhelm Weitling. K. Arthur Bailey, a member of the Church of Humanity, president of the congress and of Typographical Union No. 6, and prominent land reformer, delivered the main address. Long-time Democrat John Commerford was there, as was his associate in the land-reform movement, Lewis Ryckman. Ira B. Davis of the Protective Union delivered an address, declaring that "you must remake society on a basis where proprietor and laborer are united in the same person."[43] Gilbert Dean and Benjamin Price of Mechanics' Mutual Protection were there as well. More than fifty organizations had sent representatives: stonecutters and marble polishers, bakers, butchers, and confectioners, grocers' clerks and dry-goods clerks, coopers, dyers, saddlers, sail makers, cordwainers, laborers, and porters.

The revival of unionism involved both continuities and new departures. Whereas the General Trades' Union, like the Workingmen's Party before it, located the causes of the distress of the working classes largely in politics, the newer unions understood the dilemmas of workers as centrally socio-economic in origin. "It is useless for us to disguise from ourselves," read the address of the Journeymen Printers in 1850, "the fact that, under the present arrangement of things, there exists a perpetual antagonism between labor and capital."[44] There were still organizations that united master and journeyman, and these called for greater understanding between the classes and their ultimate reconciliation, but there were fewer than a generation before, while unions of wage workers flowered.

At the same time, the independence and equality that earlier workingmen hoped for and the rejection of the industrial system as immoral persisted. Organized workers continued to insist that the "system of competition" was "subversive of morality, religion, and virtue," operating only to the benefit of "capitalists, monopolists, and tyrants" whose "only God is Gold."[45] Bakers argued that the system "enriches the selfish at the expense of the unfortunate, and causes those to be oppressors *who wish to be just*."[46] The contrast of the "independent mechanic" with the "wage-slave" and notions of liberty and natural right also remained meaningful. The bakers asked how, "weary and exhausted after his week's unnatural toil," a man would have the energy to "study Nature and Nature's God."[47] When omnibus drivers organized a union in 1851, they resolved that they regarded "the equality of rights and opportunities as the only basis upon which Society can rest and be productive of happiness, virtue, and freedom"; their union would be "the only safety against a system of slavery whose ultimate effects are plainly shadowed forth as worse than chattel bondage."[48] Strikes and increased wages were not only to better the material condition of workers and "prevent the growth of an unwholesome aristocracy" but also "to bring labor up to its proper elevation and take that position which God intended man should fill – truly independent of his fellows, and above the position of a mere 'wage slave.' "[49]

For its part, the Industrial Congress insisted, with its president K. Arthur Bailey, that "political action on measures designed to elevate the condition of the industrial classes is the surest, speediest, and most effective plan for effecting the exodus of the producing classes from the oppressions and grievances under which they are suffering."[50] Edward Mallon of the tailors reminded workingmen that "there was one weapon the workingmen had in their hands by which they could triumph over capitalists and money . . .

It was more powerful than the gun or the chain behind the barricades of Paris. It was the ballot."[51] Though some labor representatives wanted "unionism pure and simple," the Congress, like the General Trades' Union before it and Evans and others during the 1840s, put forward a program for the protection of labor and of workerist reform. In addition to land reform and ten-hours legislation, the Congress wanted abolition of the contract system and the establishment of a minimum wage on public works, supervisors to be men who had served apprenticeships rather than "political creatures," and job security based on merit rather than partisan affiliation. Further, the Congress demanded that the city establish district surveyors to oversee landlords and rents and enforce a housing code. Like the statements of newly organized unions, the platform of the Congress embraced both continuity with the voice of industry of the 1830s and new ideas. In opposing contract labor and demanding a minimum wage on public works and in supporting ten-hours legislation, the Congress was simply repeating the demands written in *The Union*. The demand for land reform represented the impact of the radicals on both the operation of the Congress and on labor itself.

In the mayoral election of 1850, the Whigs ignored the Congress and its platform, and nativists like Thomas Whitney denounced it. Only the Democratic candidate responded positively. The *Tribune* carried his letter, which endorsed abolition of the contract system and proposed a housing code. The candidate, however, promised more than he or his party was willing to deliver. The contract system involved profits for too many to be given away, and landlord legislation was anathema to the city's property holders for some time to come. At the same time, the party saw the existence of the Industrial Congress as a threat and moved quickly to infiltrate it and disable it from within, as well as making concessions to coopt it from without.[52]

The result was that labor was restive in the party's ranks, not only because the party did not deliver workerist reform but also because of elitist intraparty practices (it will be recalled that democratic intraparty organization was one of the strong appeals of the Know-Nothing Party). In 1850, there were four wards with insurgent labor-land reform tickets, the ninth, tenth, sixteenth, and seventeenth.[53] In the tenth, it was announced that "if Sanford L. Macomber is not elected to the Assembly from this ward, then its Working Men will not have done justice to themselves."[54] In the nineteenth, independents declared: "No more primary meetings – no more packed conventions – no more club law – no more obstacles to direct voting."[55] In the same year, congressional candidate James Brodes, editor of the *Express*, was denounced for failing to pay union-scale wages, and printers urged that his candidacy be defeated.[56] And when the compromise of 1850 was being debated, "a group of working men in the eighth ward temporarily took control of a Tammany meeting and urged that the group work to abolish wages slavery 'before we meddle with Chattel Slavery.' "[57]

These insurgencies were not particularly important. In the middle years of the decade, however, when depression put thousands out of work, the platform of the Industrial Congress – though by then the Congress itself had ceased to function – became the program of the unemployed. Their demonstrations were supplemented by electoral efforts. Both the clamor of the demonstrations and electoral organization pushed Democratic leaders to make concessions in the direction of workerist reform.

The winters of 1854 through 1857 were hard ones in New York. The great inflation of 1851–2 was followed by mass unemployment in the middle years of the decade. Although other places suffered as well in 1856 and 1857, the depression was longer and more devastating in New York than elsewhere. As in the depression twenty years earlier, union treasuries were quickly depleted by the expenses of maintaining members out of jobs, and union organization deteriorated. The printers, for example, estimated having lost two-thirds of their membership by 1858.[58]

The unemployed were not silent. Each winter, beginning in 1854, the city witnessed mass meetings of the unemployed – meetings as large as 20,000 in City Hall Park, Washington Square, and Tompkins Square. At these meetings all manner of remedies were discussed. A suggestion to raid food stores – or destroy them – was shouted down. Though it was admitted that the wealthy were trying to relieve suffering, private charity was declared both inadequate and degrading. Instead, unemployed workers demanded activity on the part of the city government. Like the Industrial Congress before them, the unemployed demanded that the government abolish the contract system for public works and that it increase public works to provide employment, without partisan preference and with a guaranteed minimum wage. One suggestion was to expand work on Central Park; another was that the city build apartments on its own land, a plan that promised to provide employment, low-income housing, and income to the city treasury. It was demanded – as it had been 100 years before – that the export of grain be curtailed. Workers asked the common council to enact an injunction against evictions so that the homes of the unemployed and their families would be safe. The basic and essential demand, however, was "bread or work," the slogan on the placards of those who marched to City Hall in 1857.[59]

The demonstrations were accompanied by electoral efforts in 1854 and 1855. In the earlier year, Ira B. Davis and others organized the Practical Democrats, a group James Gordon Bennett credited as "an organization of some importance." Its platform (which candidates were asked to endorse or reject) included the range of familiar demands, from land reform to the purification of primaries, abolition of the contract system for "work which can be conveniently done by the authorities," the improvement of city lands by the construction of residential and commercial buildings the city would own and rent, and the divorce of banks from politics.[60] In 1855 the same platform, with the addition of a strong antinativist plank, was put forward under the aegis of the Workingmen's Provisional Committee, also organized by Davis. This time the Workingmen's group nominated tickets, and though the independent slate did not appear on the ballot most of the names turned up on one or another Democratic slate.[61]

Radicals and unionists were prominent both in the demonstrations of the unemployed and in the electoral efforts of the Practical Democrats and the Provisional Committee. Land reformers William West and William Arbuthnot provided leadership in each of these efforts.[62] George Adam and William Rowe, also national reformers, participated in the third-party efforts.[63] Joining them in the attempts to create a workerist third party were Thomas Baker, a cordwainer's delegate to the tailors' support meetings; D. C. Henderson of the Porter's Protective Association; Eben Morgan of the Brass Finishers; Benjamin Price of Mechanics' Mutual Protection and the House Carpenter's Protective Association (who had also worked in land-reform efforts); and Havilah Smith, also of the House Carpenter's Protective Association.[64]

The Democracy was no more indifferent to these pressures and threats than it had been to the Industrial Congress. In 1855, Democratic Mayor Fernando Wood offered in his annual message a general endorsement of the demands of the unemployed, though he offered no specific program for their relief (and in fact vetoed one measure for workingmen's relief passed by the council).[65] By 1857, popular pressure had persuaded him to act more boldly. Echoing the words of the unemployed themselves, Wood argued that

> in the days of general prosperity they labor for a mere subsistence, while other classes accumulate wealth, and in the days of general depression they are the first to feel the change, without the means to avoid or endure reverses. Truly it may be said that in New York those who produce everything get nothing, and those who produce nothing get everything.

Wood proposed that the city issue a special construction stock to finance the purchase of foodstuffs, which would be used to pay those employed on public works. The public works themselves were numerous: the improvement of Central Park; the construction of a new reservoir and some firehouses; the usual grading, paving, curbing, and cleaning of streets; and dock repairs.[66]

The Democratic platform in the same year resolved to make "such amendments to the banking system of this State as may effectively and permanently check the spirit of extravagant speculation" to "give to the laboring and

industrial classes the important advantage of uninterrupted employment"
and to relieve "the inevitable distress of the working classes" by pursuing
public works.[67] Democratic voters were often reminded to vote for those
who would, when in command of public employment, treat their workers
fairly, or of a candidate's efforts to provide employment particularly in
times of distress,[68] and that the party was best understood as the "hard-
working Democracy."[69]

There was enormous opposition to the workingmen's demands and to
the city government's response to them. The *Evening Post* editorialized that
the idea that the state should provide work was

> one of the most monstrous doctrines ever broached in revolutionary
> France ... It is the duty of the people to relieve the poor and to succor
> the distressed. That is a Christian duty, not a political duty ... [70]

"It is not," said the editors of the *Post*,

> for our municipal rulers to undertake to anticipate the ways of provi-
> dence ... the whole system of taking charge of any class of laboring
> men ... is a wrong one. Our government ... has never entered into
> any obligation to find people employment or food. Despotic govern-
> ments do incur such obligations ... But our republican system of gov-
> ernment professes to leave every channel of industry open ... [71]

The *Times* agreed, arguing that

> Fortune, to be sure, showers her favors unequally. Some succeed and
> some fail – but no one thinks of blaming his neighbor for his bad luck.
> The successful owe pity, and when necessary, relief, to their less for-
> tunate brethren. The former owe it as a moral obligation, but the latter
> cannot demand it as a right.[72]

Wood himself was denounced for arousing class hostilities. "To render
any class or set of men responsible for the existing state of things," the
Herald editorialized, "is obviously to ignore the first principles of political
economy ... "[73] John A. Dix agreed that "the assumption that those who
have everything produce nothing, while it is unfounded in fact, is calculated,
by misleading the uninformed, to create mischievous prejudices, and to
disturb the very foundations of society."[74] The Association for Improving
the Condition of the Poor was outraged at Wood's political demagoguery,
claiming it could only lead to "anarchy and lawlessness," blaming "for-
eigners" for introducing the idea of a right to subsistence, and seeing in
these ideas "a darker omen for all the classes of the community than had
frowned upon it from the suspension of banks and the closing of factories."[75]

There was even opposition to Wood within the Democracy. John Van
Buren "condemned ... Wood's message to the Common Council ... rec-
ommending the distribution of meat and flour to workingmen, as a demagogical attempt to array the poor against the rich, which resulted in mobs

and rioting."[76] In November of 1857, a meeting was held at the Merchants' Exchange to denounce Mayor Wood (for corruption), though some of the same men had been present at a dinner in May lauding Wood for his defense of "municipal rights" against the state legislature.[77] By 1858, Wood had been expelled from Tammany Hall and had organized Mozart Hall to compete with it.[78]

There were answers to arguments against relief from the platforms of those who addressed the unemployed and from the press that supported Wood. To the claim that workers' demands sprung from foreign ideas, it was responded that this was simply an old tactic, "to keep you in a divided condition so that you cannot concentrate your action for the benefit of yourselves and fellow workmen."[79] To the argument that workingmen should patiently await the natural workings of the laws of political economy, William West argued that it was obvious that "private capital is insufficient to satisfy the demands of labor. Unless you, therefore, substitute the public for private capital, in the employment of these thousands of idle workmen, it must be apparent that the men cannot live except upon charity . . ."[80] The notion that government could not or had no right to help the unemployed was declared "a species of sophistry that is as insulting to our self-respect as disgusting to our intelligence and discrimination."[81] The *Irish News* was more blunt: "When famine stares fifty thousand workmen in the face – when their wives and little ones cry to them for bread, it is not time to be laying down state maxims of economy, quoting Adam Smith, or any other politico-economical old fogy."[82]

The same arguments were mobilized in support of Wood's mayoral candidacies in 1857 and 1859. Of Wood's reform opponent, it was said that "we know that he will not do anything for the poor until he is obliged to, because if he does not frown on the people he will not be worshipped by the money gods of Wall Street and the aristocrats of this city."[83] "As for Fernando Wood," his supporters argued, "the poor man was as honored by him as the rich . . . [The] one great crime of Fernando Wood was this – that he said no man should starve while there was wealth in New York . . . when poverty comes, give the poor man work, and not alms."[84] "He has not, like his antagonist, been cruel to foreign-born citizens and intolerant" of their religion.[85] "The question," said James McGuire at a workingmen's meeting in Steuben Hall, "is labor as against capital, for at the present time it is capital against labor; but we are determined that it shall be no longer. We mean to make labor the plaintiff and capital the defendant."[86] Ira B. Davis was an ardent supporter of Wood, appearing at meeting after meeting offering his endorsement. In a long speech in the 1857 campaign, Davis contrasted Wood with his reform opponents:

> As Workingmen [Davis said], we are not prone to be invidious, or to indulge in arraying class against class. There are periods, however, when

it becomes necessary, in vindication of ourselves, that we should reveal our thoughts in this particular ... The organs of the opposition are every day reminding their readers of the great respectability of those of whom the Wall Street meeting [in support of the reform candidate] was composed. They tell us that it was made up of merchants, bankers, brokers, and speculators ... With regard to the bankers, brokers, and money changers, we are told from sacred authority, that the respectable and ancient prototypes of these improved modern vocations were whipped from the temple they polluted with their presence ... From ... the occupations these men follow, and the practices they pursue to obtain wealth, we must see that it is not their objection to the personal character of the Mayor which has invited this opposition ... strange as it may appear, the Mayor has to withstand the pelting of this pitiless storm for the mere announcement of a truth, or an admitted axiom of political economy, namely: "That those who produce everything get nothing, and those who produce nothing get everything."[87]

At other meetings, Davis explained Wood's support of the platform of workerist electoral efforts and the demands of the unemployed. The opposition, Davis insisted, were united "for the purpose of defeating our Mayor, because he practically sympathizes with the poor." The same men, Davis was quick to point out, did not object when the state government bailed out the banks, and thus they were guilty of a double standard: "What would be virtuous in them would be a crime in Mayor Wood or the workingmen."[88]

Wood's concessions to workerist reform, in combination with his solicitousness of the immigrant vote (described in the last chapter), won him the mayoralty in 1859 at the head of his Mozart Hall organization. Wood outpolled the Tammany candidate in fifteen of the city's twenty-two wards and tied in another three. The workingmen's support was important. One of the few wards Wood failed to carry was the sixth – the most Irish ward in the city and the one that housed Tammany Hall. Wood succeeded in carrying five wards in which native-born voters outnumbered immigrant voters.

This made Mozart Hall the strongest political organization in the city. In 1860, the state Democratic convention resolved that "we regard New York City as the stronghold of the Democracy in the Empire State, as represented by her delegates ... from Tammany and Mozart Hall – [the] former for the antiquity of her organization and devotion to Democratic principles, and the latter for her indomitable energy and firm adherence to the Democratic cause." If here was an inference that Tammany's power lay in the past, the *Herald* made that inference explicit: The "old Indian squaw," Bennett wrote, "has lost all her prestige and her power ..."[89] In 1860, those in the state who supported Douglas would have to buy Wood's support by sharing the spoils with Mozart Hall.[90]

The successes of Fernando Wood and Mozart Hall offered lessons that were not lost on the Tammany organization. To build a reliable majority, the party needed to fortify opposition to Know-Nothings, temperance, and Black Republicans with clear appeals to the working classes. Veteran Tammany man John Cochrane argued in 1859 that "a heavy weight" of responsibility rested upon "the financial portion of the Democratic party"; what was required was "action on the part of the moneyed classes, in such a manner as should prove to the working men of the Democratic party that the sympathy of those who held the purse strings in their hands was not wanting to them."[91] "Democratic Workingmen's clubs," "permanently established in the wards," began to make their appearance early in the 1860s.[92] If the Republican mayor in 1863 was opposed to helping workingmen avoid the notorious conscription act, the Democratic common council was not, and over the course of the war the city spent millions paying exemption fees for those who chose not to serve.[93]

The working classes whom the Democracy claimed to represent were very different from the "industrious mechanic" who had fought the Revolution, elected Jefferson, and taken issue with the party platforms of the Jacksonian era. While the Painite ideology of the artisans of the Age of Jackson saw the causes of inequality as centrally political – and insisted that there was a common good government could pursue – the working classes of the 1850s diagnosed the causes of their distress as social and economic. For the most part, they abandoned the notion of the common good, and with it hopes for a society of mutually recognized rights and obligations between classes. Although the desire for social familism was at the heart of the nativist movement in New York, the labor movement of the 1850s was distinguished by the admission that there was a "perpetual antagonism between labor and capital." The militance of this position was not an innovation. As Dawley argued, "the militance of the factory worker is hard to imagine without the legacy of artisan protest ..."[94] The identity was new – substantially more proletarian than in the Age of Jackson, the working classes of the 1850s had a different sense of class than their forebears, and this identity was announced by labor spokesmen at the workplace, in the neighborhood, and in politics. Like the industrial working classes elsewhere, the working classes in the United States at midcentury had forsaken collective actions resisting the advance of the industrial system in favor of the union, the strike, and the political campaign.

Alongside these transformations in the working classes were important elements of continuity. The most straightforward of these was the appearance of labor advocates and radicals whose political activities spanned the antebellum period: John Commerford, George Henry Evans, Gilbert Vale, and others. Although their ideas were surely more coherent and sophisticated – as well as more radical – than the great majority of the working classes, these men were important voices in the antebellum era. They and others fashioned a "workerist" politics and a platform that I have termed here "workerist reform." Like Philadelphia's radicals, New York's radical leaders "were effective organizers because of their remarkable ability to relate to the inarticulate."[95] Drafting the demands so popularly voiced in the depressions of the 1850s, they helped to make the unemployed – as the working classes more generally – a political force.

A second element of continuity was the persistent vitality of republicanism and the principles of equality and rights in the popular culture of the working classes. This is not surprising, for republicanism accords a special place to common men. Like the yeoman and artisan under the mixed constitution, the working classes were liberty's best defenders, the "bone and sinew" of the republic.

A third element of continuity was the distinctive sense of justice that for an earlier era E.P. Thompson termed "moral-economic." Fernando Wood's relief proposals were as obviously right and just to the unemployed as they were obviously demagogical to his opponents. The repudiation of railroad bonds provided, in the West, the same opportunity for "demagoguery" by politicians and righteous indignation on the part of businessmen. In difficult economic times, when the taxes necessary to redeem the bonds were oppressive, it seemed only right not to pay them – though bankers and railroad men saw justice in the obligations of the contract.[96] If their social betters viewed these demands as the product of "foreign" and even "communistic" doctrines (and they did), from a popular point of view they were simply the obvious course for a government in which the poor stood on an equal footing with the rich.

These changes and continuities may be summarized by saying that, in the antebellum years, popular republicanism and a persistent morality, colored by a new sense of class identity, were adapted to the realities of industrial society to produce a distinctive working-class voice in local politics. The concerns of the working classes, their values, demands, and world view, gave rise to the workingman's advocate, made an imprint on the Democracy, and shaped the character of the boss. These developments were not confined to New York. For example, journalists Michael Walsh and Levi Slamm found a counterpart in Pittsburgh's Lecky Harper, who denounced "the unholy and unjust attempts of . . . capitalists to crush and destroy the souls and bodies of men, women, and children."[97]

Similarly, a new rhetoric and new demands were found everywhere the new working classes labored. In Trenton, a Workingmen's Union was organized by union members to question candidates for political office on a long list of state and national demands. Although in some places such efforts were ignored, in Trenton not a candidate for office failed to endorse the general agenda of labor demands.[98] During the great shoemakers' strike in New England, congressional candidates in Lynn contributed to the strike fund. In the same city, a Workingmen's Party was organized to put in the mayor's office a man who would keep the police out of labor disputes and, himself a worker, demonstrate that the working classes were capable of self-government. Successful then and again later in the century, supporters of the Workingmen's Party could support the Republicans in national elections but balked at supporting for local government those who claimed that "in our free states property is constantly changing hands."[99]

In Newark, Philadelphia, and Baltimore, as well as New York, the depression of the 1850s brought demands for public works and public relief, demands that would have been "inconceivable sixty years before."[100] Even without the kind of successful third-party effort organized in Lynn, these demands won concessions from city governments and pressured politicians into a kind of primitive welfare-state-ism. In New York, Fernando Wood's relief program, a thousand jobs a day in Central Park in the depression years of the 1850s, and in the next decade, the city's response to the draft riots, were all concessions to working-class grievances. In Baltimore, the city government enacted make-work programs constructing city parks in the depression of 1860-1.[101] In Boston, Nativist mayor Jerome Van Crowninshield Smith opened soup houses in the depression winter of 1855. Earlier, he had proposed that the city appoint physicians to offer health care to the poor.[102] In Philadelphia, Mayor Richard Vaux supported relief and expansion of public works to aid the unemployed in the depression years of the 1850s.[103]

Finally, the 1850s witnessed in New York and elsewhere the appearance of the boss. Militant, "hard-fisted," and tough, the character of the boss reflected the "indefatigably autonomous culture" of the working classes[104] as his stance claimed to serve their interests. Some, as described in the last chapter, were nativists – Joel Barker in Pittsburgh, Joel Sutherland in Philadelphia, and Henry Winter Davis in Baltimore. Politicians' efforts to build organizations meant they associated themselves with the gangs and fire companies of the "dangerous classes." Even Vaux, himself a "gentleman Democrat," nevertheless ostentatiously associated with gangs.[105] As Weber wrote, the "American Boss . . . *deliberately* relinquishes social honor."[106]

The workingman's advocate, the boss, and local parties, then, all bore the imprint of the working classes. Like other social forces, though, their political will was mediated by the rules of the political order and disciplined by the logic of electoral politics. The boss, for example, despite the concessions and despite the militance of his stance, was more politician than workingman's advocate; electoral victory was more compelling than the solidarities of class. Although party success required, on the one hand, endorsing some working-class demands, it required on the other resources for organization building and ties to state and national governments. As a result, if labor leaders wanted to be rid of "political creatures" on public works (the term "civil service" had not yet been invented), politicians wanted employment they controlled. For that purpose, craft skill was a less important virtue than political loyalty. If the demonstrations of unemployed wanted welfare-state-ish entitlements, it was clearly in the interest of politicians to dispense these instead as favors of the boss or the organization. Alternative political organizations of the working classes (for example, the Industrial Congresses or insurgent workingmen's factions)[107] were always to be opposed. More broadly, to the extent that the working classes themselves had goals (like ten-hours legislation or the Homestead Act) that were beyond the capacity of local government, they were driven by their minority status in the general population to join the major parties. So if the Democracy was the "true home of the working classes" in New York City, it was surely not a labor party. Indeed, rather than making of the party a workers' party, the party made of the workers, Democrats.[108]

7 A house of power in town

A HISTORICAL EXPLORATION of city government in the United States reveals a set of recurrent if not constant themes: corruption and extravagance, the sacrifice of the public weal to private ends, the abuse of patronage. These outrages are denounced, evils bemoaned, opportunities seen and taken, scurrilities unmasked, men in office declared unfit, and defenders of the common good put forward and defeated with depressing regularity. Yet by accounts both contemporary and retrospective something in particular, something extraordinary and surely something worse, happened in the antebellum city. By the 1850s, reformers were declaring that the issue was not who would govern the city but whether the city could be governed at all.

Some elements of this "ungovernedness" are readily apparent. The antitemperance riot of 1857 and the mass demonstrations of 1854–57 marked a dramatic escalation in political protest and collective violence. There was more bribery and more talk of corruption than in the prior two decades. The institutional coherence of the city government was torn by the interventions of the state legislature. Factionalized parties offered voters three, four, five, or six slates to choose from, and the tabulated votes in some wards significantly exceeded the size of the registered electorate.

In addition to the popular causes of disorder, there was disorder among the leading men of New York's economic and political life. For the better part of the antebellum period, there were broad areas of agreement among politicians and men of wealth. Within the second American party system, politicians and men of wealth created an amicable division of labor, the former organizing grass-roots support and running for office and the latter providing funding for the parties and being active in the councils of party governance and the maintenance of ties to the state and national parties. When the second American party system dissolved under the impact of national divisions, the discipline that bound plutocrats and politicians to one another dissolved with it.

At the same time, the expansion of city government increased both the temptations and the possibilities for career politicians to go it alone. Seeing their opportunities and taking them, career politicians alienated their erstwhile partners, and plutocrats responded by launching the City Reform movement. That movement was a declaration of war on politicians by men of wealth, a war that the plutocrats decisively lost at the polls. Thus the 1850s witnessed the emergence of the characteristic antagonists of American city politics, the boss and the reformer.

PLUTOCRACY AND POLITICS AGAIN

In 1860, reflecting on a decade of corruption and misrule, Horace Greeley asked why New York City could not return to government by the few, the "best citizens." "Our city is fearfully misgoverned and despoiled, and Corruption has been growing worse for years," Greeley argued, "mainly because her substantial citizens ... have too generally neglected or slighted their public duties." The wealthy, he went on to say, had been allowed to abandon the ship of state for too long and should be pressed back into service.[1] Similarly, Henry J. Raymond lamented in the *Times* that businessmen were too busy making money to pay attention to politics. When August Belmont and others formed the Fifth Avenue Hotel Committee in October of 1859, James Gordon Bennett's *Herald* applauded the "revolt of the awakened respectability and integrity of the Democratic Party in New York" against "the atrocious tyranny of ruffian plunderers" from Tammany Hall.[2]

Later observers have sometimes thought, as the newspapermen did, that the conflict and insurgency of the 1850s might have been avoided, and the order and community of the older city restored, if the "best men" had not turned from public to private pursuits.[3] Indeed, the exodus of the wealthy from politics is a familiar theme in the accounts of antebellum cities. Robert Dahl presented one version of this theme in *Who Governs?*, which argued that patricians, entrepreneurs, and ex-plebes successively governed the city.[4] Sam Bass Warner, Jr., saw the emergence of the career politician in Philadelphia as a part of a more general process of specialization and the division of labor. Businessmen turned their attention to national and regional matters as the larger economic environment became more relevant to profit making; as "businessmen abandoned the city's affairs and its politics new specialists assumed their former tasks."[5] Gabriel Almond's historical study of New York documented a continuous decline in the status of New York City's officeholders from the late eighteenth to the early twentieth centuries. Almond found that, although New York's wealthy men in the pre–Civil War period were not as decadent as their postwar successors, neither were they as public spirited as their forebears. Wealthy New Yorkers were active in philanthropic organizations of various kinds, but "the wealthier groups of New Yorkers ... engaged in politics hardly at all,"[6] and in fact "developed an attitude of contempt for politics."[7] Documenting again the retreat of men of wealth from office holding, Edward Pessen concluded that "rich men appear to have gained what they need from municipal government without exercising direct influence over it."[8] Finally, when Frank Otto Gatell sought to investigate the partisan affiliations of New York's wealthiest men, he discovered that "only a few were lured into participating in political meetings."[9]

Despite the unanimity of these studies, a nagging doubt remains. Histories of nineteenth-century enterprise and party histories seem to share a familiar list of names. An effort to concretize the sense of *déjà vu* bears fruit: Patronage beneficiaries and saloonkeepers aside, it would be hard to find *any* group of New Yorkers more politically active than the rich. Compiling a list of New York's wealthiest men in 1828, 1845, and 1856, and comparing it to the list of politicians I constructed from party histories and newspaper accounts, I found that of the city's wealthiest 470 men, 103 – or 21 percent – were active in party politics.[10] Although this finding is, on the basis of past studies, a surprise, it is very probably an understatement of the political activity of wealthy men. For one thing, the list of politicians is obviously incomplete. Second, the representation of wealth in politics would be greater if the activity or representation of families or firms rather than individuals was examined. Although the individual Thornes, Rhinelanders, Schermerhorns, and Schiefellins on the list of the wealthiest were not politically active, among their uncles, brothers, sons, in-laws, and business partners were men who devoted a good part of their energies to politics.

Who were the wealthy partisans? The 103 wealthy partisans represent all the important sources of wealth, and are not very different from the apolitical men of the same class. Included among the partisans are industrialist James P. Allaire; shipbuilders William Webb and Henry Eckford; bankers Stephen Allen, Saul Alley, J. Q. Jones, James Gore King, and Edward Prime; manufacturers Alonzo Alvord, William Colgate, and Peter Cooper; financiers John J. and William B. Astor and August Belmont; merchants William H. Aspinwall, Philip, John, and Isaac Hone, Samuel Judd, Moses Grinnell, Anson Phelps, and A. T. Stewart; and men of diversified interests like Samuel Ruggles and George Law. Peter Cooper is one of the very few men on the list who was a self-made man. The entrepreneur-industrialist who, as Robert Dahl saw, was taking the reigns of office up when the patricians were laying them down simply did not have as much money as the men on this list. Mayors Havemeyer, Harper, and Fernando Wood, for example, were affluent men, but they were not possessors of fortunes on the scale of the Grinnells, Posts, Schieffellins, Primes, and Astors.

The politically active among the wealthy were a minority group, but it is clearly not the case that only the extraordinary man of wealth took time from making money to engage in politics. The retreat from office is, to be sure, marked: In the years from 1828 to 1840, 32 of these men ran for office (and more had held office before 1828), whereas in the years from

1850 to 1863 only 12 did so. There was no comparable retreat from party politics, nor was there a retreat into a single party. If all the affiliations of wealthy partisans are examined (some changed parties and are counted more than once here), 51 were Democrats, 30 were Whigs, 2 were Workingmen, 11 were American Republicans or Know-Nothings, 22 were Reformers, 10 were Republicans, and 4 were men who ran for office before 1834 and therefore cannot be properly said to have had a party affiliation. Looking only at that affiliation that lasted longest does not change the distribution much: The 103 partisans included 46 Democrats, 25 Whigs, 6 nativists, 18 Reformers, 4 Republicans, and the 4 men without party identification.

The predominance of Democrats here is in part an artifact of the longevity of that party, and a better sense of party affiliations and shift in affiliations can be gained by looking at the figures for partisanship by decade. In the 1830s, plutocrats, like the city's electorate, favored the Democrats: Of the 20 men with party affiliations between 1834 and 1840, 12 were Democrats and 8, Whigs. In the forties, and probably beginning in the late 1830s, with the revolt of the conservative Democrats against the removal of deposits in 1838, plutocrats distinguished themselves from the electorate as a whole by favoring the Whigs 16 to 9. This finding accords well with Frank Otto Gatell's affirmation of the "basic assumption" of "olden times" that the Whigs were the party of wealth,[11] though the party's hold on them may not have been as great as the "basic assumption" claimed. In the 1850s, particularly as the struggle for control of the national government grew intense toward the end of the decade, the Democrats experienced a new infusion of wealth, claiming 17 of the very wealthy to the 4 Republicans and one die-hard Whig.

This Democratic predominance did not mean unity, for during most of the 1850s New York's wealthy partisans were as much affected by the disarray of the national party system as were the career politicians. Philip Foner has emphasized the bipartisan efforts of the wealthy during the decade before the Civil War to stop, in George Templeton Strong's words, "Billy Seward and his gang of incendiaries who wanted to set the country on fire with Civil War."[12] Foner's *Business and Slavery* demonstrates the fear of "black Republicanism" among New York's business leaders, their desire to avert a break with the South, and their bipartisan efforts to maintain the Union. The other side of support for the Missouri Compromise, the Union Safety Committee, the petitions to Washington, the assurances to the South, and the great Castle Garden Meetings was a series of partisan efforts to which Foner is less attentive. For, finally, the fate of the Union depended on who ran the national government. Only twice, in the state elections of 1850 and at the last moment, in the presidential election of 1860, did this unity transform itself from the meeting ground to the electoral ticket. For most of the 1850s, men of wealth like other men differed on the best candidate and the party to implement their consensus. John A. Thomas, Myndert Van Schaick, and Prosper Wetmore worked for William Marcy's nomination for the presidency on the Democratic ticket in 1852; Belmont worked for Buchanan; "steamboat Democrats" supported Douglas.[13] Whigs Ketchum, Grinnell, and Minturn hoped Webster would be the candidate of the Whigs; Henry Brevoort, Shepherd Knapp, and Hugh Maxwell worked for Fillmore.[14] In 1856, some former Whigs were so fearful of Republican victory that they supported Buchanan,[15] Ruggles and other die-hard anti-Republican Whigs worked for Fillmore.[16] In city contests, Francis B. Cutting, Thomas Suffern, and John Anderson supported the Hard Shells,[17] and Edward Phillips and Royal Phelps the Soft Shells.[18] Ruggles and others worked to keep the Silver Grey Whigs alive. The greatest number of wealthy partisans however, twenty-two, worked for the Reformers in city contests.

Wealthy men helped their parties in a variety of ways. Men of wealth could demonstrate their support of partisan efforts by being present at party meetings. At public meetings, the parties generally appointed a group of vice-presidents and secretaries. These positions of honor were ways to advertise who supported the party. At the same time, from this honorary vantage point the man of wealth could demonstrate his approval of the democratization (such as it was) of intraparty processes, thereby proving themselves Gentleman Democrats. Stephen Whitney and John L. Lawrence were prominent in this role at Whig meetings in the 1840s, and John G. Rohr and James P. Allaire served as vice-presidents of meetings of Whig mechanics![19] Saul Alley and John L. Graham in the 1830s, Henry Brevoort in the 1840s, and Isaac Lawrence and George Law in the 1850s were among those who supported Tammany in this way.[20] J. C. Green and George Folsom lent their energy and prestige to the emergent Republican Party;[21] Solomon P. Townsend and Anson Phelps showed their approval of the Temperance Party in 1854, and in the succeeding year Phelps appeared at a Know-Nothing meeting.[22] George Law also played an active role in the Know-Nothing organization, and the earlier nativist party, the American Republicans, also had the help of wealthy men. Edward Prime, Thomas Woodruff, and Waldron Post helped found and endorsed the American Republicans. In addition, Post and one of the Schieffelin brothers ran for alderman on the American Republican ticket.[23]

Men of wealth also acted as ward leaders and organizers for their parties. In the 1830s, wealthy men commonly served as chairmen of ward meetings. Though this kind of activity on the part of the wealthy declined, in the 1840s we find Richard Carman organizing for the Whigs in the twelfth ward,[24] and Jonathon I. Coddington[25] and Francis B. Cutting[26] worked for Tammany in the wards in the 1840s and 1850s, respectively. In general, until the appearance of the City Reform League in the 1850s, when wealthy men once again took to ward organizing, few of the wealthy are found at ward meetings outside of the first, second, third, and fifteenth wards (where many of them lived) after 1840.

Wealthy men were prominent, however, in citywide organizing and in maintaining communications with party members elsewhere in the state or in Washington. Philip Hone and Samuel Ruggles were indefatigable workers for the Whigs in this capacity, and the Whigs could also claim Robert Minturn, Hamilton Fish, the Hones, Richard Blatchford, and Simeon Draper. Similarly, the Democrats relied over the antebellum period on James Boorman, Moses B. Taylor, James R. Whiting, William B. Astor, Anson Phelps, Myndert Van Schaick, Alexander T. Stewart, Francis B. Cutting, Peter Cooper, and, toward the end, August Belmont. Men like Hone, Ruggles, Verplanck, Cooper, and Grinnell were exceptional in the consistency and prominence of their political roles. Of the 100 men examined here, perhaps 20 were consistently politically active over a long period; a few, like George Law or Charles Henry Hall, changed affiliation often and were opportunistic; the majority were active over periods of about ten years.

In addition to their time, organizing ability, and status, wealthy men could of course give money to their parties, money that was needed for broadsides and newspapers, campaign and travel.[27] Thurlow Weed tells the story of a trip to Albany, conducted with the greatest secrecy, so that Minturn, Grinnell, Draper, Blatchford, and James Bowen could deliver $8,000 to aid Weed in securing a Whig victory Upstate.[28] In 1838, Grinnell, Blatchford, Wetmore, and others hired an estimated 200 Philadelphians to vote for the Whigs in New York City.[29] Henry Eckford offered to buy the state legislature to ensure Crawford's victory in the presidential campaign of 1824.[30] And much later, in 1859, August Belmont organized the Democratic Vigilant Association to unify the power of wealth and coerce faction-ridden Democratic politicians into line.

If, then, businessmen had abandoned older roles of patrician social leadership, and they were heavily involved in the newer forms of gaining and maintaining fortunes, they had not abandoned politics. The attachment of wealthy men to the parties is only surprising because the contrary tale has been told so many times. Even a little reflection argues that the idea that the wealthy could renounce partisan activity in the antebellum period does not square with common sense. The parties were vehicles for fixing tariffs, chartering banks, managing the currency, securing or abandoning investments in land at the frontier, and making the hinterland accessible through internal-improvement programs. Parties, for the wealthy as for others, were the institutions through which allies were or were not secured and government moved or not moved in desired directions. Men of wealth could not abandon politics for profits, if only because the latter depended in part on government policy. Moreover, among the wealthy as among citizens in general there were those who cared passionately about democracy or republicanism, religion, slavery, or the immigrant presence. To further these values, they engaged in party politics.

Although wealthy men funded parties, organized ties with state and national party organizations, and pressed for a nationally oriented political life in the city, the work of running for office, grass-roots party organizing, and a good part of local governance were left to career politicians. At the same time, politicians and wealthy men insisted, contrary to the facts of their association, that they were not the same men at all. It is not difficult to speculate on the incentives underlying this insistence. For the politicians, the same decline of deference or even outright hostility to wealth that made wealthy men poor candidates and organizers was an incentive to emphasize their own distinctiveness and their likeness to their supporters. For the wealthy, in a general situation of low stateness, and in repeated particular situations of scandal, theft, and sacrifice of the common good to private gain (in which the wealthy were as often as not implicated), there was every reason to trumpet their contempt for politics. In the 1830s and 1840s, this made for an amicable division of labor between men of wealth and career politicians. Their tasks were different, but they shared an orientation to federal and state levels of government that wed them to the parties of the second American party system and, as a result, to one another. There was, however, tension in this division of labor, and in the 1850s that tension became open conflict. In that decade, there would be intense efforts to capitalize on the distinction between the wealthy and politicians. The "best men" would put their virtue to the service of the City Reform movement, and politicians would use their popularity to coerce wealth and attempt independence of party. The conflict between career politicians and men of wealth shaped the city politics of the 1850s.

THE SECOND AMERICAN PARTY SYSTEM AND THE ROAD TO REFORM

In the 1830s and 1840s, politicians and plutocrats created an amicable division of labor. Politicians organized the machinery of local party politics and political life in the wards, mobilized grass-roots support, and held most local offices. Men of wealth funded the parties, worked to maintain ties with the state and national party apparatus, and worked in the citywide councils of party governance. Politicians and men of wealth were bound together by their shared commitment to the second American party system. For men of wealth, the policies associated with party politics in the state and nation were the politics of importance. Gideon Lee and Prosper Wetmore, for example, were Jacksonians because their "democracy and their interests had coincided in enthusiastic support of the Jacksonian assault on the 'monster monopoly.' "[31] In 1838, many wealthy Democrats became

Whigs in opposition to Van Buren's Independent Treasury proposal.[32] Banks, internal improvements, tariffs, and trade were all the business of state and federal government. There were things at stake in the city – franchises and real estate, for example – but for the most part partisan dominance in the city was a means to state and national goals.

There was good reason for career politicians to share that orientation, for the patronage resources of city government had not kept pace with the growth of the electorate. In the 1780s and 1790s, when the electorate numbered about 4,000, the number of appointees – put thoroughly to use by the Federalists – was about 1,500.[33] Fifty years later, politicians faced an electorate of 40,000 with perhaps 2,000 jobs.[34] For the most part patronage was divided among the aldermen, each of whom was responsible for maintaining party organization in his ward. Readily available patronage resources were regarded as inadequate, and council members attempted various strategies in an effort to increase the number of city employees. A Whig council in the 1840s passed an ordinance to reduce the salaries of the 1,000-man municipal watch in order to increase the number of watchmen without increasing the budget. The watchmen, of course, immediately protested. Threatening to ensure Whig defeat if their salaries were not restored, the men presented the council with a petition of 3,860 signatures to demonstrate the public support they had and succeeded in regaining their former rate of pay.[35] In 1850, the Whigs attempted the same ploy with Customs House employees, with a similar lack of success.[36] For their part, the Democrats increased the pace of work on the Croton Aqueduct in the 1840s, giving rise to the term "pipe laying" to refer to public work undertaken for partisan purposes. The Democrats also tried, unsuccessfully, to use the fire department in a partisan way (see Chapters 4 and 6). These strategies were not only clumsy in their particular application but also generally contentious. Workers resented being made "political creatures" and wanted government to be an exemplary employer by recognizing skill rather than partisanship, limiting the work day to ten hours, and paying good wages.

The less contentious means to increase the patronage at the disposal of local politicians was partisan control of the state or federal government. The state appointed port wardens, judges, surrogates, county clerks, weighers of merchandise, measurers of grain, and other inspectors of commodities, totaling perhaps 1,400 New York City jobs controlled by the state government in the late 1830s.[37] The national government had even larger resources at its disposal. The great prize was the Customs House. From a partisan point of view, the Customs House's attraction lay in its staff of 750 appraisers, clerks, weighers, inspectors, and the like. These were relatively well-paying positions that could be and were filled by men with some grade-school education and "rather humble origin."[38] That employment there had a four- rather than a one-year tenure was also attractive. As a result, the

Customs House was an important concern of New York politicians for nearly the whole of the antebellum period. When, for example, Jackson appointed a collector not approved of by the local Democratic organization, and who did not use jobs to build it, C. C. Cambreleng wrote to the president that "we have driven from our ward meetings a body of strong republicans who for twenty or thirty years have been the back-bone of our party."[39] There were in addition 1,500 civilian jobs at the Brooklyn Navy Yard, and jobs controlled by the U.S. Marshall in the city, the subtreasurer, and the postmaster, all federal appointees. In 1853, the federal payroll in the city totaled 1.5 million dollars. In the same year, Customs House employees contributed nearly $7,000 to the Tammany treasury.[40]

None of these benefits were available if one's own party was not in power, and the existence of a significant state and even larger federal payroll in New York was a tremendous incentive to local politicians to mobilize the electorate along national lines. In this, they were in perfect agreement with those who provided partisan warchests, with nativists who wanted immigration restrictions, with those who had become convinced that general prosperity was dependent on national policy, and with organized labor desirous of ten-hours legislation and other forms of relief not in the power of local government. The success of the parties at mobilizing the electorate along national lines may be seen in turnout statistics. Voters consistently turned out in larger numbers for presidential (even, according to partial data, congressional) elections than they did for local ones. On average, the presidential elections of 1836 through 1848 drew 15 percent more votes from the city than mayoral elections. The vote for governor, though it was smaller than the vote for president, was also greater than the vote cast for mayor in the 1830s and 1840s. In the 1850s, these gaps would be appreciably narrowed (See Figure 2).

If there were good reasons for politicians and men of wealth to share a national orientation, there were also tensions between the things politicians needed to do to get elected and the policy preferences of the wealthy men with whom they were in partnership. The partnership gave rise to a series of unpopular policy positions. Politicians of both parties denounced landlords, but neither party supported legislation for a residential building code. Neither party supported popular demands for democratized control of the city's school system, nor did either party support workingmen demanding an end to contract labor. Both parties agreed with the view that charity undermined independence and caused vice and that government should retreat from economic management and the offering of succor to the unfortunate.

At the same time that these were the official positions, the behavior of politicians was at variance with them in response to popular pressure. Thus, if in their role as aldermen it was agreed to cut back on charity, as politicians the same men offered it. If as officials they insisted that state legislation like the Maine Law had to be enforced, as politicians they refrained from doing so. If officials of city government denounced disorder and rowdyism by gangs and fire companies, as politicians they offered patronage to gang leaders and joined the fire companies themselves. While both parties endorsed governmental frugality, both parties engaged in pipe laying. This divergence of behavior from policy was early evidence that, by forsaking the offices of government and distancing themselves from the populace, the wealthy had lost control of city government. There was more direct evidence as well. Loss of control of public policy was demonstrated by Seward's successful promotion of the common-school system and by Fernando Wood's outrageous relief proposals.

More concretely, loss of control of public policy was evidenced in the rapid growth of the city budget, which endangered the security of wealth against taxation and the security of investments in city bands against overissue and overspending. The dimensions of the city budget are not altogether clear (and the standard source on the history of New York's finances argues that this is no accident), but the general outlines of the situation are. First, the tax rate was rising. In 1853, after making appropriations beyond the originally proposed budget, the Common Council raised the rate from $.97 per $100 to $1.23. The reform council of 1853–4 succeeded in lowering the rate, but by 1856 it was $1.38, by 1857, $1.56, and by 1863, $2.03.[41]

While taxes were going up, the tax revenue and the fees collected by the city accounted for a shrinking proportion of the city's income. In the 1830s and 1840s the city sold Croton Aqueduct and other special bonds to fund large projects, but beginning in 1843 the city sold bonds to meet current expenses as well.[42] In the 1850s, these revenue-anticipation bonds accounted for greatly increased proportions of current "income."[43] In 1844, the tax levied (when the rate was $.86) covered 67 percent of all expenditures.[44] In 1853, the tax covered 49 percent of the city's expenditures; in 1856, the levy covered 32 percent of the city's expenditures.[45] In 1844, revenue-anticipation bonds covered 27 percent of the city's expenditures;[46] in 1853 and 1856 the figures were, respectively, 32 percent and 47 percent.[47] Small wonder that reformers argued the city was having trouble selling its bonds.[48]

Wealthy men also lost direct access to the profitable areas of government that were franchised or regulated. It is this aspect of the loss of control that readers of urban history are most familiar with, for the most frequent cry of the reformer is "corruption!" In the 1850s, the accusation of corruption meant in particular taking bribes. If "much of what we consider . . . corruption is simply the 'uninstitutionalized' influence of wealth in a political system," and if, as Namier pointed out, "no one bribes where he can bully,"[49] then corruption itself is testimony to the loss of control of government decisions. Bribery, of course, was an old story in the city and an older one in the state legislature. Indeed, some of the men who became prominent in the reform movement were themselves involved in efforts to bribe the city council. In the 1850s, however, politicians seemed to stop playing by the rules. The council of 1852–3 took bribes and then did not deliver contracts.[50] They and their successors made deals and subsequently upped the ante. Offices were sold and the buyer not appointed. The "best men" could honestly react with horror when men "guilty of dishonesty in business" were nominated for office in a city that "looked to commerce for its lifeblood."[51] The council of 1852–3 may at least be credited with a fine sense of how to add insult to injury: If the Sixth and Eighth Avenues railroad franchise had to be illegally bought, the Third Avenue railroad franchise was granted to a group of men who were prominent not in business, but in politics.[52]

None of this passed unnoticed. As early as 1845, there was concern that uncontrolled city spending and the issue of revenue-anticipation bonds be curtailed. It was thought at the time that the concentration of power in the common council, the nearly powerless role of the city's executive, and the absence of executive departments were responsible for overspending. As a result, there was a flurry of reform activity in the city in the mid-1840s, including a charter-reform convention, to reorganize the city government. Nothing came of this effort,[53] and in April 1849 Robert Jones (a former Whig alderman of the fifth ward counted as one of the city's wealthiest men in 1845) chaired a meeting at Vauxhall Gardens. Cambridge Livingston served as secretary; Joseph Blunt, later a prominent Republican, and Democrat James B. Murray were speakers.[54] Ward meetings were held as well,[55] and a petition was drawn up and taken to the state legislature, demanding reorganization of the city government. The legislature passed the new charter, and it was ratified by the city's electorate later in the same year.

The new arrangements created by reformers with the assistance of the state legislature did not provide any relief from corruption, overspending, and demagoguery and indeed made things worse. Reformers wanted to remove powers from the city council; they were assisted by the state legislature because the legislature, largely Republican, wanted to remove patronage resources from Democratic hands. These joint efforts succeeded in constraining the power of the city council, but at the cost of shattering the institutional coherence of the city government and increasing entrepreneurial opportunities for politicians.

The charter revisions of 1849 created ten (later seven) municipal departments with elected commissioners. Throughout the 1850s, citizens elected seven "little mayors": the comptroller; the street commissioner; the commissioners of repairs and supplies, streets and lamps, and the almshouse; the counsel to the corporation; and the city inspector (whose province was public health).[56] Appointment of the police was moved from the aldermen to the office of the mayor.[57] Later the influence of the best men in combination with Republican dominance of the statehouse led the state government to create a series of commissions with appointed chiefs. The metropolitan police board (discussed in Chapter 5), the Central Park Commissioners, and the Croton Aqueduct Board were removed from the control of the city government and made available to Republican partisans. The Board of Education had been separate from the city council for some time. Each of these boards made up its own budget and demanded funds from the city council.[58] To further reduce the fiscal control of the city council, the legislature in 1857 made the Board of County Supervisors distinct from charter officials and arranged for it to be bipartisan.

The multiplicity of relatively independent city departments provided opportunities for enterprising politicians to create their own organizations, and in doing so to make themselves independent both of the parties and of partnership with men of wealth. It was not possible, when each of the independent departments was run by an elected official, to coordinate their policies. The functioning of the almshouse – whether criteria for relief were stringent or relaxed, whether inmates were exploited or not – depended on who was almshouse commissioner. The work life of city employees (whether they would be subject to political taxes, whether there would be much work or little, whether foremen would be knowledgeable workmen or political "creatures," and the size and certitude of the paychecks) depended on who was elected commissioner of repairs and supplies, who was appointed to the Central Park Board, and who ran the street department (that last, according to the *Times*, the "El Dorado of municipal offices"). Candidates boasted of their generosity or Americanness and accused others of bigotry, partisan abusiveness, or tight-fistedness. Emphasis on personality fueled the disintegration of parties, already factionalized by national differences. Thus the 1850s and 1860s witnessed a series of entrepreneurial efforts by men declaring themselves anti-Tammany Democrats. Daniel F. Tiemann, who was the reform candidate for mayor in 1857, could bring a part of the Democratic organization with him to the reform effort because he had been an alderman and also an almshouse governor.[59] John McKeon, who organized the "McKeon Democracy" in 1862–3, had been alderman, district attorney, and almshouse governor.[60] Henry W. Genet, who tried to take Tammany over from within, had built his own "ring" of supporters in a career as alderman, president of the board of aldermen, and county clerk.[61] The most successful of these insurgencies, of course, was that of Fernando Wood.

The efforts of reformers to diffuse the powers of the common council and the efforts of upstate Republicans to gain control of certain institutions of municipal governance were both made more intense by the fact that the expansion of city government had as its natural concomitant the expansion of resources available for organization building in the city. Entrepreneurial efforts by politicians were inviting prospects not only because of the increased independence of municipal departments but also because the pot was much larger than it had been five or ten years before. Central Park alone, for example, employed as many as 1,000 men a day.[62] By 1858, Isaac Fowler was writing to a friend, "It is hardly necessary . . . to tell you that city patronage is greater than the Customs House."[63] Three years later, a Tammany official declared: "No man should have power in this state if that power is to be swayed by the authorities in Washington."[64] Things had changed a great deal since the days when Cambreleng complained to Jackson. It was now possible for the first time to build an elegant house of power in town, and politicians were working away at it. Legislative intervention having failed to bring city government under control, the reformers decided to move into that house themselves.

THE ELECTORAL BATTLE JOINED

The electoral effort to reform city government had its origins in the 1850s. Having tried and failed to reform city government by imposing charter changes enacted by the state legislature, men of wealth took to the hustings. There can be no doubt that the City Reform effort was the project of men of wealth. For the first time in a generation, not only the candidates and meetings chairmen, but also the ward organizers and ward candidates were chosen from the city's very wealthiest men. If plutocrats had participated, in unobtrusive ways, in the second American party system, the reform movement would be their very own.

It was not to be a successful movement. The reformers were crippled by their own partisan attachments, and they were unable to gain a mass following. Thus they were, ultimately, forced to negotiate a modus vivendi with the opposition. This earliest of reform campaigns, the campaign of the 1850s, paved the way to the achievement of that modus vivendi by demonstrating that the "best men" could not reclaim city government for themselves.

Beginning in March 1853, and continuing through the local elections in November, the City Reformers held mass meetings citywide and in the wards. The initial meeting was held March 5 in Metropolitan Hall.[65] Peter Cooper was declared president and would be a leader of municipal reform for nearly two decades to come. Cooper argued along lines that will be familiar to the reader from Chapter 2: The city suffered a "despotism in its midst" because of an inadequate separation of powers in the structure of its government. The meeting's vice-presidents were then appointed, and the list was an impressive one indeed. It included the shipbuilder William

Webb; president of the Merchants' Exchange Simeon Baldwin; William Colgate; James Boorman; Myndert Van Schaick; leading nativist Thomas R. Whitney; Gerald W. Kipp, William B. Crosby, and Peter Stuyvesant, representing the Old Knickerbocker Committee; William Henry Stagg and Gerardus Cushman of the immense Novelty Works; merchants Henry Grinnell, Moses Taylor, George Griswold, and William Whitlock, Jr.; two of the Harper brothers; George Butler, editor of the *Journal of Commerce*; and *Times* editor Henry J. Raymond. Also among the vice-presidents were representatives of the workers at Webb's shipyard, Jacob Westervelt's shipyard, and the Novelty Works. A series of speakers, including the foreman of the grand jury, Henry Erben, then elaborated the reformers' complaints and plans. They denounced extravagance, high taxes, and corruption, placing particular blame on career politicians and the undemocratic party structures that supported them. They argued that New York's solid mechanics had been "driven away from New York by unjust taxation," causing Westchester and other places to thrive, and only by a lowering of the tax rate could businesses and citizens be persuaded to stay. A series of resolutions embodied the program of the reformers: amendments to the city charter to further separate executive, judicial, and legal functions and to increase the restrictions on contracting debt and authorizing expenditures; and a change in the date of municipal elections from November to December, so that they would not coincide with national and state elections. As remedies to the evils of party, the reformers proposed in addition that the system of party nominations be abolished, and that the city be redistricted (with one set of districts for electing members of the lower legislative house in the city and another set for electing the representatives to the upper house) to undercut the party organization based on wards. Finally, a legislative committee was appointed to draw up legislation and present it to the state legislature. The committee represented the elite of even this meeting's estimable vice-presidents, as well as some additions, Henry Grinnell, Henry Erben, Aaron Vanderpoel, Martin Zabriskie, Thomas Suffern, and George Butler being among those chosen (an indication of Know-Nothing influence here is that Thomas Whitney, author of *A Defense of the American Policy*, was also chosen). The petition was duly presented, a modified version passed as a set of proposed charter amendments, and these were approved by the electorate in a special election in June.[66] By November, however, the reformers had decided that these changes were not enough, and in the fall of 1853 they organized to win the vote.

At mass meetings, the reformers repeated many of the arguments already illustrated here and in Chapter 2. In the wards as at the mass meetings, lists of nominees and vigilance committees included very wealthy men, some of whom had formerly played partisan roles and others of whom appear for the first time in electoral politics. Royal Phelps worked for the reformers in the eighteenth ward,[67] Moses Beach in the sixth, [68] Alexander Stuart and Horace Waldo in the third,[69] Henry Erben and long-time nativist and Mechanics' Mutual Protection leader William Tucker in the eighth, [70] and Alfred Pell in the twenty-first.[71] In the eighteenth ward as in the eighth, alliance with the Know-Nothings was public. Aaron Vanderpoel and Royal Phelps ceded their nominations to the school board to make room for the nativists, "a powerful organization already existing in the ward."[72] This Know-Nothing support was crucial to the party's initial success. In 1853, the reformers elected thirteen of twenty-two aldermen; in 1854 and 1855, when Know-Nothing alliances were public or the Know-Nothings fielded different candidates, reformers carried only two wards.[73] In the same years, respectively, the municipal reform candidates for the mayoralty polled 26 percent and 5 percent of the vote.

In 1857, the reformers were again successful. Some of the provocations to reform sentiment in 1857 have already been described: the anti-metropolitan-police disturbances represented once again the failure to control city politics from the outside; workingmen's demonstrations in 1854, 1855, and 1857 provoked responses that in retrospect seem to border on the paranoid but at the time were thought to be well-grounded; and the mayor's support of workingmen's demands was simply outrageous. Respectable men viewed the workers' speeches as "seditious"; George Templeton Strong described city hall as "under siege" in 1857.[74] In November, federal troops under the command of General Scott were sent to protect the Customs House and armory from the workingmen.[75] Degler argues that in this situation "the propertied class began to see the possibility of America's going the road of Europe – with a working class arrayed against the institutions of property and capable of excitement against the state itself."[76] At this moment, the mayor let them down: On October 22, Fernando Wood proposed that the city council take extensive measures to relieve the plight of the unemployed.[77] On November 14, at a large meeting at the Merchants' Exchange, Wood was denounced for corruption.[78]

Until 1856, the list of Wood supporters had been impressive. For his handling of various issues in the years 1855 and 1856, Wood had received public support from, among others, William B. Astor, William Aspinwall, Moses Taylor, Royal Phelps, Stephen Whitney, James and Fletcher Harper, William Havemeyer, and reformers Peter Cooper and Robert Minturn.[79] After the fall of 1857, many of the same men opposed him. The November meeting at the Merchants' Exchange in 1857 boasted the presence of Peter Cooper, a former supporter, and in addition Simeon Chittenden, Henry Nicoll, Hickson W. Field, and shipping merchant Robert L. Taylor.[80] Though Wood managed to secure the Tammany nomination later in the year, important party politicians denounced him for stirring up class feeling.[81] Prominent Democrats William Havemeyer, John McKeon, and John Van Buren joined reformers in support of their candidate – also a Democrat, Daniel F. Tiemann – and he won.[82]

At the next mayoral election, "the awakened respectability and integrity of the Democratic party in New York" formed themselves into the Fifth Avenue Hotel Committee. The committee included many who had been present at the great reform meeting of 1853: James Lee, Royal Phelps, Emmanuel B. Hart, Samuel J. Tilden, Myndert Van Schaick, and James B. Murray. In addition, there was impressive representation of the city's wealth. August Belmont, Schuyler Livingston, William S. and William C. Wetmore, Francis B. Cutting, Gulian Verplanck, Benjamin Whitlock, Watts Sherman, C. V. S. and Judge James I. Roosevelt, and others joined in resolving that "if Democrats who are businessmen content themselves with sighing and groaning over the state of things, ... and did not act with decision and energy, the ruin of the party was inevitable."[83] "Tammany Hall," Bennett editorialized, "has nothing to hope from them. It must die from want of funds."[84] Tammany nominated gentleman Democrat William F. Havemeyer, and, perhaps for the first time, mass Democratic rallies were held in Wall Street. Republican Joseph Hoxie remarked on this union of wealth and poverty, "Wall Street and Five Points ... embraced. The millenium must be close at hand." For their part, Republicans, declaring an equal commitment to reform – and displaying, if not quite so impressive an array of wealth, a more than respectable collection of rich reformers[85] – nominated George Opdyke. Fernando Wood won the election under the banner of his own organization, Mozart Hall. In 1861, a bipartisan "People's Union" nominated Opdyke, who defeated both the Tammany candidate and Wood;[86] in 1863, reformers supported C. Godfrey Gunther, a candidate of non-Tammany Democrats, who defeated the Tammany and Republican candidates.[87]

THE REFORM DILEMMA

The reformers' electoral success in the aldermanic election of 1853 was deceptive. The most obvious way in which this is so is that once Know-Nothings left their semicovert place within the reform alliance it became clear how much of "reform" strength was owed to the nativist organization. The success of 1853 was deceptive in a broader sense, however. It suggested that men of wealth could transcend their partisan commitments and that, if they were diligent and well-organized enough, they could mobilize the electorate behind their program of reform. This was incorrect on both counts, and the pattern of reform successes shows the conditions under which reformers could themselves transcend party and the conditions under which they could win. Reformers mounted truly bipartisan efforts only when national issues were temporarily off of the agenda: 1853, 1857, and 1861 were all postpresidential election years. However genuinely reformers may have desired to sever the ties between local and national politics, they could do so neither for the organizers of parties nor for themselves. Although in 1853, 1857, and 1861 wealthy men could gather at a single meeting and support a reform candidate, in 1856, 1859, and 1863 they could not. In 1859, though campaigners called for attention to the city and its severance from national concerns, the division of wealth was well explained in the newspapers. On the Republican side, Greeley argued:

> In 1857, we formed the majority of the voters who elected Tiemann. But now, in 1859, we stand at once for the Republican cause and for the welfare of the City ... The prize to be gained is the honor and prosperity of this great metropolis, and an honest use of the patronage of the City Government in the great struggle of 1860, instead of the perversion to the corrupt and corrupting services of our deadliest foe.[88]

Hiram Ketchum might declare, at a mass meeting in favor of Havemeyer, that "it was nothing to us in our corporate capacity, whether slavery was extended or not"[89] and argue that a vote for Havemeyer was a vote for reform, but the Fifth Avenue Hotel Committee explained itself differently. "It has long embarrassed conservative men of worth, standing, and responsibility in the community, to know precisely how to act," for they opposed both the corruption of Tammany and "the infamous disunion program" of Seward.[90] In the face of the great national importance of the Democratic Party, they could only regret the neglect of men of substance to control it in the city and resolve to select its local candidates.[91] The alternatives, after all, were allowing the city to become "a political spoil of the abolitionists"[92] or to be ruled by "the ruffian plunderers of Tammany Hall."[93]

The latter alternative suggests how illusory the reform victory of 1853 was. Unlike the 1840s, in the 1850s if the city was to be governed by nativists or antinativists the electorate would resoundingly endorse the latter. By the mid-1850s, New York was a Democratic city; by 1860, overwhelmingly so. Between 1856 and 1863, Democratic factions taken together never accounted for less than half the vote. The same returns suggest that about a third of the electorate would, with John Cochrane, vote for the devil himself if he had Tammany's endorsement (Republicans could count on the support of just over a quarter of the electorate). Reformers could win only if some portion of that Democratic strength was with them, or if the nonreform Democratic vote was split. In 1857, although Wood retained the official Democratic nomination, both the party's "respectable element" and important Tammany politicians supported Tiemann, himself a Democrat. In 1863, when the reform-supported candidate won, he was the candidate of a Democratic faction, the "McKeon Democracy."[94] In 1861, wealthy Democrats supported Opdyke, and Democratic voters were still divided between Tammany and Mozart halls – Opdyke won with 34 percent of the vote.

One wonders how the champions of municipal reform felt about this. Michael Frisch writes that when, in the 1870s, wealthy reformers in Springfield, Massachusetts, responded to the depression by proposing a new charter, and voters defeated it by an enormous majority, "the reformers were stunned. They felt they had honestly been trying to design a way for democracy to survive the new demands of city government."[95] Frisch goes on to say that rather "than finding in the charter reform a confirmation of the public power, [voters] saw it as enshrining only another, more powerful and potentially more dangerous form of particularism."[96] In New York, James Gordon Bennett for one argued against the reformers on similar grounds. The election of their candidate, he argued, "will amount to a new lease of power to the sixty irresponsible gentlemen who have attempted to lord it over the common council during the past year, and may be considered as a guarantee that the administration of the city affairs will be taken still further out of the hands of the authorities . . ."[97]

Just a few years after embarking on an electoral campaign to regain control of the city government, then, the reformers realized that they could not themselves move into the city's house of power. The Fifth Avenue Hotel Committee petitioned Tammany to make a deal not only to carry the city against the Republicans but also because Democratic reformers like Cooper and Havemeyer had learned that their independent quest for office was doomed to failure. As Havemeyer himself explained some years later, respectable men were simply a nuisance in politics, and any one popular machine politician was worth forty of them.[98] Popular hostility to "exploiters," "speculators," and the "sixty irresponsible gentlemen" was only a part of the reason.

The City Reform platform offered little to the city's voters. In our own time of tax revolt, for example, the appeal to taxpayers made by the reformers has a popular ring that is misleading. New Yorkers whose assessed valuation was below $1,000 did not pay taxes at all. Boyd's tax list for 1856–7 has about 33,500 entries, including individuals, businesses, and estates on which taxes were paid. Subtracting an estimate for businesses, widows, and estates, there were perhaps 25,000 individual taxpayers in the city – between a third and a half of the electorate. The reform council of 1853 succeeded in lowering the tax rate by nearly 20 percent, but they were not rewarded at the polls, for there were simply not enough taxpayers to deliver a reward. Appeals denouncing the "dangerous classes" and demanding law and order had a double edge. On the one hand, many citizens were surely desirous of a decrease in the crime rate and an end to collective violence. On the other hand, the denunciation of the "dangerous classes" was also an attack on popular organizations – the gangs and the fire companies. Moreover, large-scale collective violence, like the temperance riots of 1857, had not only popular participation but also broader popular support – after the antitemperance disturbances, not a soul could be found to testify against rioters. Six years later, the common council quickly conceded that the draft rioters, if excessive, had had good cause to protest.[99] The reformers also campaigned against "tyrannical" party practices. Democratizing intraparty practices might well have gained the reformers a following (as it did, it will be recalled, for the Know-Nothings), but the reformers did not themselves offer a participatory party structure. The distance between the City Reform program and popular sentiment is perhaps best symbolized in events around the election of 1861. Those who supported City Reform candidate Opdyke formed a taxpayers' association; the Democrats responded by forming a rentpayers' association.[100]

The slogan "retrenchment and reform" made manifest the tensions in the partnership of plutocrat and politician and made explicit a conflict in values between the respectable element and the dangerous classes. The conflicts ranging reformers and the "respectable element" on the one side and career politicians and the "dangerous classes" on the other involved both ideological and material stakes. The ideological stakes were those of laissez-faire and contract versus the moral economy. The material stakes were the obvious ones of bond markets, taxes, and franchises for the plutocrats and relief and employment for the working classes. Since government authority offered ideological sanction and government policy distributed material benefits, the conflict was a contest for control of the city government.

On the side of wealth, there was increased faith in the market and its logical counterpart, skepticism of government activity. Businessmen portrayed themselves not only as society's economic leaders but also as liberty's most faithful defenders. Charles dePeyster Ogden, for example, argued that "despotism and tyranny have been first opposed and eventually hurled down by commercial influence."[101] Unlike the Whigs, who had supplemented celebration of the virtues of the "commercial class" with an insistence that government play a role of intervention and coordination, reform (and Republican) spokesmen claimed that the common good naturally flowed from the pursuits of the business community. Like the *Journal of Commerce*, they urged "every man" to "look out for himself" and saw in the laws of the economic system the work of the Creator. Even so ardent a labor advocate as Horace Greeley wrote that "the relations of labor and capital present a vast theme . . . [and] Government cannot intermeddle with them without doing a great mischief."[102] If the poor were taught "habits of frugality, temperance, industry, and self-dependence," the market would bring them rewards just as it brought rewards to their social betters.

On the popular side, these were precisely the views that led to the denunciation of the "industrial system" as immoral and "selfish." As Paul Gilge wrote, "the elite had one vision for the new urban order while the plebeian culture held steadfastly to the traditions which opposed that vision."[103] At the same time that men of wealth were expressing faith in the market, elaborating an ideology of individualism, and insisting on the sacredness of the contract, a different view of justice persisted among the working classes. Fernando Wood's relief proposals were as obviously right and just to the unemployed as they were obviously demagogical to men of wealth, and more than any other issue in New York they brought to the fore the conflict between the persistence of moral-economic views in the electorate and the emergence of laissez-faire views among the city's elite. The rough ways of gangs, fire companies, or neighborhoods resisting the enforcement of temperance legislation could only aggravate the fear that when "the laboring classes are contaminated, the right of suffrage becomes the engine of destruction."[104] In the same years, rapidly expanding and precariously financed municipal budgets, unobtainable franchises, and rising tax rates testified to elite loss of control of municipal governance.

Little wonder that businessmen sought to regain control of the city government. Reform was as much the logical product of nineteenth-century society and politics as was the boss; reformers, like bosses, appeared in city after city. In Pittsburgh, worry about city finances led to the formation of an Independent Citizens' Ticket in 1850.[105] Soon after, Cincinnati reformers reorganized city government to the commission form.[106] In Baltimore, opposition to corruption and the prominent association of the governing Know-Nothing Party with violence at the polls led to the organization of a City Reform Association.[107] In Boston in 1855, a Committee of Sixty organized a Citizens ticket to provide "economical, honest, and businesslike" administration; after one term, they found themselves derided as "self-constituted, secret, and irresponsible."[108]

The same situation that forced businessmen to wage campaigns for office made it very difficult for them to win. New York's reformers, like reformers in Springfield, Boston, and Baltimore, were seen to embody "another particularism" rather than a common good. Like the Paterson industrialists described by Herbert Gutman, New York's merchants, financiers, and employers "met with unexpected opposition from nonindustrial property owners, did not dominate the local political structure, and learned that ... [their] leadership"[109] was not automatically accepted. Indeed, at crucial moments these men found themselves simply lacking moral and political authority. The divergence in social and political sensibilities at midcentury meant that businessmen, if they were dominant, were not hegemonic. Gramsci argued that " ... even before attaining power a class can (and must) 'lead' ... "; the exercise of that leadership presupposes an "intellectual and moral unity"[110] that midcentury cities did not enjoy.

New York City's politicians stood squarely in the center of these diverging social sensibilities. In the antebellum years, their autonomy and importance increased in equal pace with an expanding suffrage and deepening social dissensus. In the same years, the growth of local government increased the resources available to politicians for institutionalizing their autonomy both from their erstwhile patrician partners and from the national party system. On the one hand, they organized diverse social forces into reliable political majorities. On the other, their very ability to organize that majority forced the Reformers to bargain with them. When "Wall Street and Five Points . . . embraced" it was the beginning of an accommodation between plutocrats and politicians, between the "best men" and the "dangerous classes," that made machine politics a livable arrangement for everyone and ensured that efforts at reform were only intermittent for decades to come. The same embrace revealed that although city politics had acquired a rhythm, form, and pattern of its own, bosses and reformers alike maintained a stake in the national party system. So it is that parties join social force and dominant group, political faction and governance. This is just what one would expect in a society where community did not come naturally, but was a product of politics.

8 The Democracy

By THE OUTBREAK OF THE CIVIL WAR, New York had been transformed from an eighteenth- into a nineteenth-century city. Its citizens bore little resemblance to the mechanics and merchants of 1830. Its political leaders were a group of self-made men attempting to govern the sprawling and diverse metropolis that had replaced the smaller and more intimate city of patricians and Liberty Boys. The government they provided was not the paternalistic one of their forebears, but an increasingly bureaucratized and growing set of municipal organizations. When reformers spoke of that "juggernaut," the political machine, it was a recognition that urban political life had become more autonomous both of social structure and of the national political context in which it was embedded.

City politics had acquired distinctive qualities of its own, qualities that, refined and institutionalized, would be the hallmark of American urban politics for nearly a century to come. The characteristic conflict of the nineteenth- and early twentieth-century American city, the conflict of bosses and reformers, had already taken shape. The Democracy claimed the loyalty of the overwhelming majority of the city's voters. The expansion of municipal government placed at the party's disposal resources adequate for organizing that majority, and the politicians they elected, into a disciplined and centralized organization. How did this transformation – the appearance of characteristic contestants for urban power, the creation of a majority, and the development of a distinctive and autonomous city politics – come about?

In part, the new arrangements of urban political life were a remaking of long-standing habits. Chapter 4 showed that the practices of career politicians attempting to gain followers were adaptations of the patrician style of political leadership. As wealthy men withdrew from officeholding, career politicians joined fire companies and distributed assistance much as the patricians had. For the patrician, those activities were part of a larger role of social, economic, and political leadership, civic leadership closely bound up with the communal life of the ward, in which the line between the public and the private spheres was indistinct. For the career politician, the goal

146

was party dominance as well as individual electoral success, yet the means were the time-tested ones of friendship to the poor and the working man and "multiplied conveniences" for the ward. The career politician began where the merchant patrician left off; the boss was immanent in the career politician.

Since the politician had neither the larger role nor the civic social relations to build upon, and since his aim was the creation of partisan as well as personal support, his effort was of necessity an effort to rebuild the ward as a politically meaningful place. He did so by trying to give primarily social organizations like gangs and social and civic organizations like militia and fire companies a partisan role. For their part, gangs, fire companies, and militia companies resisted the loss of autonomy that went along with partisanship. Patronage controlled by the city government was dispensed on a ward basis, but since there was little of it, patronage and the ambivalent allegiance of social and civic organizations to the parties provided at best a shaky organizational basis for party life. In the 1850s, Fernando Wood's success was associated with two innovations aimed at making the ward a politically meaningful place. First, Wood was the first politician to attempt to deliver on the promise of the ward-based common-school system. His organization, Mozart Hall, held nominating conventions in the wards for electoral slates for ward school boards. To do this was not only to increase the political significance of the ward but also to deliver concretely on the Democracy's often-voiced commitment to cultural pluralism, putting the party behind parents and against the citywide school board for the first time. Second, it was in response to Wood's success that the Democracy created "workingmen's clubs," "permanently established in the wards." Here was the beginning of the clubhouse as a social institution independent of the saloon and liquor grocery, a place of fellowship and likemindedness, and a recognition of the political salience of class.

These two developments were the ward counterparts of the construction of a majority, a majority forged on the twin bases of class and ethnicity. In the 1840s, it was briefly possible to construct a different majority bound by nativism, mutualism, and Whiggery. The growth of the immigrant population and the resurgence of the union movement meant that that majority could not last (though elsewhere such majorities were built more successfully), and Democratic preponderance was fashioned from appeals to ethnic and religious "civil liberties" and to the "hard-working masses." The first of these was hardly Tammany's initial inclination. The Democrats, like the Whigs in the early 1840s, recognized that a viable party required significant support from the native-born, and this recognition kept the Democrats (with the exceptions of Daniel Pentz and Michael Walsh) from backing the Catholic position on the school question. As the *Irish News* admitted, the Democrats, like the Whigs, had "anti-adopted citizens and anti-Irish views and prejudices." In the wake of the nativist–Whig alliance, however, the Irish were solidly in Democratic ranks and committed nativists had joined the Whigs. Over the succeeding decade, the Democrats had opportunities to reinforce immigrant loyalties. The revival of nativism in the 1850s, under the aegis of the Know-Nothings, met loud and consistent denunciation from the Democratic Party. The party was also militantly opposed to temperance legislation. These positions enabled the Democrats to trumpet their virtue as the party of "political equality warring against the spirit of exclusiveness and proscription," the party of "universal toleration."[1]

The Democracy's other claim to voter support was its self-characterization as the "true home of the working classes." The Democrats portrayed themselves as the rightful inheritors of Jefferson, champions of the political freedoms of common men. In the Age of Jackson, the Democrats sought out labor leaders to display at their meetings (as the Whigs did), sent Workingman Ely Moore to Congress, and subsidized a worker-oriented newspaper, the *Plebeian*. As Chapter 6 explained, the changing character of the working classes pressured the Democrats to accommodate working men in new ways. Thus, in the 1840s the party accommodated itself to the career of Michael Walsh, and in the 1850s they did not, like the Whigs, ignore the formation of the Industrial Congress. Late in the same decade, the Democrats echoed the denunciations by the unemployed of "speculators," "exploiters," and "parasites," and Mayor Wood affirmed the claim of the unemployed to assistance from their municipal government. Here, as in refusing to enforce temperance legislation, and as in creating new dimensions for political life in the ward, Wood showed his skill for constructing a majority. Though Wood himself was forced out of Tammany Hall for his "demagoguery," the Democrats took the lessons of his success to heart.

The working classes and the immigrants were of course largely the same people. In the vision of society the Democracy voiced, the party was their instrument and the party, the immigrant, and the worker were bound together in a single "we" against the "they" who mistakenly thought themselves respectable. By 1860, Democratic loyalty embraced and elaborated the ties of class and ethnicity, the "unterrified Democracy" insisting that parties "were the great implements of freedom," that "Tammany [has] stood a political lighthouse … amid the darkness and gloom of the political world."[2] Against the incursions of the state legislature, against the "sixty irresponsible gentlemen," against temperance advocates who wanted to class "everyone who is possessed of social qualities" with "felons and law breakers"[3] stood the "hard-working Democracy," without which "there is no means of opposition – there can be no combined and uniform effort."[4] By 1860, *Democratic* solidarity embraced cultural affinities, class loyalties, and political demands.

The creation of Democratic solidarity was fraught with provocations to the respectable element. Democratic politicians ostentatiously associated themselves with gangs, fire companies, and collective protest, deliberately, as Weber put it, relinquishing social honor. The reformers recognized this in their struggle against party and partisanship. The distaste for the boss was particularly strong among those reformers, like Phelps and Harper, who were also associated with nativist politics or the temperance movement, and in the antebellum period efforts at municipal reform were openly tied to nativism and Protestant and temperance preaching. These cultural antagonisms, however, were not the heart of the reform impulse. Opposition to "muscle" and the "dangerous classes" involved more than dislike of immigrants and drink; it was also a campaign to regain control of city government – to manage its finances and franchises and to restrain it to the role of efficient administration.

Corruption – the subordination of the public weal to private ends – was not new to city government in the 1850s, but the men who controlled it were. Career politicians not only threatened the investments of financiers in city bonds and the pocketbooks of the wealthy through taxation, they also overthrew the monopoly of wealthier men on profitable undertakings like the street railways. They were not even, as I suggested in the last chapter, honest about their corruption – a bribe paid not ensuring a contract delivered.

Wealthy men had not only lost control of city government, they had also changed. Like the working classes, men of wealth were developing a more modern outlook on government and politics. Fernando Wood's relief proposals brought into the open the conflicts between party principle and political practice that had coexisted, sub rosa, with the partisan division of labor between politicians and men of wealth. Like the repudiation of railroad bonds in the West, Wood's proposals heightened the fear that "when the laboring classes are contaminated, the right of suffrage becomes the engine of destruction." As a result, once the reformers realized they could not win elections without Democratic aid, their effort became an effort to discipline the Democrats, refusing funds until the party nominated "suitable candidates." Thus, for the moment, "Wall Street and the Five Points embraced."

The appearance of the boss and the reformer in the place of a two-party system echoing national divisions meant that for the first time city politics had a distinctive and autonomous life of its own. The discontents and issues that plagued the second American party system intermittently in the 1830s and 1840s moved to center stage in the 1850s. In part, this was because of the collapse of the national party system. Yet, once the party system was reestablished nationally, it did not again subordinate city politics as the Whig–Democratic contest had. There were two reasons for this. First, more than in 1830, the city was a socially distinctive place. The mechanics of the Age of Jackson had much in common with shopkeepers, liberals, and farmers in rural areas, commonalities on which political alliances could be based. Wage laborers were not so fortunate and their alliance, through the Democracy, was a more indirect and tenuous one. Their demands, as well as the presence of Catholics and immigrants in large numbers, did much to make the city a distinctive political arena. Second, by 1860 the urban party system was not dependent on state and national parties for organization-building resources. The Customs House remained a political plum for many decades to come, and the donations its workers made to the Democratic treasury were a great assistance to Tammany Hall. The employees of the city, however, were even more numerous, enabling the Democracy to declare its emancipation from Washington and to survive the long years of Republican domination of the national scene.

In complex ways, then, long-standing habits, ethnic affinities, class antagonisms, municipal expansion, and the dynamics of electoral conflict conspired to create an American city politics. The boss, the reformers, the majority, and patronage resources were securely in position by the election of Lincoln.

Still divided in 1860, New York's Democracy had tasted but not yet feasted on the fruits of majority loyalty and expanded municipal resources. Although the opposition of boss and reformer, the majority, and the autonomy of city politics were the hallmarks of urban political life for nearly a century to come, the materials at hand had yet to be constructed into a political machine. That work of construction was an elaboration and institutionalization of the chaotic elements of the city of the 1850s. Although the maintenance of a majority continued to rest on the twin allegiances of ethnicity and class, the ward became the central arena for the maintenance of voter support. The machine required above all organization and discipline among Democratic politicians, discipline that was lacking in the late antebellum era of factionalism and entrepreneurship. That organization and discipline enabled, over time, the negotiation of a modus vivendi with the respectable element. In each of these respects, William Tweed was the logical successor of Fernando Wood. The years of Tweed's activity in the party reveal both what had been accomplished in the antebellum era and the work that remained to be done.

Tweed's career in politics began in 1850, and stylistically as well as chronologically it was part of the antebellum era. Tweed, like the patrician and the career politician of the 1830s and 1840s, was prominent in one of the city's volunteer fire companies, and his first forays into electoral politics began in the same ward as his company and his home, the seventh.[5] Like the reformer who saw in the close association of politician and voter in the neighborhood the basis of partisan loyalty, Tweed recognized that the local school, the local party, and the neighborhood clubhouse were the building blocks of a majority organization. In his first post with citywide importance, as a member of the school board, Tweed worked to persuade the board to refrain from Protestant proselytizing by seeking a devolution of power to the ward school boards.[6] Similarly, one of Tweed's first acts as a power in the party was to make the ward organization a more participatory if not substantively democratic one.[7] The spatial development of the city assisted the effort of making the ward a politically meaningful place, for as ethnic groups became more segregated in the years following the Civil War the ward party organization could more and more take on a cultural affinity to its constituents. The ethnic politics with which the machine is so closely associated found its basis after the Civil War in the ethnic neighborhood and the party clubhouse that shared its culture.[8]

The auxiliary of these efforts was a party stance designed to maintain the twin allegiances of class and ethnicity. The generosity and sympathy of the patrician and career politician took shape in the 1860s as "Boss Tweed's Welfare Program." As a member of the New York State legislature in the late 1860s, and more particularly its Senate Committee on Charitable and Religious Societies, Tweed arranged for the appropriation of state funds for denominational schools, orphanages, hospitals, and dispensaries. Of $1,893,000 appropriated for expenditure in New York City, $1,396,000 went to institutions operated by the Catholic church. Not only the ultimate recipient of these monies, but also the sheer size of the appropriation, was quite an innovation. In the dozen years preceding Tweed's sojourn in the state senate, the state had spent under $2.2 million; during the three years Tweed spent in Albany, $2.225 million was appropriated by the legislature at the direction of Tweed's committee.[9] Appended to the "welfare program" were strategic public appearances at a variety of ethnic functions, like the dedication of the Hebrew Orphan Asylum, that reinforced the persona of the boss as a friend of the immigrant.[10]

There were also efforts to maintain the allegiance of the voice of industry. One of these was the assistance given to workingmen in avoiding the Civil War draft, an effort in which Tweed was prominent, along with the paying of bounties to men who chose to enlist. Another was the rhetorical recognition of the "contest ... between capital and labor." In 1868, the party sounded like this:

> We are united. We believe in our cause. It is the cause of constitutional liberty, of personal rights, of a fraternity of States, of an economical government, of one currency for all men, rich and poor...and the protection of American labor...[Our candidate] is a friend of the poor, the sympathizer with the naturalized citizen, and the foe to municipal oppression in the form of odious excise and all other requisitional laws...Is not the pending contest preeminently one of capital against labor, of money against popular rights, and of political power against the struggling interest of the masses?[11]

In the depression winter of 1873–4, the Democracy declared itself, as it had in 1857, in favor of relief and public employment for those in need.[12]

The latter-day Democracy accommodated itself to John Morrissey much as Democrats of the 1840s learned to live with Michael Walsh. Though a self-made man of considerable affluence, Morrissey as a politician presented himself as a friend of the working man. Morrissey contributed $5,000 to a relief fund for those in the shipbuilding industry who were striking for an eight-hour day in 1866 (and organized labor endorsed his congressional candidacy later in the year), and he insisted that workers on municipal projects be paid decent wages. Even more than Walsh, Morrissey was tough (his initial monetary success was from prize fighting), and like Walsh he refused to adopt a middle-class demeanor when his fortunes rose.[13] Finally, not only did workingmen, with the assistance of some liberal allies, particularly in the field of public health, succeed in getting tenement-code legislation passed, they also, eventually, succeeded in their demand that the city government refrain from intervening in labor disputes.[14]

Tweed, like Wood, operated in the years Martin Shefter has termed the era of "rapacious individualism." Unable to discipline his fellow party politicians, Tweed was compelled to alter the city charter to concentrate effective power in a small number of officials who composed his "ring."[15] To add to the resources at their disposal Tweed, again from his position in the state legislature, did away with the state-run commissions that so angered Fernando Wood and replaced them with municipal departments for police, fire fighters, public health, and parks whose commissioners were appointed by the mayor.[16] Yet outside of his few associates – who of course shared in the profits of their positions of authority – Tweed had only the bribe and the payoff with which to make other politicians his allies. Thus what order there was among party politicians was, like the welfare program, expensive. The lengths to which Tweed went to finance both welfare and centralization led to his downfall at the hands of the "wisest and best citizens" in 1871.[17]

The reformers, like the bosses, took up after the Civil War where they had left off before it. Many of the same men were again prominent, including Peter Cooper (and later his son Edward and his son-in-law Abram Hewitt) and William Havemeyer.[18] Reform late as early was associated with nativism, opposition to Tweed's subsidy of Catholic schools forming the leitmotif when the dominant theme was outrage over the unscrupulous marketing of city bonds.[19] Tweed was deposed by indictment rather than opposition at the polls: As Seymour Mandelbaum pointed out, the "men who could depose the king could not themselves ascend the throne and lead" in 1871[20] any more than they could in 1859. Moreover, reformers who were Democrats had partisan commitments to maintain, and for the rest of the century independent reform candidates were only put forward when no national election was at hand.

Thus the end of the Tweed era was also the beginning of an accommodation between boss and reformer. The man who led the party in Tweed's wake, John Kelley, pioneered both the institutionalization of intraparty discipline and the accommodation with reformers. The first was a prerequisite both to party rule of the city and to negotiation; the latter was an agreement to maintain the city government's fiscal soundness.[21] The accommodation of boss and reformer with one another was not without its coercive element. Those in the financial community could abort the worst disasters by threatening to make city bonds unmarketable; bosses could coerce (or woo) men of wealth by adjusting tax assessments and the like.

The legacy of the antebellum years, then, was a set of arrangements that organized and disciplined politicians and also accommodated both the "dangerous classes" and the "respectable element." If the accommodation between bosses and men of wealth was a tense one, between politicians and the "hard-working masses" the accommodation was equally two-edged. Nativism was anathema, charity and the "welfare program" were forthcoming. The brief years of the legislatively enacted "welfare program" were an anomaly, for charity remained a personal favor from the boss, a private matter rather than a right or an entitlement. Municipal employment was plentiful, but the primary requisite was political loyalty rather than skill, despite the campaign of organized workers against the partisan abuse of municipal employment. Rhetorical support for the workingman was not political support for union organization or decent wages (though bosses did not use police to help employers). Like ethnic politics, class rhetoric offered the symbolic rewards of status more often than programmatic results. So from time to time after the Civil War as before, the Irish, or the Germans, or a workingman's group rose up in insurgency against Tammany Hall.[22] These no more placed their leaders on the throne than the reformers. The machine was a set of arrangements that maximized the power and autonomy of the boss.

Despite his ascendancy, the boss remains an elusive figure, sometimes denounced as a demagogue, rogue, or thief, at other times lauded as a Robin Hood, defender of the immigrant, and cultural symbol of the political triumph of the common man. The Fernando Wood who was the "friend of the working man" was also a demagogue, the open-hearted William Tweed an embezzler, the efficient Mayor Daley a power broker. When account is taken of the social forces among whom the boss mediated, the compromises he orchestrated, and the city he governed, it can be recognized that ambiguity is fundamental to the boss and the machine he organized. The ties of the boss to the dangerous classes and to the respectable element were equally strong, and his autonomy from each of them equally important to his continued ascendancy. The institutional arrangements of machine politics organized social force, political faction, dominant group, and government. The "unterrified Democracy" provided a "community of many."

Machine politics was of course not peculiar to New York City. The machine was the characteristic form of government in the cities of the United States; the boss and the reformer were the most prominent urban antagonists for nearly a century. The central elements of that characteristic politics appeared in the antebellum years, when city politics acquired a form and rhythm of its own. Career politicians tied themselves to popular clubs, gangs, and institutions in their efforts to build party organization. The growth of municipal government meant an expansion of patronage and other organizational resources. "Bosses" organized followings in Pittsburgh, Philadelphia, Baltimore, and Boston. Reformers campaigned against "extravagance" and "corruption" in Boston, Cincinnati, Philadelphia, Baltimore, New York, and Springfield. For the most part, bosses organized the many and reformers the few.

The style and constituency of urban majorities varied from place to place. In New York City, the Democracy's majority was built on a militant workerist stance and assertive ethnic and immigrant loyalties. The "unterrified Democracy" was both the "true home of the working classes" and the defender of their cultural liberty and diversity. Similarly, in Lynn and Trenton militant workers' organizations informed the style of local politics and underlay the organization of majorities (though in these cities ethnic pluralism seems not to have been at issue).[23]

In contrast to this militant style of politics was a style of local politics that may be termed "mutualist." Here the unity of master and journeyman was updated to include employer and wage worker. Whiggish, Republican, and nativist, mutualist politics insisted on the primacy of American interests and the subordination of class divisions. In New York in the 1840s, the mutualist style in politics was the province of Whigs and American Republicans who (like their counterparts in Philadelphia) wished to "knit up" their "social sympathies once again" but formed only a minority of the city's electorate. In Providence, Pittsburgh, and Newark, it was possible to organize mutualist majorities.

Three things particularly favored mutualist politics. First, in Providence there were continued property restrictions on the franchise.[24] Since artisans were at the center of mutualist politics elsewhere, it seems likely that excluding their social inferiors from the electorate made the organization of a mutualist majority more likely. The second might be called "ostentatious paternalism," employer reinforcement of social familism. Even wealthy Democrats in New York who wished to rout the "demagogues" from the party recognized that "action on the part of the moneyed classes" was required to "prove to the working men that the sympathy of those who held the purse strings...was not wanting to them."[25] In Providence, the lavish display of charitable efforts on the part of wealthy men in the depression of the 1850s was accompanied by reminders that those who provoked class hostility in the United States were out of place. The *Providence Daily Journal*, denouncing "bread or work" agitation in New York City, insisted that "their rhetoric draws a separation between the different classes whom the laws of nature and a just political economy have made mutually dependent."[26]

The third facilitator of mutualist politics was the tariff. The tariff was the policy cement of the view that labor and capital shared the same interest, and mutualist politics, generally Whig and then Republican, trumpeted the tariff as the best protection of American labor from English competition. The national platform of the Republican Party in the elections of 1856 and 1860 was largely devoted to other matters, but local and working-class Republican partisanship was hardly based on a desire to destroy the "peculiar institution." Rather, in some places the possibility of the Homestead Act, quiet concessions to nativism, and more generally the tariff were the basis of working-class attraction to the party. Pittsburgh and Newark provide examples of the transition from Whiggery to Republicanism by such accommodations to the changing working classes. In Newark, the tariff was "sacred," and Whigs and later Republicans never abandoned the rhetoric of the mechanics as "the very blood and muscle of society."[27] In Pittsburgh, tariff, Homestead, and "free labor," carefully wedded to racist and anti-Catholic sentiment, provided enough economic promise to win the city for the Republicans.[28]

There were other political styles in local politics, though without the power of a national partisan presence they were inevitably short-lived. There were more than a few nativist politicians who, like the militants, based their appeal on a strong sense of class; a hard-fisted, tough self-presentation; and close association with rough supporters. Joel Barlow Sutherland in Philadelphia, Joel Barker in Pittsburgh, and Baltimore's Know-Nothing regime serve as examples.

Further study is required to document the styles of local politics at midcentury and to account for their distribution across cities. A number of hypotheses are suggested by what is already known about political change in antebellum cities. For example, differences in the organization of the cultural division of labor (that is, differences in class structure, differences in national origins, and differences in the relation of one to the other) should bear some relationship to the constituencies of militant or mutualist political styles and the prominence (or absence) of nativist politics. New York and Baltimore provide obvious contrasts: New York's artisans formed the central constituency of a mutualist American Republic Party, whereas Baltimore's wage workers organized in the militant Know-Nothing Party to express hostility to ruling Catholics. In other places, like Lynn and Providence, ethnicity seems less important in politics.

Cities also differed in their institutional arrangements at the beginning of the antebellum period. Although the coastal cities shared a set of local political institutions, the inheritance of Midwestern cities is less well known. Nevertheless, the leadership styles of manufacturer and merchant entering the industrial era contributed to the shape of political life everywhere. The "ostentatious paternalism" of Providence (or Harper and Brothers), for example, provided an experience to support mutualist political claims. By contrast, the withdrawal of New York's men of wealth from communal roles provoked the city's workers to turn from private expectations to militant public demands. As paternalist leadership styles on the part of merchants and industrialists became less common (and in places where that style was less common), the role of politicians grew in importance. The habits on which politicians might draw, and available resources for organization building, however, varied from city to city.

The larger context of national politics also informed the different patterns of local political life. Tariff, "free trade," internal improvements, and the like always had differential appeal across regions, and after 1850 region loomed increasingly large in the national party system. Imminent national crisis could only reinforce New York's Democracy, while "free soil" was bound to be more salient in Pittsburgh and Milwaukee than the cities of the coast. As political parties were the central vehicle of urban dependence and permeability in the antebellum era and beyond, national partisanship and local politics remained connected even as local political life acquired more autonomous form and rhythm.

Across the differences in local political styles, there was a striking set of common changes. Everywhere, political leaders were tireless in their efforts to promote particular visions of society in order to create reliable majorities. Although local political life bore the imprint of the working classes and other social groups, it also reflected the successes of political leaders at creating partisan solidarities. In the creation of these solidarities, the various styles of local politics incorporated a sense of class and a vision of the relations betwen classes. For many voters that sense was reinforced by ethnic solidarities or cultural interests (as when the New York Irish voted Democratic both because the Democracy was the "true home of the working classes" and because it protected their "right" to drink). As one might suspect where ethnicity and class were themselves so closely related, "class" and "ethnicity" were not always loyalties in competition with one another. Rather, they were often politically reinforcing loyalties.

Nowhere did urban politicians succeed without softening the hard line

156

of the national parties, and the common theme of these concessions was to ameliorate the harshness of the "industrial system." In the cities I have termed "mutualist," these concessions took the form of continued paternalism. Elsewhere, successful urban politicians supported one or another form of primitive, sub rosa, or informal welfarism. In New York and Philadelphia, Democrats supported public works in times of distress. In Baltimore, urban reformers did the same. In Boston, it was a nativist boss who offered relief and public-health reforms.

Most important, American cities shared a future of machine politics, and central features of that politics existed by the election of Lincoln. The persona of the boss began to appear when the patrician retired from popular political leadership. The boss rose to the center of city politics at a moment when the political aims and values of the "best men" and the "hard-working masses" were most seriously at odds and when ethnic pluralism was an objective but not an accepted fact. The institutional arrangements of machine politics, in creation and in triumph, accommodated the social forces of a city that no longer created a "natural" community. The boss, the reformer, the clubs, and the majority appeared in the antebellum era and dominated city politics for generations to come.

"Ultimately," Hartz wrote, "for all the magical chemistry of American life, we are dealing with materials common to the Western world."[29] Yet since machine politics was the characteristic form of city government in the United States, any persuasive account of the origins of machine politics is bound to be linked to the distinctive patterns of American political development. This account of machine politics has embraced both these premises by arguing that in the antebellum city the magical chemistry of American life consisted of the reaction between materials common to the Western world and the franchise, and that the products were machine politics and municipal reform.

Machine politics requires explanation because, although New York's Democracy created a "community of many," at its creation machine politics was not what anyone (with the possible exception of machine politicians) wanted. Working-class leaders demanded something resembling a local welfare state and that government hire on the basis of skill rather than employing "political creatures." Catholic immigrants wanted government to stop assisting Protestant proselytizers and to assist parochial education. Reformers wanted small, efficient, honest government. Probably not a few citizens simply wished that things might be as they had been a generation before.

Because machine politics was not what anyone wanted, it would be wrong to see it as an "institutionalization" of some particular set of values. From a great historical distance, it seems that political cultures give rise to political institutions rather like meadows grow wildflowers. Closer examination reveals the contingencies and gaps between popular cultures and institutionalized political life. Indeed, the moments when communities can purposively design institutions to embody their values (for example, the Constitutional Convention of 1787) are rare. By contrast, machine politics, like most political institutions, was the product of inheritance and incrementalism, conflict, inadvertence, and compromise. Thus machine politics is not properly understood as the "institutionalization" of working-class ethics, ethnic solidarity, or neighborhood loyalties, nor can it be accounted for by describing it as an admirably designed mechanism for social control (though it may well be true that machine politics bears some relation to each of those values).

Machine politics began to take shape in the antebellum years, when the cities of the United States lost their last resemblance to the eighteenth-century municipality and acquired the central elements of the nineteenth-century urban political order. In those years, two momentous developments transformed the American political economy. The beginnings of industrialization reorganized the ways in which people got, spent, and labored, while white manhood suffrage posed the challenge of organizing the many into political life. The first of these developments provoked conflicts and changes that the United States shared with its industrializing contemporaries; the second created a distinctive setting in which social sympathies might be "knitted up again" and a peculiarly American urban polity take shape.

In the United States, as elsewhere, the social revolution accompanying the industrial revolution encompassed changes not only in getting and spending, but also in people's relationships to one another and the values they wished to see government affirm. In place of advocating a "well-regulated society," merchant, industrialist, and financier began to reject "what the rich owe the poor" and embrace laissez-faire ideology. There was, moreover, an organized effort to persuade the working classes and the poor to Protestantism, "self-dependence," and greater industriousness, frugality, and temperance. In the same years, the working classes became more diverse as wage workers increased in numbers and the artisanate dwindled in size. Artisans in particular denounced the "industrial system" as immoral while new and old working classes shared an ethic bearing a strong resemblance to Thompson's "moral economy" of the poor. This resilient sensibility, popular republicanism, and new sense of class identity among the city's wage workers combined to produce a distinctive working-class voice in local politics. Men of wealth withdrew from those leadership roles in which public and private were hardly differentiated, leaving charity to professionals and community to politicians. More broadly, the erosion of old ties, the creation of new solidarities, and increased ideological diversity provided the themes of New York's political life in the antebellum years. In a variety of ways, then, the "social revolution" undermined the institutions of the old political order.

Simultaneous with the "social revolution" were important changes in the organization of political life. The abolition of remaining property barriers to the franchise broadened access to politics and posed the challenge of mobilizing the many. The creation of the second American party system changed the organization of political competition. The "Jacksonian Revolution" combined adptations of old political habits with political innovation to meet these challenges.

As important as these adaptations were the ways in which politics structured social conflict to its own logic and discipline. Expanded suffrage provided greater access to political life, giving common people additional resources and so empowering the many. The ballot, party insurgency, and popular organizations were added to petition, protest, muscle, and disorder, and these older resources were put to use in new arenas. Early in the antebellum era, the political resources of the working classes were used to pressure career politicians to behave as patricians had, and for further democratizing reforms. Later, they were used to demand that politicians endorse unionism, to protect (or assail) the civil liberties of immigrants and Catholics, and, perhaps most important, to gain welfare concessions from local government. The result (in addition to the concessions) was a boss who relinquished social honor – or, to make Weber more precise, a boss who relinquished social status in order to be popularly honored. Equally, the political power of common people made would-be patricians and reformers dependent on the boss, forcing (as it were) Wall Street to embrace Five Points.

The politicization of social conflict also raised the stakes of disagreement. To cultural difference was added the power and authority of government; to charity, sanction; to union, liberty and rights. The results were, first, an intensification of social conflict where the symbolic stakes of "status politics" were added to cultural issues, and, second, more complex social dissensus as "rights" and "liberty" were added to drink and religion. Equally important, to school, church, and union were added patronage, opportunism, party leadership, campaign finance, and public office. These provided incentives and goals that made the boss – despite his forfeiture of social honor – politician as well as (and often more than) workingman's advocate or immigrant's friend. More broadly, the rules, incentives, and goals of electoral politics created gaps between electors and elected, social desires and public policy, society and political order. The ways in which republicanism fell short of democracy were as visible in the city as anywhere else; the result was a set of urban institutions that "created community" yet were not what anyone wanted.

The logic and discipline of elections provoked the creation of alliances among social forces and politicians to create majorities, and these alliances took shape under partisan banners. Through the Democracy, New York's workingmen were allied with Southern planters; through Pittsburgh's Republican party, workers joined forces with farmers, nativists, and the middle classes. At the same time, social cleavages not being a datum, and parties being little more epiphenomenal to social forces than political institutions to social will, the configuration of party choices offered to voters determined different coalitions and alliances from place to place, time to time, and party to party. Whigs, Republicans, American Republicans, and Know-Nothings may have borne resemblances to one another, but they were not the same; some Whigs had no stomach for nativism, some Democrats could not abide Catholics, and many from each party favored democracy over elitism in the matter of public education. Parties not only reorganized social forces, they also created new solidarities and social identities as they promoted holistic visions of society. The result was a political universe of Democrats and reformers where a century before were merchants and mechanics.

The cities of the antebellum United States inherited institutions created in the eighteenth century by mechanic and merchant, a political order of liberty, rights, and the mildest of mercantilisms. The momentous events of the early nineteenth century – the expansion of suffrage and the onset of industrialization – made the old urban order contentious and unworkable. The cultural setting made political retreat by once again restricting the suffrage unthinkable (as, for a long time to come, it meant that expanding suffrage to women and blacks was out of the question). The same culture provided enduring language and values for political life. Electoral politics provided rules for resolving social conflicts and so influenced the character of the resolutions. The "social revolution" creating an industrial society made the old political life of mechanic and merchant unworkable. The reorganization of the economic order undermined long-standing habits, provoked new solidarities, and provided themes of social and political conflict.

Politics being epiphenomenal to neither culture nor structure, these developments did not themselves determine the institutional arrangements that came to be. Urban citizens (and many who were not, precisely, citizens) argued, compromised, voted, protested, fought, and organized to replace the old political order with a new one. Like other generations, they made history, but not under conditions of their own choosing. Alternatively, it may be said that culture and structure, placing limits on workable alternatives and providing rules for the resolution of social conflict, made politics the art of the possible.

What was possible in 1860 was the rather equivocal arrangements of machine politics. This new order, the legacy of the antebellum era, lasted until the conflicts of liberty and drink, immigrant and native, laissez-faire and social welfare, "respectable element" and "dangerous classes" were fought on national as well as local ground. Until then, machine politics provided a setting for urban history making. Embracing both adaptations of long-standing political habits and innovations for making political community out of social disorder, machine politics was the logical creation of an industrializing society with widespread suffrage and the historical creation of the cities of the United States.

Notes

Abbreviations for frequently cited periodicals:

EP   *Evening Post*
JC   *Journal of Commerce*
NYG   *New York Gazette*
NYH   *New York Herald*
NYT   *New York Times*
NYTr   *New York Tribune*
TU   *The Union*

1. A city in the republic

1 Samuel P. Huntington, *Political Order in Changing Societies* (New Haven, Conn.: Yale University Press, 1968), p. 11: "In a complex society community is produced by political action and maintained by political institutions." Quentin Hoare and G. N. Smith, eds., *Selections from the Prison Notebooks of Antonio Gramsci* (New York: International Publishers, 1971), p. 55: "The modern state substitutes for the mechanical bloc of social groups their subordination to the active hegemony of the directive and dominant group ..."

2 Edward Banfield and James Q. Wilson, *City Politics* (New York: Vintage Books, 1963), pp. 40–1. There is no evidence whatever that these are reasonable characterizations of white Anglo-Saxon Protestant and immigrant political cultures, or even of bosses and reformers (both of whom had selfish as well as collective interests and motivations). Banfield and Wilson also provide the most widely accepted definition of machine politics, characterizing the machine as "a party organization that depends crucially upon inducements that are both specific and material." It follows that the machine "is apolitical: it is interested only in making and distributing income ... to those who run it and work for it. Political principle is foreign to it, and represents a danger and a threat to it." Hence machine politics is associated with corruption and patronage. Because specific, material inducements are never plentiful enough to be distributed to all voters, machine politics is also associated with personalistic leadership and the camaraderie and loyalty of the clubhouse. The artful combination of clubhouse solidarity and material rewards creates a well-disciplined and centralized political organization reaching from city hall to the city's wards and precincts and claiming the majority of the city's electorate. Although any party may use patronage and friendship, or exhibit centralized and hierarchical organization, political machines governed the cities of the United States for nearly

a century by delivering majorities over and over again. (ibid., pp. 115–21). Generations of municipal reformers have opposed machine politics with admirable persistence; bosses and reformers have been the Siamese twins of American city politics.

3 Nathan Glazer and Daniel Patrick Moynihan, *Beyond the Melting Pot*, 2d ed. (Cambridge, Mass.: MIT Press, 1970), pp. 221–9.

4 Sam Bass Warner, Jr., *The Private City: Philadelphia in Three Stages of Its Growth* (Philadelphia: University of Pennsylvania Press, 1968), pp. 54–6. Warner offers a more complex account of the antebellum reordering of Philadelphia. He is concerned throughout *Private City* with the limits a political culture of privatism set on the objects of urban government. Although these limits were always dysfunctional, Warner argues, the colonial city was small enough that its communal nature overcame them. Urban growth and concomitant spatial differentiation brought the latent dysfunctionalism of the city's political culture to the surface. Without gathering places in which the neighborhoods of the city could focus, the city suffered a loss of community. Urban residents responded to this loss of community by organizing a host of clubs and associations. These were incapable of nourishing "effective and inclusive community growth," but they did provide a basis for "ethnic politics." Although I appreciate Warner's articulation of the "culture of privatism," for the antebellum period his emphasis on cultural continuity obscures important developments having to do with the changing definitions of "public" and "private." In addition, as I argue in the text, I see more than "ethnic politics" in the 1850s. I also take issue, in Chapter 7, with Warner's understanding of the political role of men of wealth.

5 Walter Hugins, *Jacksonian Democracy and the Working Class* (Stanford, Calif.: Stanford University Press, 1960), pp. 151, 29.

6 *NYH*, 1 April 1837.

7 *NYH*, 24 November 1857.

8 Chilton Williamson, *American Suffrage from Property to Democracy, 1760–1860* (Princeton, N.J.: Princeton University Press, 1960).

9 Morton Horwitz, *The Transformation of American Law, 1780–1860* (Cambridge, Mass.: Harvard University Press, 1977).

10 Huntington, *Political Order*, p. 10.

11 Oscar Handlin and Mary Flug Handlin, *Commonwealth: A Study of the Role of Government in the American Economy: Massachusetts, 1774–1861* (Cambridge, Mass.: Harvard University Press, 1969). Louis Hartz, *Economic Policy and Democratic Thought: Pennsylvania 1776–1860* (Chicago: Quadrangle Books, 1968).

12 Hartz, *Economic Policy*, pp. 308, 177–8.

13 Handlin and Handlin, *Commonwealth*, p. 225. Cf. Horwitz, *Transformation*, p. 253: "Law, once conceived of as protective, regulative, paternalistic, and, above all, a paramount expression of the moral sense of the community, had come to be thought of as facilitative of individual desires and as simply reflective of the existing organization of economic and political power."

14 Hartz, *Economic Policy*, pp. 177–8, 314.

15 Douglas Yates, *The Ungovernable City: The Politics of Urban Problems and Policy Making* (Cambridge, Mass.: MIT Press, 1977), p. 34.

16 For a general consideration of this issue, see Leonard Binder et al., *Crises and Sequences in Political Development* (Princeton, N.J.: Princeton University Press, 1971). Rheinhard Bendix has argued in particular that the sequencing of industrialization and democratization has tremendous consequences for how

politics works and what its issues are. For the United States, Bendix claimed that political rights softened the sense of deprivation among the newly created working classes. See his *Nation Building and Citizenship* (New York: Wiley, 1964), especially pp. 61–74. The emphasis here, by contrast, is not on the consequences of democratization on consciousness in the short run, but on the consequences of democratization for the arena in which social conflicts were resolved. The setting of course had profound effects on class consciousness in the long run. See my "Becoming American, The American Working Classes before the Civil War," in Ira Katznelson and Aristide Zolberg, eds., *Working Class Formation: Nineteenth Century Patterns in Western Europe and the United States*, forthcoming.

17 Louis Althusser, *For Marx* (New York: Vintage Books, 1970). Nicos Poulantzas, *Political Power and Social Classes* (London: New Left Books and Sheed and Ward, 1975).

18 For suggestions on such an implicitly comparative structural framework see Poulantzas, *Political Power*, pp. 147–57.

19 E.J. Hobsbawm, *The Age of Revolution 1789–1848* (New York: New American Library, 1962), p. 46.

20 Even so modern a writer as John Stuart Mill characterized class relations by saying that "the rich should be *in loco parentis* to the poor." See Rheinhard Bendix, *Work and Authority in Industry* (Berkeley: University of California Press, 1956), p. 57.

21 Ibid., pp. 74–5. In New York City, the common council cited the "zealous investigations" of "able individuals" in "England and this country" to the effect that charity diminished "the industry and economy of the poor" and promoted "a lamentable dependency." New York City Board of Aldermen, *Documents*, vol. 4, doc. 57 (1838), pp. 445–9. The best-known villain of this ideological piece is of course Malthus, who declared "the poor cannot, in the nature of things, possess the *right* to demand" employment and maintenance. Bendix, *Work and Authority*, p. 83.

22 *JC*, 1 February 1838, p. 2.

23 E.P. Thompson, "The Moral Economy of the English Crowd in the Eighteenth Century," *Past and Present* 50 (February 1971), pp. 76–136. Although Thompson formulated the notion of "moral economy" to describe eighteenth-century crowd behaviors, it seems only sensible to use the same appellation for later behaviors exhibiting the same values and demands. Indeed, there is even a family resemblance between Thompson's "moral economy" and "from each according to his abilities, to each according to his needs." For a consideration of the moral economy in eighteenth-century America, see Eric Foner, *Tom Paine and Revolutionary America* (London: Oxford University Press, 1976), chapter 4. The same notions of morality and good I am calling here "moral-economic" underlay the substantive justice of eighteenth-century law. See Horwitz, *Transformation*, pp. 161–73.

24 Charles Tilly, Louise Tilly, and Richard Tilly, *The Rebellious Century: 1830–1930* (Cambridge, Mass.: Harvard University Press, 1975), pp. 50–5. For similar observations of changing collective behaviors in the United States, see Paul Gilge, "Mobocracy: Popular Disturbances in Post-Revolutionary New York City, 1783–1829," Ph.D. dissertation, Brown University, 1980; and his "The Baltimore Riots of 1812 and the Breakdown of the Anglo-American Mob Tradition," *Journal of Social History* 13:4 (Summer 1980), pp. 547–64.

25 Hobsbawm, *Revolution*, p. 248.

26 *NYH*, 19 October 1842, p. 2.

27 The world view of the working classes "was powerfully connected with and reinforced by what may be called Jacobin consciousness – the set of aspirations with which the French (and also before it the American) Revolution had imbued the thinking and confident poor." Hobsbawm, *Revolution*, p. 249; see also E. P. Thompson, *The Making of the English Working Class* (Harmondsworth, England: Penguin, 1970), chapter 16; and William H. Sewell, Jr., "Artisans, Factory Workers, and the Formation of the French Working Class, 1789–1848," in Katznelson and Zolberg, eds., *Working Class Formation.*

28 Adam Przeworski and John Sprague, "A History of Western European Socialism," paper presented at the Annual Meeting of the American Political Science Association, Washington, D.C., September 1977, pp. 22–3.

29 Paul Kleppner, *The Cross of Culture: A Social Analysis of Midwestern Politics, 1850–1900* (New York: Free Press, 1970), p. 36.

30 Ibid., p. 47.

31 Przeworski and Sprague, "European Socialism," p. 25; compare Huntington, *Political Order*, p. 10: Political "institutions ... give new meaning to the common purpose and create new linkages between the particular interests of individuals and groups."

32 Przeworski and Sprague, "European Socialism," p. 26.

33 V.O. Key, *The Responsible Electorate* (New York: Random House, 1966), pp. 1–2.

34 Kleppner, *Cross of Culture*, p. 47.

35 H.H. Gerth and C. Wright Mills, eds. and trans., *From Max Weber: Essays in Sociology* (New York: Oxford University Press, 1958), p. 194.

36 Huntington, *Political Order*, p. 91.

37 Ibid., p. 9.

38 In the period under examination here, the crucial case in point is charity. As a private matter, it was a "Christian duty," as a public matter it was an entitlement, a "right" signifying that the poor were blameless.

39 Alan Nevins and Milton Halsey Thomas, eds., *The Diary of George Templeton Strong*, 3 vols. (New York: Macmillan, 1952), 2:331.

40 *Address of the General Executive Committee of the American Republican Party of the City and County of New York to their Fellow Citizens (ARP Address)* (New York, 1843), p. 5.

41 See, for example *The Crisis! An Appeal to Our Countrymen on the Subject of Foreign Influence in the United States* (New York: 201 Broadway, 1844).

42 *NYH*, 17 January 1838, p. 1.

43 Edward Mallon of the tailors, *NYH*, 9 August 1850.

44 Peter Cooper in *NYT*, 3 November 1854, p. 3.

2. The chronicles of party

1 *EP*, 30 September 1828, p. 2.

2 *Sentinel*, 12 September 1832, quoted in Walter Hugins, *Jacksonian Democracy and the Working Class* (Stanford, Calif.: Stanford University Press, 1960), p. 28.

3 *EP*, 1 November 1828, emphasis added.

4 For these views in Massachusetts and Pennsylvania, respectively, see Handlin and Handlin, *Commonwealth*, and Hartz, *Economic Policy*.

5 For the rhetorical oppositions of eighteenth-century political thought, see Bernard Bailyn, *The Ideological Origins of the American Revolution* (Cambridge, Mass.: Belknap Press of Harvard University Press, 1970); for suspicion of

laissez-faire, see Foner, *Tom Paine*, chapter 5, and Gary B. Nash, *The Urban Crucible: Social Change, Political Consciousness, and the Origins of the American Revolution* (Cambridge, Mass.: Harvard University Press, 1979). Nash reports that "unrestrained competition . . . was thought of as a prescription for chaos and corruption" (p. 32). For consensus on the commercial republic, see Alfred Young, "The Mechanics and the Jeffersonians: New York 1789–1801," *Labor History* 5 (1964):247–69, and Staughton Lynd, "The Mechanics and New York Politics, 1774–1788," *Labor History* 5 (1964):225–46.

6 *Working Man's Advocate*, 8 May 1830; quoted in Seymour Savetsky, "The New York Workingmen's Party," M.A. thesis, Columbia University, 1948, p. 79.

7 *New York Sentinel and Workingman's Advocate*, 16 January 1830. Quoted in John R. Commons, *History of Labour in the United States*, 4 vols. (New York: Macmillan, 1926), 1:233. See also Edward Pessen, *Most Uncommon Jacksonians: The Radical Leaders of the Early Labor Movement* (Albany: State University of New York Press, 1967), pp. 120–3.

8 William H. Hale, *Useful Knowledge for the Producers of Wealth, Being an Inquiry into the Nature of Trade, the Currency, the Protective and Internal Improvement Systems, and into the Origin and Effects of Banking and Paper Money* (New York: George H. Evans, 1833), p. 15; *Workingman's Advocate*, quoted in John R. Commons et al., *A Documentary History of American Industrial Society*, 10 vols. (Cleveland: Arthur H. Clark, 1910), 5:49. Clinton Roosevelt, *The Mode of Protecting Domestic Industries* (New York: Benjamin H. Tyrell, 1889 [orig. pub. 1831]), also argued that the ultimate effect of the banking system was likely to be despotism. For Roosevelt and Hale, England represented nothing so much as a liberty-loving people enslaved by a national debt. Roosevelt saw the same process closer to home: "Look at any town six or eight years after a bank has been established in it, and see if industry has not sown and cunning has not reaped the fruit in the shape of deeds and bonds and mortgages held by bankers . . ." (p. 32). For both Roosevelt and Hale, moreover, the English had a stake in undermining the American experiment in republican government and were attempting to do so by funding the national debt.

Workingmen also argued that the inflation caused by bad currency raised the prices of American goods, vitiating the protective effects of the tariff. Hard currency would protect both the workingman's income and his market.

9 Roosevelt, *Mode*, p. 34. With respect to temperance, the same author wrote, "We have often desired that our friends in the temperance cause, would look into the effect of want of hope in real things, in causing the mind to wander to artificial stimulants to find what they desire . . . Our decided impressions are, that if we secure to industry its fair reward, and render men happy physically, we destroy the strongest inducements to immorality . . ." See ibid.

10 G.H. Evans in *Working Man's Advocate*, quoted in Hugins, *Jacksonian Democracy*, p. 179.

11 Roosevelt, *Mode*, pp. 10–11.

12 *EP*, 21 November 1834, quoted in Hugins, *Jacksonian Democracy*, p. 148.

13 William Marcy, quoted in ibid., p. 35.

14 *EP*, 1 November 1828.

15 *EP*, 8 January 1828.

16 *EP*, 3 November 1820, p. 2.

17 Quoted in Jerome Mushkat, *Tammany: The Evolution of a Political Machine, 1789–1865* (Syracuse, N.Y.: Syracuse University Press, 1971), pp. 123, 125.

18 *EP*, 2 January 1828.
19 *EP*, 9 March 1831, p. 2.
20 *EP*, 1 November 1830, p. 2; 9 March 1831.
21 *NYH*, 19 October 1842.
22 *EP*, 8 March 1831, p. 2.
23 As for example, by the Democratic Young Men of the fifteenth ward, who defined monopoly as "all exclusive privileges, or powers, or facilities, for the accumulation of wealth, or the exclusive use and enjoyment of the bounties of providence secured to individuals or combinations of men by legislative enactments, the free and uninterrupted enjoyment of which are denied by the laws to other members of the same community" (Hugins, *Jacksonian Democracy*, p. 149).
24 Jackson's veto message, quoted in Edwin C. Rozwenc, ed., *Ideology and Power in the Age of Jackson* (Garden City, N.Y.: Doubleday, Anchor Books, 1964), pp. 198–9. It was not the other way around, as Arthur Schlesinger's *The Age of Jackson* (Boston: Little, Brown, 1945) argues. Schlesinger presents "The Credo of the Workingmen" in chapter 11, after his discussion of the bank war and hard money. His presentation as well as his text argue that the Workingmen were inheritors of Jacksonism. Yet even Schlesinger's footnotes reveal that Workingmen's "Jacksonism" happened *before* Jackson. This is particularly true of the theory of hard money (see, for example, Hale, *Useful Knowledge*, and Roosevelt, *Mode*). Finally, while some Workingmen became Jacksonians, others, as I will argue below, did not. For Jacksonism, by turning to small government and a radical emphasis on equality, turned away from another element of Workingmen's faith, that "the object of all policy is to bind all the members of the families which constitute society, into one common interest; so that instead of reciprocally injuring themselves, they should mutually assist each other in their daily and social wants" [Ely Moore, *Address on Civil Government, Delivered Before the New York Typographical Society, February 25, 1847* (New York: B. R. Barlow, 1847), p. 23].
25 Quoted in Fitzwilliam Byrdsall, *History of the Loco-Foco or Equal Rights Party* (New York: Burt Franklin, 1967 [orig. pub. 1841]), p. 139.
26 Ibid., p. 157. This was nothing new in the history of the world: "The world has always abounded with men, who, rather than toil to produce the wealth necessary to their subsistence, have contrived to strip others of the fruits of their labor, either by violence and bloodshed, or by swaggering pretensions of exclusive privileges."
   "It is, however, chiefly by this latter mode of robbery, that the working classes of modern times are kept in debasement and poverty. Aristocrats have discovered that charters are safer weapons than swords; and that cant, falsehood, and hypocrisy serve all the purposes of a highwayman's pistol, while they leave their victims alive and fit for future execrations" (ibid., p. 135). And cf. the veto message: "It is to be regretted that the rich and powerful too often bend the acts of government to their selfish purposes" (Rozwenc, ed., *Ideology and Power*, p. 198).
27 Rozwenc, ed., *Ideology and Power*, p. 41.
28 Ibid., p. 139.
29 Ibid., p. 73.
30 Ibid., p. 148. These thoughts were elaborated on many occasions, for example, in 1836: "A disordered currency (inseparable from the present system of banking or the issue of 'paper money') is one of the greatest political evils as it undermines the virtues necessary for the support of the social system." Ob-

viously, the system was *immoral*: It brought wealth to those who had not labored, it benefited the rich at the expense of the poor, and it taxed necessities rather than financing government out of surplus. Isaac S. Smith, an upstate Locofoco, declared, "All wealth is an accumulation of surplus labor, from which alone the expenses and burthens of government should be borne. No person possessing mental or physical ability, can have a *moral* right to consume that which he does not in some manner contribute to produce"; the Locofocos declared themselves on another occasion "opposed to all bank charters ... because we believe them founded on, and as giving an impulse to, principles of speculation, at war with good morals." By contrast, it was maintained, "the principles of Democracy, and the principles of morality, are one and the same" (Moses Jacques in eighth-ward aldermanic campaign speech). Ibid., pp. 75, 50.

31 Meeting of Democratic Mechanics, 18 October 1842; reported in *NYH*, 19 October, 1842, p. 2.

32 *NYTr*, 27 March 1845, p. 2. "If our Seamstresses cannot stand a competition with our country women, who make shirts for 11 cents each, how will they be benefitted by throwing open our market to all the world, when shirts are made in England for three farthings or a cent and a half each?" (Ibid.). Greeley did admit that "the extent of [the tariff's] power to benefit the Laborer is limited by the force and pressure of domestic competition, for which Political Economy has as yet devised no remedy."

33 Calvin Colton, *Junius*, Tract VII (March 1844), quoted in Rozwenc, ed., *Ideology and Power*, pp. 352–3.

34 *NYH*, 3 April 1847, p. 2; 3 April 1838, p. 1.

35 *NYH*, 9 April 1849, p. 2.

36 Peletiah Peret, *New York American*, 28 October 1834, quoted in Elliot R. Barkan, "The Emergence of a Whig Persuasion: Conservatism, Democratism, and the New York State Whigs," *New York History* 52 (1971):387.

37 Colton, *Junius*, Tract VII, quoted in ibid., pp. 388–9.

38 *New York American*, 2 November 1847, quoted in ibid., p. 378.

39 *New York Courier and Enquirer*, 3 May 1839, quoted in ibid., p. 385.

40 "In such a country as the United States or England, the great commercial class, like Samson under the portico of Dagon's temple, cannot be struck down without pulling the idolatrous fane with him in the general crash. Miserable, ignorant, dirty, rum-drinking politicians may talk and jeer at the mercantile classes as they please. Let the political power at Washington strike to the earth the spirit of commerce, and in a few months that unchained spirit will start up, in tenfold strength, and tear the miserable democratic rags from the filthy back of power, and kick it to perdition. Why is this so? It is the supremacy of mind, genius, talent, and industry, over avarice, fanaticism, hypocrisy, drunkenness, and folly ... Among the great *commercial class* – and by this term we mean the merchant, farmer, banker, broker, or mechanic, who is educated, intelligent, and understands the principles of doing business – among the great commercial class is the ultimate and sovereign power of this country" (*NYH*, 1 April 1837, p. 2). It followed that "the nomination of a wealthy man for mayor was but a just response to the claims of the merchants of this commercial metropolis to a share in the government of a city to whose wealth, prosperity and industry, the merchants have so largely contributed" (*NYH*, 1 November 1850, p. 1). Whigs had their doubts too. The *American Review* wrote, in 1845, that "we have more conscience than heart, and more propriety than either" (quoted in Rozwenc, ed., *Ideology and Power*, p. 54).

41 To the tenth-ward Clay Club, 23 March 1843, quoted in Barkan, "Whig Persuasion," p. 385.
42 *NYTr*, 10 June 1848.
43 *Albany Evening Journal*, 8 September 1837, quoted in Barkan, "Whig Persuasion," p. 391.
44 *NYTr*, 6 April 1842, p. 2.
45 *NYTr*, 25 January 1844, p. 2, quoted in Commons, *Documentary History* vol. 7, pp. 37–8.
46 *NYH*, 5 April 1845, p. 2.
47 *NYH*, 17 January 1838, p. 1.
48 Ira M. Leonard, "New York City Politics, 1841–1844, Nativism and Reform," Ph.D. dissertation, New York University, 1965.
49 *NYH*, 9 April 1844, p. 1.
50 Thomas R. Whitney, *A Defense of the American Policy As Opposed to the Encroachments of Foreign Influence, and Especially to the Interference of the Papacy in the Political Interests and Affairs of the United States* (New York: DeWitt and Davenport, 1856), p. 68; see also pp. 92–3 and his chapter 17.
51 Ibid., p. 325. See also pp. 16, 17, and 31ff. for the contrary case of France.
52 *ARP Address*, p. 5.
53 See, for example, *The Crisis*, p. 62. For nativist evidence that immigrants were illiterate or unschooled, see, for example, *The Crisis*, p. 37; *ARP Address* ("the majority ... are ignorant, superstitious, and vicious"). For further references to the authoritarian backgrounds of immigrants see *The Crisis*, p. 62, and Samuel C. Busey, "Immigration, Its Evils and Consequences" (New York: n.p., 1856) quoted in Edith Abbott, ed., *Historical Aspects of the Immigration Problem, Select Documents* (Chicago: University of Chicago Press, 1926), pp. 503, 507. It was, moreover, argued that immigrants could not transcend their attachment to their country of origin to form allegiance to the United States (*The Crisis*, pp. 52, 61, 63, 71; Whitney, *Defense*, p. 135; Abbott, *Historical Aspects*, p. 510). Finally, Washington, Lafayette, and others were quoted to the effect of agreement with nativist sentiments – most of the quotes quite apparently and outrageously out of context. See, e.g., *The Crisis*, title page.
54 This was an old argument, going back to before the Revolution. In the eighteenth century, it was also an argument that had considerable historical or empirical weight – the only republics in the world, it was frequently pointed out, were Great Britain, the United States, and, briefly, the Netherlands, all of which were Protestant. In its most sophisticated form, it anticipated modern arguments about political socialization (see, for example, the *Independent Reflector*, 19 July 1753). Most of the time, in somewhat less sophisticated form, the same meaning remained. Thus, it was not argued that Catholics were, for example, clannish, but rather that they were taught to be obedient and unreflective, not even permitted to read the Bible for themselves. How could such men shoulder the responsibilities of enjoying the franchise in a republic?
55 Whitney, *Defense*, pp. 90, 98, 100.
56 *ARP Address*, pp. 5–7; on immigrant competition in the labor market, see Whitney, *Defense*, pp. 169–70. This argument was made more prominently in the late 1840s in the newspaper the *Champion of American Labor*. The *Champion* claimed to be a "family paper, devoted to the intellectual and social improvement of the laboring classes" (8 April 1847). The paper criticized Democrats for stirring up class feeling, but pointed out that the wealthy could only prove their good will toward working men and women by supporting immigration restriction (8 April 1847, p. 1).

57 *The Crisis*, p. 56.
58 Whitney, *Defense*, pp. 56–60.
59 Ellen Dwyer, "The Rhetoric of Reform," Ph.D. dissertation, Yale University, 1977, pp. 222, 256.
60 *NYH*, 8 April 1843, p. 2.
61 *NYH*, 28 March 1845.
62 6 April 1844, quoted in Leonard, "Nativism and Reform," p. 437.
63 *NYT*, 11 November 1854.
64 *Sketches of the Speeches and Writings of Michael Walsh: Including His Poems and Correspondence Compiled by a Committee of the Spartan Association* (New York: Thomas McSpedon, General Agent, 1843). See also Workingmen's view in Roosevelt, *Mode*, p. 34.
65 John Cochrane, quoted in *NYH*, 3 November 1854.
66 *NYH*, 3 November 1854, p. 1.
67 *NYH*, 10 April 1846, p. 2.
68 On Free Soil, see *NYH*, 27 October 1854, p. 4, and 29 December 1859, p. 4. On union, see *NYH*, 30 October 1854, p. 4, and 25 October 1854, p. 4. On abolitionism, see *NYH*, 30 October 1854, p. 4, and 25 October 1854, p. 4.
69 *NYH*, 31 October 1856, p. 4.
70 Hiram Ketchum, quoted in *NYH*, 2 December 1859, p. 4. See also *NYH*, 30 October 1857, p. 1.
71 *NYH*, 1 November 1852, p. 5.
72 *NYH*, 28 October 1854, p. 8.
73 Municipal Reform Committee address in *NYH*, 18 October 1854, p. 1. Further: "The regular conventions have been so often packed to force on the people objectionable nominees, that the word 'regular' has lost its charm. Reflecting men naturally begin to consider what a man's party predilections have to do with his administrative ability. Once it was a favorite theory that the election of local officers on party grounds, served as a check to bad legislation, by including incumbents of opposing politics to watch each other. But we have lately seen this theory exploded, by witnessing the remarkable spirit of concord and fraternity with which Whigs and Democrats in office unite to further their personal ends."
74 James R. Whiting (reform mayoral candidate) in *NYH*, 30 October 1856, p. 1.
75 Peter Cooper in *NYH*, 18 October 1854, p. 1.
76 *NYH*, 1 November 1852, p. 5.
77 *NYH*, 27 November 1857, p. 4.
78 *NYH*, 4 November 1856, p. 4 (editorial); and 28 November 1857, p. 1, quoting Fernando Wood.
79 *NYH*, 30 October 1856, p. 4; see also *NYH*, 22 November 1861, p. 2.
80 "Assuredly the greatest of the many great deceptions which are foisted into public notice at the present time is the so-called reform movement ... It seems to have been the aim of the municipal reforms to retard the cause they pretend to advance." Their amendments will simply grant "a new lease of power to the sixty irresponsible gentlemen who have attempted to lord it over the common council during the past year, and may be considered a guarantee that the administration of city affairs will be taken still further out of the hands of the authorities ..." (*NYH*, 4 November 1854, p. 4).
81 Wood, quoted in *NYH*, 28 November 1857, p. 1; and see "How New York is Going to be Punished," *Harper's Weekly*, 28 March 1857, p. 194.
82 Article on Democratic Ratification Meeting, *NYH*, 1 November 1852.

83 Article on Democratic Ratification Meeting, *NYH*, 24 November 1857. See also Wood, quoted in *NYT*, 29 May 1857, p. 5: "Upon this occasion it is not only a right but a duty for the people of New York, irrespective of birth, class, or party, to resist and denounce the gross usurpations which have been perpetuated by their tyrant master at the State Capital."

84 Wood in *NYTr*, 16 October 1850, p. 1. Workers argued that since public works were labor intensive, the lowest bidder for a public-works contract was necessarily the employer who paid the lowest wages. Workers therefore demanded an end to the contract system, and that laborers on public works be hired directly by government.

85 *NYH*, 30 October 1854, p. 4.

86 New York City Board of Aldermen, *Documents*, vol. 22, p. 9.

87 *NYH*, 14 January 1856, quoted in Carl N. Degler, "Labor in the Economy and Politics of New York City, 1850–1860: a Study in the Impact of Early Industrialism," Ph.D. dissertation, Columbia University, 1952; see also *EP*, 10 November 1857, and *NYTr*, 10 November 1857.

88 *NYTr*, 28 December 1863, p. 1.

89 *NYH*, 27 November 1861, p. 5.

90 *NYH*, 27 November 1861, p. 4.

91 Article on Opdyke Ratification Meeting, *NYH*, 2 December 1859, p. 4.

92 *NYTr*, 28 December 1863, p. 4.

93 *NYH*, 23 November 1861, p. 5; see also *NYH*, 27 November 1861, p. 4.

94 *NYH*, 24 November 1857, p. 1.

95 *NYH*, 28 November 1857, p. 1.

3. Fellow citizens

1 New York State, secretary of state, *Census of the State of New York for 1855* (Albany: Charles Van Benthuysen, 1857), calculated from pp. 117–18.

2 Alan Nevins, ed., *The Diary of Philip Hone, 1828–1851* (New York: Dodd, Mead, 1936), p. 41.

3 This description is based on examination and summary of the manuscripts of the U.S. census of 1850, schedule 6, the census of manufactures.

4 Calculated from the 1855 census, pp. 110–11, 117–18.

5 Edward Pessen, *Riches, Class, and Power Before the Civil War* (Lexington, Mass.: D. C. Heath, 1978), p. 177.

6 Peter Temin, *The Jacksonian Economy* (New York: Norton, 1969), p. 174. For 1855–7, see George W. Van Vleeck, *The Panic of 1857: An Analytical Study* (New York: AMS Press, 1967).

7 Robert G. Albion and Jennie Barnes Pope, *The Rise of the New York Port, 1815–1860* (New York: Scribner, 1970 [orig. pub. 1939]), pp. 56–62.

8 Ibid., pp. 67–8.

9 Philip Foner, *Business and Slavery, the New York Merchants and the Irrepressible Conflict* (New York: Russell and Russell, 1968), p. 4.

10 Ibid., pp. 164–7.

11 Degler, "Labor," p. 3.

12 Ibid., pp. 4–8.

13 Ibid., p. 96.

14 Pessen, *Riches*, p. 35. Harry James Carman, *The Street Surface Railway Franchises of New York City*, Studies in History, Economics and Public Law, vol. 88, no. 1 (New York: Columbia University Press, 1919), p. 78.

15 Albion and Pope, *Rise*, pp. 245, 248, 249.

16 See ibid., chapter 12 passim.

17 Pessen, *Riches*, p. 67.

18 Ibid., p. 35. Gustavus Myers, *History of the Great American Fortunes* (New York: Random House, Modern Library, 1937), p. 114. The opportunities for making profits from real estate can be grasped by examining the assessed value of real estate in the city in 1833 – $114 million – and in 1855 – $337 million. Assessed valuations were of course lower than actual values [James Valentine, *Manual of the City of New York for 1857* (New York: McSpedon and Baker, 1857), p. 185]. Unofficial estimates suggest that the value of land and buildings doubled between 1833 and 1836. See Marvin Meyers, *The Jacksonian Persuasion: Politics and Belief* (Stanford, Calif.: Stanford University Press, 1960), p. 111.

19 Carman, *Surface Railway*, p. 23; Pessen, *Riches*, p. 35.

20 Albion and Pope, *Rise*, pp. 67, 315. August B. Gold, "A History of Manufacturing in New York City, 1825–1840," M.A. thesis, Columbia University, 1932, p. 46.

21 Ibid., p. 121.

22 Ibid., p. 112.

23 Nevins and Thomas, *George Templeton Strong*, 2:478.

24 See, for example, John H. Griscom, *The Sanitary Condition of the Laboring Population of New York* (New York: Harper and Brothers, 1845); Report of the Commissioners of the Almshouse, in New York City Board of Aldermen, *Documents*, vol. 4, doc. 32 (1837), pp. 226–7.

25 For this reason, I have avoided using newspaper reporting or editorials as measures of "public opinion." If indeed there was something that might reasonably be called "public opinion" in the 1850s, newspapers played a much greater role in shaping than in voicing it.

26 I am indebted for circulation figures to Michael Schudson. For the influence of the press, see Paul O. Weinbaum, "Mobs and Demagogues," Ph.D. dissertation, University of Rochester, 1974, pp. 94–6.

27 Census data are not adequate to construct a table for 1835 comparable to the table for 1855. Totaling the occupations listed in the *New York Annual Register* shows that 35.5 percent of those listed in the *City Directory*, and 66 percent of those with occupations placing them in the working classes, were artisans. However, the *Register–Directory* count includes only about half the city's labor force, and doubtless those left out were predominantly wage workers I or II. Although there are great discrepancies among the classifications systems used by social historians to discuss the transformation from artisan to wage workers, no one has claimed that this process was very far underway before the 1830s.

28 Helen Sara Zahler, *Eastern Workingmen and National Land Policy, 1829–1862*, Columbia University Studies in the History of American Agriculture, no. 7 (New York: Columbia University Press, 1941), p. 71; Commons, *Documentary History*, 8:243–62.

29 Pessen, *Riches*, p. 105; Albion and Pope, *Rise*, p. 290.

30 George W. Sheldon, *The Story of the Volunteer Fire Department of the City of New York* (New York: Harper and Brothers, 1882), p. 156.

31 The Rev. Joseph Tuckerman, describing Philadelphia in 1830, quoted in David Montgomery, "The Working Classes of the Preindustrial American City, 1780–1830," *Labor History* 9 (1968):7.

32 John R. Commons, et al., *History of Labour in the United States*, 4 vols. (New York: Macmillan, 1926), 1:357–80.

33 Commons et al. emphasize the role of merchants in bringing competitive pres-

sure to bear on artisans, as well as making "incursions of capital." *History of Labour*, vol. 1, chapter 3. Compare Marx, *Capital*, 3 vols. (Moscow: Progress Publishers, 1971), vol. 3, chapter 20.

34 *New York Evening Journal*, 18 February 1840, quoted in Hugins, *Jacksonian Democracy*, pp. 54–5.

35 *National Trades' Union*, 1834, quoted in ibid., p. 55.

36 Sean Wilentz, *Chants Democratic: New York City and the Rise of the American Working Class, 1790–1850* (London: Oxford University Press, forthcoming), offers a description of the contractor and the ambitious master in chapter 3.

37 Commons, *History of Labour*, pp. 444–5.

38 Jacob Abbott, *The Harper Establishment, or How the Story Books are Made* (Hamden, Conn.: Shoe String Press, 1956 [orig. pub. 1855]), passim. Quotes are from pp. 60, 70, 130, 82, 44.

39 J. Henry Harper, *The House of Harper, A Century of Publishing in Franklin Square* (New York: Harper and Brothers, 1912), chapter 2.

40 *JC*, 7 February 1838, p. 1.

41 Wilentz, *Chants Democratic*, chapter 3.

42 Commons, *Documentary History*, 8:223–6; George A. Stevens, *New York Typographical Union Number 6* (Albany, N.Y.: J. B. Lyon, 1913) pp. 7–10.

43 Commons, *Documentary History*, 8:226–31.

44 Stevens, *Typographical Union*, chapter 1, provides an account of the labor movement in 1850, sketching the formation of these unions.

45 Stevens, *Typographical Union*, pp. 16–17.

46 For unions among the building trades in the 1830s, see Hugins, *Jacksonian Democracy*, p. 58; and Commons, *Documentary History*, 5:214, 279, 8:287. For the 1850s, see Stevens, *Typographical Union*, pp. 4–7.

47 Quoted in Degler, "Labor," p. 263.

48 Ibid., p. 262.

49 This is a quote from the journeymen printers, ibid., p. 258.

50 Stevens, *Typographical Union*, chapter 1.

51 See her second chapter in "The 'Bloody Ould Sixth': A Social Analysis of a New York City Working Class Community at Mid-Nineteenth Century," Ph.D. dissertation, University of Rochester, 1973, especially tables II-3 and II-5, showing the disadvantaged situation of the Irish and the relative situation of other groups in 1819.

52 Degler, "Labor," p. 9; Pernicone, " 'Bloody Ould Sixth,' " p. 97.

53 Degler, "Labor," p. 9.

54 Calculated from *Manufactures of the United States in 1860, Compiled from the original Returns of the Eighth Census Under the Direction of the Secretary of the Interior* (Washington, D.C.: Government Printing Office, 1865), pp. 379–85.

55 Gary Lawson Browne, *Baltimore in the Nation* (Chapel Hill: University of North Carolina Press, 1980), pp. 178–84.

56 Bruce Laurie, *Working People of Philadelphia 1800–1850* (Philadelphia: Temple University Press, 1980), pp. 15–27.

57 Bruce Laurie, Theodore Hershberg, and George Alter, "Immigrants and Industry: The Philadelphia Experience, 1850–1880," *Journal of Social History*, vol. 9, no. 2, 1975, p. 234.

58 Susan E. Hirsch, *Roots of the American Working Class: Industrialization of Crafts in Newark, 1800–1860* (Philadelphia: University of Pennsylvania Press, 1978), p. 37.

59 Ibid., p. 35.

60 Ibid., p. 48.
61 Oscar Handlin, *Boston's Immigrants, 1790–1880* (New York: Atheneum, 1968), pp. 74–80; appendix table XII, pp. 250–1.
62 Michael Holt, *Forging a Majority: the Formation of the Republican Party in Pittsburgh, 1848–1860* (New Haven, Conn.: Yale University Press, 1969), pp. 29–30.

4. The second American party system

1 Michael Wallace, "Changing Concepts of Party in the United States: New York, 1815–1828," *American Historical Review* 74:2 (December 1968), pp. 453–91.
2 Ronald P. Formisano, "Deferential-Participant Politics: The Early Republic's Political Culture, 1789–1840," *American Political Science Review* 68:2 (June 1974), pp. 473–87; quote is from p. 484.
3 Schlesinger, *Age of Jackson*.
4 Frank Otto Gatell, "Money and Party in Jacksonian America: A Quantitative Look at New York City's Men of Quality," in Stanley N. Katz and Stanley I. Kutler, eds., *New Perspectives on the American Past* (Boston: Little, Brown, 1969), pp. 256–71.
5 Lee Benson, *The Concept of Jacksonian Democracy: New York as a Test Case* (New York: Atheneum, 1969).
6 On Chandler, see Thurlow Weed, *Autobiography of Thurlow Weed*, ed. Harriet A. Weed (Boston: Houghton, Mifflin, 1884), p. 408; Board of Aldermen, *Documents* 6:976; *NYH*, 22 October 1854. On Clannon, see Hugins, *Jacksonian Democracy*, pp. 17, 19, 92; the Politicians' List constructed by the author (see Chapter 7, n. 10 below).
7 On McLean, see Hugins, *Jacksonian Democracy*, p. 119; Politicians' List. On Odell, see Hugins, *Jacksonian Democracy*, pp. 70, 71; Commons, *Documentary History*, 5:214, 322.
8 On Darling, see Hugins, *Jacksonian Democracy*, p. 93. Harris was a candidate in the first ward. See Politicians' List; Commons, *History of Labour*, 1:242, n. 41. On McPherson, see Hugins, *Jacksonian Democracy*, p. 93. Clinton Roosevelt, the author of a pamphlet quoted in Chapter 2, managed to have the endorsement of both parties when he ran for the state assembly in 1836. Ralph Wells, perhaps the wealthiest of the Workingmen, was a broker who by "1834 ... had become the principal orator for the newly christened Whig Party"; Hugins, *Jacksonian Democracy*, p. 92.
9 As supporters of Clay gained coherence with the approach of the 1832 presidential election, Tammany's margin of dominance was decreased throughout the city. Their most dramatic loss of support by 1832 was in the eighth and ninth wards, where Workingmen had been strongest. Of the five wards that most strongly supported the Workingmen, three elected Whig aldermen in 1834. When voting for mayor, however, wards that had supported the Workingmen seemed to favor the Democrats: The correlation between the Workingmen's vote of 1829–31 and the average Democratic vote, 1838–43, is .60.
10 Kleppner, *Cross of Culture*, p. 36.
11 Benson, *Jacksonian Democracy*, pp. 200, 146, 185.
12 Ibid., p. 146.
13 Ibid., p. 185.
14 Ibid., chapters 7 and 8. Data are offered for upstate counties; analysis of New York City is anecdotal.

15 Benson, *Jacksonian Democracy*, p. 167, n. 4, assumed that the percentage of the foreign-born population that was Irish was the same in 1845 as in 1855, though the later date was postfamine and the earlier date prefamine. As a result, Benson assumes that there were at least 20,000 voters born in Ireland. In 1855, the Ireland-born constituted 27.9 percent of the city's population; in 1845, all the citizens born in Great Britain constituted 26 percent of the population. Between 1850 and 1860, the Ireland-born constituted 96 percent of the immigration from Great Britain (disembarking in New York); from 1831–40, 73 percent; from 1841–50, 64.5 percent. There is every reason to believe, then, that New York was a much more Irish (as it was a much more immigrant) town in 1855 than in 1845. Two alternative estimates of the Irish vote may be calculated as follows: The 1855 census provides the number of naturalized voters as well as the number of naturalized citizens. The proportion of naturalized voters to naturalized citizens varied little from ward to ward, around a median of 46 percent. Since census takers counted as "naturalized" not only men who had become citizens, but also their wives and children born overseas, the figure of 46 percent seems intuitively satisfactory. Forty-six percent of the nonalien foreign-born population of 1845 produces the generous estimate that 31,038 voters of an electorate of 63,297 were foreign-born. If these were distributed as disembarking passengers, then 17,000 were Irish, 6,500 were non-Irish Britons, and 5,600 were German. A more straightforward estimate would be that voters were the same proportion of the Irish population as they were of the population as a whole. This would result in an estimate that there were 12,000 qualified Ireland-born voters in 1845. The actual vote, of course, was considerably smaller than the qualified electorate.

16 Under a variety of specifications, multiple regression results consistently show that the percentage of children in private schools is strongly related (negatively) to the Democratic vote. When this variable is included in the equation none of the other variables examined are significant at the 5 percent confidence level. In most specifications the only other variable with a t-statistic greater than 1.0 is the percent British, which enters with a negative coefficient, suggesting that the greater the percentage of British (largely Irish) immigrants in a ward, the lower the Democratic vote. The small number of data points and high levels of collinearity among the independent variables limits the usefulness of multivariate analysis. Therefore, regression results are not shown in detail here.

17 Leo Hershkowitz, "The Native American Democratic Association in New York City, 1835–36," *New York Historical Society Quarterly* 46 (1962):41–60.

18 David Brion Davis, ed., *Ante-Bellum Reform* (New York: Harper & Row, 1967); for an account of these values as "industrial morality," see Paul Faler, "Cultural Aspects of the Industrial Revolution: Lynn, Mass., Shoemakers and Industrial Morality, 1826–1860," *Labor History* 15 (1974):367–94.

19 In Upstate New York, for example, Benson found that "particularly among workers associated with the textile, iron, and other industries affected by foreign competition ... significant, and clearly perceived relationships ... were believed to exist among government action on the tariff, party policy, and material interests"; p. 161.

20 Brian Joseph Danforth, "The Influence of Socio-Economic Factors upon Political Behavior: A Quantitative Look at New York City Merchants, 1828–1844," Ph.D. dissertation, New York University, 1974.

21 The first two men were Whig Simon Clannon, who was rapidly leveling himself up out of the working classes (see n. 6), and John Windt. Windt was a journeyman printer who was interested in reform and radical politics, soon had

his own press, and was only briefly associated with Tammany. Hugins, *Jacksonian Democracy*, discusses Windt, pp. 74ff. The cartmen were Robert Millicken, Stephen Halsted, and Andrew Jackman; New York City Board of Aldermen, *Documents*, vol. 7 (1841), p. 93. Jackman was a Democratic aldermanic candidate, and Millicken appeared at a Whig mechanics meeting (*JC*, 7 February 1838, p. 2); Halsted was present at the same meeting. The butcher was William H. Cornell, who appeared at the Tailors' Support Meeting in August 1850 (Commons, *Documentary History*, 8:303) – though perhaps as a Tammany infiltrator – and was the seventeenth ward alderman and a Democrat in 1851 (and assistant alderman in 1845).

22 Slamm appears in almost every account of Tammany Hall; see Hugins, *Jacksonian Democracy*, pp. 69 ff.; Commons, *Documentary History*, 5: 262, 293, 318, 6:265. Robert Townsend was a delegate from the Journeymen Carpenters to the GTU but seems to have left the organization when the carpenters organized a strike. He was active, at different times, in both parties and by 1839 had a patronage position courtesy of Tammany. See Hugins, *Jacksonian Democracy*, pp. 70 ff.; Commons, *Documentary History*, 5:318, 6:197. On Odell, see n. 7 above. On Beatty, see Hugins, *Jacksonian Democracy*, p. 68; Commons, *Documentary History*, 5: 219, 223, 322. On Scott, see Hugins, *Jacksonian Democracy*, p. 70, and Commons, *Documentary History*. Scott is prominent throughout the documents of the General Trades' Union, 5:219, 256, 6:196. Moore is the most studied of these men, and like Slamm appears in every account of Tammany. See Hugins, *Jacksonian Democracy*, pp. 63 ff., Mushkat, *Tammany*, p. 158; Commons, *Documentary History*, 6:192; Pessen, *Most Uncommon*. Commerford was often in the papers as a labor advocate and is given space in most accounts of antebellum labor in New York. Historians are very much in need of a Commerford biography. See Hugins, *Jacksonian Democracy*, pp. 73ff; Commons, *Documentary History*, 6: pp. 193, 196, 255–6; 7:305, 8:302; Degler, "Labor," pp. 157 ff.

23 For Joseph Tucker, see Commons, *Documentary History*, 8: 217. Tucker ran for the eighth ward aldermanic seat on the Whig ticket in 1834 and won. For George Clark, see ibid., 8: 288, 321; Clark ran for twelfth-ward alderman on the Whig ticket in 1849 and won. For William Tucker, see ibid., 7: 217; and *JC*, 7 February 1838, for his prominence at a Whig meeting. Later he was associated with the nativist movement (as were all the Mechanics Mutual Protection leaders), running for eighth ward alderman on the American Republican ticket in 1844 and 1845 and losing both times.

24 For Gregory, see Commons, *Documentary History*, 8: 287, 301; Stevens, *Typographical Union*, p. 7. Gregory ran for alderman three times on the Whig ticket, winning in 1850. For Cameron, see *NYTr*, 5 April 1843, p. 2; Commons, *Documentary History*, 5:233. For White, see Commons, *Documentary History*, 8:289. Like MMP, the House Carpenters' Protective Association was a secret order, "having rites, ceremonies, grips, signs and passwords"; Stevens, *Typographical Union*, p. 4. White was a Whig assembly candidate in 1849 and 1850.

25 For Bowie, a Democrat who succeeded in leveling himself upward, see Hugins, *Jacksonian Democracy*, p. 68; Commons, *Documentary History*, 5:214, 219, 318, 6:196. He served on the publishing committee of *The Union*, *TU*, 28 April 1836, p. 3. In 1846 and 1847, he was a Democratic assembly candidate, winning both times. Potter represented the curriers in the General Trades' Union (see Commons, *Documentary History*, 5:250) and was a Democratic assembly candidate in 1849 and 1850, losing both times.

26 Lodewick was vice-president of the Journeymen House Carpenters (see *TU*, 17 June 1836) and a Democratic aldermanic candidate. O'Neill was active in the Journeymen Boot and Shoemakers and a Democratic alderman in 1841. See Commons, *Documentary History*, 8:341.

27 For Reede, see Commons, *Documentary History*, 5:282; *NYH*, 19 October 1842. For Stewart, see Commons, *Documentary History*, 5:289. Stewart was also a Democratic assembly candidate. For Wells, see Stevens, *Typographical Union*, p. 106.

28 Ely Moore, *Speech of the Honorable Ely Moore, in Reply to the Honorable Waddy Thompson and Others* (Washington, D.C.: Blair and Rules, 1836), pp. 10–11.

29 *NYG*, 19 March 1753. See Chapter 2, notes 4 and 5, and my "Contending Views of Politics and Society in Colonial New York," Chicago, 1977 (unpublished).

30 George William Edwards, *New York as an Eighteenth Century Municipality, 1731–1776*, Studies in History, Economics, and Public Law, no. 178 (New York: Columbia University Press, 1917), pp. 69–80; see also Virginia D. Harrington, *The New York Merchant on the Eve of the Revolution*, Studies in History, Economics, and Public Law, no. 404 (New York: Columbia University Press, 1935), p. 283.

31 George William Edwards, "New York City Politics Before the American Revolution," *Political Science Quarterly* 36 (1921):586–602, 598; and Patricia U. Bonomi, *A Factious People, Politics and Society in Colonial New York* (New York: Columbia University Press, 1971), pp. 137–8.

32 Bruce Wilkenfeld, "The New York City Common Council, 1689–1800," *New York History* 33 (1952):249–73.

33 Edwards, *Eighteenth Century Municipality*, chapter 4; and Arthur Peterson, *New York as an Eighteenth Century Municipality Prior to 1731* (New York: Columbia University Press, 1917), chapter 8.

34 This is surely not to say that the eighteenth-century city was a happy community of reciprocity between high and low, or that merchants led in the public interest. Merchant councilmen dealt with city property as if it were their own to buy and sell; patrician politicians freely used a variety of economic threats to encourage artisans to vote for them.

35 Weinbaum, "Mobs and Demagogues," pp. 197–200.

36 These observations were gained by comparing the List of the Wealthy (see below, Chapter 7) with the index to George W. Sheldon, *The Story of the Volunteer Fire Department of New York City* (New York: Harper, 1882). Historians of the fire companies are unanimous in the description of company class composition deteriorating during the antebellum period. For Giles, see ibid., p. 358; for Eckford and Webb, p. 156; for Carman, p. 406; for Mead, p. 43; for the Goelet brothers, p. 398; and for Rankin, p. 61.

37 On Draper as a mob leader, see Leo Hershkowitz, "New York City, 1835-1840: A Study in Local Politics," Ph.D. dissertation, New York University, 1960, p. 51.

38 Mushkat, *Tammany*, p. 89.

39 However, the patterns of rioting and riot control were changing in this period. See Paul A. Gilje, "Mobocracy: Popular Disturbances in Post-Revolutionary New York City, 1783-1829," Ph.D. dissertation, Brown University, 1979.

40 Weinbaum, "Mobs and Demagogues," p. 177.

41 For Harper in office, see Gustavus Myers, *The History of Tammany Hall* (New York: Dover, 1971 [orig. pub. 1917]), p. 136.

42 William Oland Bourne, *History of the Public School Society of the City of New York* (New York: William Wood, 1870), p. 704.

43 Weinbaum, "Mobs and Demagogues," p. 200.

44 Pessen, *Riches*, p. 265.

45 Weinbaum, "Mobs and Demagogues," is centrally concerned with changing forms of collective violence, and argues that the increasing autonomy of mobs rather than the increased frequency or intensity of collective violence provoked concern to form a larger police department. See his chapter 1. Paul Gilge, "Mobocracy," sees changing patterns even earlier. Arguing that the mob tradition was an accepted form of political bargaining in the eighteenth century, Gilge argues that as the idea of the common good was rejected, collective violence became less acceptable (and also more violent). In this light, the food riot described below seems striking for its anachronism. Like Weinbaum, Gilge sees the creation of a professional police force as testimony to the breakdown of mutualistic class relations; p. 226. Gilge makes similar arguments in "The Baltimore Riots of 1812 and the Breakdown of the Anglo-American Mob Tradition," *Journal of Social History* 13:4 (Summer 1980), pp. 547–64.

46 *EP*, 1 November 1828, p. 2.

47 *EP*, 6 March 1834, p. 2.

48 Two of the standard accounts are Sheldon, *Fire Department*, and Lowell M. Limpus, *History of the New York Fire Department* (New York: Dutton, 1940).

49 Sheldon provides a complete list of companies, pp. 349 ff. I mapped these, using maps provided in various editions of Valentine, *Manual*, to discover their ward location.

50 Limpus, *Fire Department*, p. 161.

51 Alvin Harlow, *Old Bowery Days* (New York: Appleton, Co., 1931), p. 205.

52 Ibid.

53 There are many accounts of this incident. See, for example, Limpus, *Fire Department*, pp. 161–8.

54 Sheldon, *Fire Department*, pp. 371, 454, 156.

55 Robert Ernst, *Immigrant Life in New York City, 1825–1863* (New York: King's Crown Press of Columbia University Press, 1949), pp. 127–8. Malachi Fallon, foreman of the Black Joke Engine Company, was also commander of two independent militia companies of 1,000 men each, the Baxter Blues and the Black Joke Volunteers. Fallon was also Warden of the Tombs, proprietor of the Ivy-Green Saloon, and a lesser power in Tammany politics. The Gulick Guards were less clearly partisan, but probably Whig. See Limpus, *Fire Department*, pp. 181–2; Sheldon, *Fire Department*, p. 354.

56 Harlow, *Bowery Days*, p. 206.

57 Ibid., pp. 299–300.

58 Herbert Asbury, *The Gangs of New York* (New York: Capricorn Books, 1970 [orig. pub. 1927]), p. 30; Harlow, *Bowery Days*, pp. 195, 207.

59 Evan Stark, "Gangs," New Haven, Conn., 1974 (mimeo).

60 For locations of the gangs, see Harlow, *Bowery Days*, pp. 187–8.

61 *EP*, 27 March 1833, p. 2.

62 For an analysis of the Democratic committees, see William Trimble, "Diverging Tendencies in the New York Democracy in the Period of the Locofocos," *American Historical Review* 24 (April 1919):396–441; Anthony Gronowicz, "Revising the Concept of Jacksonian Democracy: A Comparison of New York City Democrats in 1844 and 1884," Ph.D. dissertation, University of Pennsylvania, 1981, pp. 43-4, describes ward insurgencies in 1843.

63 *Sketches of the Speeches ... of Michael Walsh*, p. 26.

64 Bray Hammond, *Banks and Politics in America from the Revolution to the Civil War* (Princeton, N.J.: Princeton University Press, 1957), p. 576.
65 *TU*, 8 June 1836, p. 2.
66 For example, Roosevelt, *Mode*, and Hale, *Useful Knowledge*.
67 New York City Board of Aldermen, *Documents*, vol. 4, doc. 57 (1838), pp. 445–9. This was quite true. In 1807, for example, the council had provided relief to sailors and others suffering from the embargo. See Gilge, "Mobocracy," p. 173.
68 *JC*, 1 February 1838, p. 2; and 31 January 1838, p. 2.
69 Byrdsall, *Loco-Foco Party*, p. 103.
70 Weinbaum, "Mobs and Demagogues," pp. 137ff., and Herbert Gutman, *Work, Culture, and Society in Industrializing America, 1815–1919* (New York: Vintage Books, 1977), pp. 60–1.
71 Bruce Laurie, " 'Nothing on Compulsion': Life Styles of Philadelphia Artisans, 1820–1850," *Labor History* 15 (1974):350.

5. Status and solidarities

1 This interpretation differs from available analyses of political nativism. For some authors, nativism provides the key to the Jacksonian party system and the antebellum city. Lee Benson used the election of 1844 to inquire into the concept of Jacksonian democracy and found ethnocultural affinities at the heart of partisanship (*Jacksonian Democracy*, chapter 8). Sam Bass Warner saw nativism as the extreme expression of a larger disorganization imposed by industrialization and immigration, a disorganization that gave rise to ethnic politics (*Private City*, chapter 7). Joseph Gusfield has argued that the relations among evangelical Protestantism, abolitionism, temperance, and nativism prefigure the Democratic–Republican opposition that came into being around the Civil War (Joseph R. Gusfield, *Symbolic Crusade: Status Politics and the American Temperance Movement*, Urbana: University of Illinois Press, 1963, pp. 56–7).

The history of political nativism in New York does not square well with these interpretations. First, even in the wake of nativist politics, ethnic alignments were not the sole organizing principle of parties in the antebellum city. Obviously the appearance of political nativism opposes immigrants to the United States–born, and Know-Nothings did not find supporters among the Catholic Irish. Yet there were so few immigrant voters in the 1840s that if most native-born voters had supported the American Republicans they would have been a very strong contender for power, rather than a weak sibling of the Whigs. On the other side of the contest, the Democracy retained the loyalty of many voters born in the United States. Thus political nativism represents something less than a reorganization of the electorate along ethnic lines.

Second, the voters who supported American Republicanism and the Know-Nothing Party were at best vague representations of the coalitions that formed the Whigs and Democrats before 1844 or the Democrats and Republicans in 1860. After the election of 1844, only six of seventeen wards retained the partisan tendencies they exhibited through 1843. Because nativism brought about such radical changes, the partisan tendencies of ethnic groups in the earlier Jacksonian era are not well measured by the election of 1844. Similarly, the wards where the Know-Nothings had strong support chose differently from one another when the choices were Republicanism or Democracy. Thus nativism is not the key either to the Jacksonian party system or to the one that succeeded it.

2 General accounts of this conflict can be found in Diane Ravitch, *The Great School Wars: New York City, 1805-1973* (New York: Basic Books, 1974), and Bourne, *Public School Society*.

3 Bourne, *Public School Society*, p. 179.

4 Ibid., pp. 479–81; Leonard, "Nativism and Reform," p. 129, for nativist endorsements; Assemblymen's List, *NYTr* 6 June 1842, 8 June 1842.

5 Ravitch, *School Wars*, p. 69; Weed, *Autobiography*, p. 501.

6 Leonard, "Nativism and Reform," p. 171, quoting *EP*, 21 March 1842.

7 *NYTr*, 8 June 1842, reported ward outcomes for this election. Unfortunately, the paper reported only whether the Public School Society ticket or the common-school ticket was victorious, or if the ward was "split," rather than reporting ballots cast. PSS victory was coded "1," common-school victory, "0," and split, ".5." Spearman correlations between PSS victory and selected variables are as follows:

Percent of children in private school	.81
Percent of churches that were	
Presbyterian and Episcopal	.67
Methodist and Baptist	−.43
Catholic	−.09
Percent foreign-born residents	.15
Average Democratic vote, 1838–43	−.71

In multivariate analysis, controlling for the percent of children in private schools, no other variables are significant.

8 The Spearman correlation between Public School Society victory and percentage of votes cast for the American Republican mayoral candidate was, for 1844, .05; for 1845, −.12; for 1846, −.43. Even this last is barely significant at the 10 percent level, but of course in the "wrong" direction if one expected voting on this issue to prefigure nativist voting.

9 Clifford Griffin, *Their Brothers' Keepers, Moral Stewardship in the United States, 1800–1865* (New Brunswick, N.J.: Rutgers University Press, 1960), p. 66; Charles I. Foster, *An Errand of Mercy, The Evangelical United Front* (Chapel Hill: University of North Carolina Press, 1960), pp. 234–5.

10 Ibid., p. 240.

11 William McLoughlin, "Charles Grandison Finney," in Davis, ed., *Ante-Bellum Reform*, p. 101.

12 Gusfield, *Symbolic Crusade*, p. 49.

13 Ibid., p. 44.

14 Paul Faler, "Cultural Aspects of the Industrial Revolution: Lynn, Massachusetts: Shoemakers and Industrial Morality, 1826–1860," *Labor History* 15 (Summer 1974): 367–94.

15 Gusfield, *Symbolic Crusade*, p. 51.

16 Clifford Griffin, "Religious Benevolence as Social Control, 1815–1860," in Davis, ed., *Ante-Bellum Reform*, p. 91.

17 This impulse to the management of others has been variously understood by students of antebellum reform. It has been argued that missionary and benevolent efforts of various kinds were the recourse of dethroned Federalists, a rearguard action for political control once rule had been denied to them. Lois Banner has shown, however, that on the whole those who funded the Protestant

crusade were not only too young to have been Federalists but also self-made men, representatives of a new rather than the old order ("The Protestant Crusade: Religious Missions, Benevolence, and Reform in the United States: 1790–1840," Ph.D. dissertation, Columbia University, 1970, p. 254). The Protestant crusade has also been seen as "the main cultural vehicle for the creation of a modern work ethic in antebellum America (John Barkley Jentz, "Artisans, Evangelicals, and the City: A Social History of Abolition and Labor Reform in Jacksonian New York," Ph.D. dissertation, City University of New York, 1977, p. 71); much as its English counterpart was directed at English workers (Bendix, *Work and Authority*, p. 68). Whatever the uses of deferential socialization at the workplace, its political advantages were terribly important *where wage workers could vote*. This issue is taken up again in Chapter 7.

18 Laurie, " 'Nothing on Compulsion,' " p. 350.
19 Griffin, "Religious Benevolence," pp. 95–6.
20 Hugins, *Jacksonian Democracy*, p. 132.
21 Even so mild a labor advocate as Horace Greeley, after reporting that "of 32,000 families in this city, recently visited by the indefatigable agents of the New York Bible Society, over 6,000 were found to be destitute of the Bible," noted pointedly that "the visitors did not report how many were destitute of bread." *NYTr*, 30 October 1850, p. 5.
22 On Harper, see J. Henry Harper, *The House of Harper: A Century of Publishing in Franklin Square* (New York: Harper and Brothers, 1912), pp. 4–7, for childhood and family; Sheldon, *Fire Department*, p. 147, and *NYH*, 5 November 1854, for temperance activity.
23 This class classification of the wards is based on a tabulation of manufacturing firms listed in the manuscripts of the 1850 census of manufacturers. Employees were classified, according to the scheme of Chapter 3, as mechanics or wage workers I. Since this is a count of employees rather than residents, it is not as reliable a portrait as one would like. However, in conjunction with contemporary commentary, secondary accounts, and the census data that are available, it seems a reasonable measure of artisan presence.
24 If in New York City nativist voting was not the political expression of conflict over neighborhoods, this does not distinguish the city from other places. Louis Dow Scisco observes that Upstate New York, taking "the interior counties as a whole there was no natural basis for a widespread nativist sentiment. Except in the towns along the line of the Erie canal, the foreign-born element was very small and not especially objectionable. In the canal towns the Irish element was more or less unpopular, and here there might be a genuine feeling of nativism, but in general the spread of the secret movement [that is, the Know-Nothing Order] was not due to actual dislikes" [Louis Dow Scisco, *Political Nativism in New York State* (New York: Columbia University Press, 1901), p. 112]. And even along the line of the canal, Know-Nothingism met with less success than it did elsewhere Upstate, where there were fewer Catholics and fewer foreign-born residents. If, in fact, we look across the states, the success of the Know-Nothings bears little relation to the presence of Catholics or to the presence of the foreign-born. For example, the Know-Nothings were quite successful in the 1855 elections in the areas along the New York–Pennsylvania border, in New York along the Hudson, and in Pennsylvania in the central and south-central counties. This last area had a population less than 5 percent foreign-born in 1860. The area along the New York–Pennsylvania border had a population that was between 5 and 10 percent foreign-born in 1860, and the counties along the Hudson varied considerably in the composition of their

population. Ray Allen Billington, *The Protestant Crusade: 1800–1860* (Chicago: Quadrangle Books, 1964 [orig. pub. 1938]), pp. 400, 401, 404.

That nativist voting in general is not related to actual immigrant presence or Catholic presence helps reconcile the logical status of anti-Catholic argument with where it found support. The argument, it will be recalled from Chapter 2, was in essence an argument about political socialization. As such, it had as much logical standing as, say, Harry Eckstein's arguments. It had, moreover, a fair amount of historical evidence behind it. After all, France, Portugal, Spain, and Austria, Catholic countries, did not have civil liberties, while Protestant Britain and the United States did (the contrary case of Belgium was not, of course, mentioned by nativists). In the counties of the west side of the Hudson, in the southwest corner of Pennsylvania (Greene, Westmoreland, Somerset, Allegheny, Lawrence, and Beaver counties), as in wards three, four, six, fifteen, twenty-one, and twenty-two, people who lived near Catholics tended less than those who did not (on the New York–Pennsylvania border, etc.) to believe that their "slavish" character made them bad citizens.

25 Scisco, *Political Nativism*, chapter 3, passim.
26 In addition to the mechanics, American Republicans had the ardent support of market men – those butchers, grocers, and the like who held city licenses to sell their goods in public markets. In what sense can these groups be understood as politically displaced or having special grievances with the parties? The market men had a clear set of gripes. Democrats were decreasing the opportunities of native-born market men by giving licenses to the Irish and moreover subjecting native-born market men to the inspection of Irish clerks, weighers, and the like. Whigs, for their part, attempted to abolish the market system altogether. Ibid., p. 30; Ira M. Leonard, "The Rise and Fall of the American Republican Party in New York City, 1843-1845," *New-York Historical Society Quarterly* 50 (1966): 164; *NYTr*, 10 April 1843, p. 2.
27 Holt, *Forging*, p. 149.
28 David Montgomery, "The Shuttle and the Cross: Weavers and Artisans in the Kensington Riots of 1844," *Journal of Social History* 5 (1972):429.
29 Bruce Laurie, *Working People of Philadelphia, 1800–1850* (Philadelphia: Temple University Press, 1980), p. 167.
30 Commons, *Documentary History*, 8:246, 249.
31 Ibid., p. 256.
32 Ibid., pp. 257–8.
33 *Champion of American Labor*, 8 April 1847, p. 2.
34 Though unlike the Mugwumps the mechanics had never had the influence they felt they lost.
35 Commons, *Documentary History*, 8:256.
36 *Champion of American Labor*, 8 April 1847, p. 2. None of these men appear elsewhere in the labor movement.
37 Montgomery, "Shuttle and the Cross," p. 439.
38 Commons, *Documentary History*, 7:259.
39 *Champion of American Labor*, 8 April 1847, p. 2.
40 Laurie, " 'Nothing on Compulsion,' " p. 357.
41 Scisco, *Political Nativism*, pp. 103–4, 107.
42 Walter Dean Burnham, *Critical Elections and the Mainsprings of American Politics* (New York: Norton, 1970), pp. 26–7, observes the relationship between realigning eras and politicized social movements.
43 See Ernst, *Immigrant Life*, pp. 167–7, and *NYT*, 30 October 1852, p. 8, for

Germans and the tariff. For German Democrats, see *NYH*, 4 November 1850, p. 1.

44 Ernst, *Immigrant Life*, pp. 170; 289, n. 69, *NYH*, 30 October 1855, p. 8.
45 Ernst, *Immigrant Life*, p. 167.
46 Quoted in *NYT*, 16 October 1852, p. 6.
47 *NYH*, 8 October 1859, pp. 4, 5.
48 On tailors and longshoremen, see Carl Wittke, *The Irish in America* (Baton Rouge: Louisiana State University Press, 1956), pp. 217–18. On laborers, see Pernicone, " 'Bloody Ould Sixth,' " p. 102.
49 In fact, of 229 antebellum labor leaders whose ethnicity could be unambiguously determined, 106 were Irish.
50 Degler, "Labor," p. 152.
51 *Irish News*, quoted in Pernicone, " 'Bloody Ould Sixth,' " p. 101.
52 Degler, "Labor," p. 148.
53 *Irish American*, 2 October 1852.
54 *NYH*, 3 November 1854, p. 1.
55 *NYH*, 3 November 1854, p. 1.
56 *NYT*, 11 November 1854.
57 *NYH*, 24 November 1857, p. 1.
58 *NYT*, 5 November 1859, p. 3.
59 James F. Richardson, "Mayor Fernando Wood and the New York Police Force, 1855–1857," *New-York Historical Society Quarterly* 50 (January 1966):19.
60 Ibid., p. 31.
61 Paul O. Weinbaum, "Temperance, Politics, and the New York City Riots of 1857," *New-York Historical Society Quarterly* 43 (July 1975):246–70.
62 Leonard Chalmers, "Tammany Hall and New York City Politics, 1853–1861," Ph.D. dissertation, New York University, 1967, p. 181.
63 Ibid., p. 186, and Degler, "Labor," p. 387. Wood's organization, Mozart Hall, held nominating conventions for school slates in 1861; *NYH*, 23 November 1861.
64 The artisans' response might usefully be thought of in terms of "negative symbolic politics." If symbolic politics are often used to ameliorate or legitimate, "symbolic crusades" may be thought of as responses to the "negative symbolism" of rhetorical abandonment by political leaders. In our own time, a comparable case might be the white blue-collar workers drawn to the Moral Majority in the wake of their rhetorical displacement by blacks among Democratic politicians. See my "The Republicans Come to Power: 1860 and 1980," paper prepared for the annual meeting of the American Political Science Association, September 1981.
65 Browne, *Baltimore in the Nation*, p. 200.
66 Ibid., pp. 200–7, and Laurence F. Schmeckbeier, *History of the Know-Nothing Party in Baltimore*, Johns Hopkins University Studies in Historical and Political Science, Series XVII, Nos. 4–5, April–May 1899, pp. 43–4.

6. The voice of industry

1 Understanding of these parties is controversial, though the debate is less prominent now than it once was. In the first view, put forward by Arthur Schlesinger, Jr., support for Jackson was based on a nascent proletariat, organized into these parties that shared with Jackson the championing of the common man. This view was opposed by Joseph Dorfman, who pointed out that Workingmen's Parties, and those that shared their ideology, were not proletarian. Dorf-

man was right; Workingmen's Party members were not proletarians. They were, however, workingmen – mechanics, men who worked in small shops, masters, and journeymen. And the Workingmen's Parties did receive the support of wage laborers in New York. See Schlesinger, *Age of Jackson*; Joseph Dorfman, "The Jackson Wage-Earner Thesis," *American Historical Review* 54 (January 1949):396–406.

2 Lynd, "Mechanics in New York Politics." Young, "Mechanics and Jeffersonians," and Young, *The Democratic Republicans of New York: The Origins, 1763–1797* (Chapel Hill: University of North Carolina Press, 1967).

3 George Henry Evans quoted in Commons, *History of Labour*, 1:234.

4 Robert Sean Wilentz, "Ritual, Republicanism, and the Artisans of Jacksonian New York," paper presented at the Annual Meeting of the Organization of American Historians, New York, April 1978.

5 George Henry Evans, quoted in Philip Foner, *History of the Labor Movement in the United States*, 2 vols. (New York: International Publishers, 1975), 1:136.

6 Commons, *History of Labour*, 1:278. On imprisonment for debt, Commons comments, "Upon this question all the workingmen of the state seemed to have been equally emphatic"; p. 281.

7 Ibid., pp. 232, 264.

8 Hugins, *Jacksonian Democracy*, chapter 6.

9 Ibid., p. 145; New York City Board of Aldermen, *Documents*, vol. 15, pt. 2, doc. 12, pp. 94–107.

10 Hugins, *Jacksonian Democracy*, p. 137.

11 The Public School Society also lobbied for a tax for the schools; agitation by the Workingmen's Party undoubtedly enhanced their case. See Diane Ravitch, *School Wars*, p. 25.

12 The remaining issues were the auction system and the franchises of the New York and Harlem Railroad. The auction system died for economic reasons. Grants to the NYHRR involved a powerful set of opposing interests, though there was considerable protest against it. Franchises to railroads were an object of labor protest throughout the antebellum period, with no success. Single-member districts were desired to increase popular control of nominating conventions; this demand was a threat to the party system, and SMDs were not established until 1847.

13 Indeed, although the attempt of employers to lengthen the working day was the immediate provocation to the formation of the Workingmen's Party, the issue was settled in New York City before the first election in which the party ran candidates. Similarly, in Philadelphia the ten-hour working day was won from private and public employers by a citywide strike. In New England, with its larger and more widely distributed factory population, ten-hours legislation received more attention, though labor nowhere achieved ten-hours legislation until 1847. Even then, antebellum laws limiting hours of work had loopholes that made them of little use, and the ten-hour workday was established in practice by economic action. It is interesting to notice, however, in relation to the question of rural allies, that of the states that passed ten-hours legislation in this period, most had a broadly based factory population. In New York State, fully 25 percent of all those engaged in "manufactures and trades" lived in New York City. New Hampshire, Maine, New Jersey, and Connecticut, which passed ten-hours legislation, had respectively 10.2, .85, .8, and 5.9 percent of their manufacturing and trades population in their largest population concentrations. And in New England, of course, the fact that many of the factory girls were daughters of farmers enhanced farmer–worker solidarity.

There are two exceptions to this pattern of where ten-hours legislation was achieved, Rhode Island and Pennsylvania. Fully 28.5 percent of the manufacturing and trades population of Rhode Island lived in Providence – but in Rhode Island the manufacturing population outnumbered the farming population (the only state in the union where this was the case); moreover, Rhode Island had just come through the reforms attendant on the Dorr Rebellion. In Pennsylvania, which also passed ten-hours legislation, 22 percent of the manufacturing population lived in the greater Philadelphia area, but Pennsylvania also had significant industrialization in the west. In Massachusetts, the state that, after Rhode Island, had the largest proportion of its gainfully employed engaged in manufactures, and in which moreover that population was spread most evenly across the state, the struggle for ten-hours legislation was intense. Workers were so successful in pledging assembly candidates to ten-hours legislation that, to preclude such candidates becoming a majority of the legislature, employers had the secret ballot repealed. They could then freely threaten to retaliate against those who voted for ten-hours candidates.

For a brief account of the struggle for ten-hours legislation see Foner, *History*, chapter 11. Figures for the concentration of the manufacturing population were calculated from the *Compendium of the Seventh [1850] Census of the United States* (Washington, D.C.: Beverly Tucker, Senate Printer, 1854).

14 Commons, *Documentary History*, 5:288, 211; and Hugins, *Jacksonian Democracy*, p. 79.

15 Social historians point to Protestantism and republicanism as the major elements of workingmen's culture and agree that "republicanism represented nothing less than a political expression of the artisan outlook." To say this is to say little more than that Jacksonian journeymen shared the elements of a political culture common to the whole society. My effort here is to show how the republicanism of artisans was distinctive. (The quote is from Wilentz, "Ritual, Republicanism," p. 8. Herbert Gutman's views are similar. See his *Work, Culture, and Society*, pp. 3–78.)

16 Commons, *Documentary History*, 5:290.

17 *TU*, 25 April 1836, p. 2. Similarly, in support of the movement for a ten-hour day in Boston, the GTU resolved that "while we indignantly deprecate the cause which has forced them to strike, viz. – the hostile efforts of their aristocratic employers, to keep them in a state of vassalage – but little better than that of the serfs of Russia – we will use our united exertions to sustain them in so good and glorious a cause." Commons, *Documentary History*, 5:253.

18 Ibid., 6:245.

19 *TU*, 28 April 1836, p. 2.

20 *TU*, 25 April 1836, p. 2.

21 National Trades' Union resolutions, 1835; Commons, *Documentary History*, 6:247.

22 In that light, the convention's resolutions take on additional meaning:

"Resolved, That as productive labor is the only legitimate source of wealth, and as the productive laborers have been deprived of the advantages of their labor by bad legislation, it behooves this portion of the community to regain and maintain, by correct legislation, what they have lost by inattention to their own best interests.

"Resolved, That hereafter it should be the first as well as the last duty of every laborer, to inform himself on the subject of his equal rights and labor to promote the good of the whole community" (Rozwenc, ed., *Ideology and Power*, pp. 126–7).

23 Commons, *Documentary History*, 6:256–7. Not that the alteration of the tariff one way or another could fundamentally change the problems of American workingmen. What was necessary was that English workingmen organize to raise their wages. See ibid., 6:222.

24 Ibid., 6:221.

25 Ibid., 4:273. It is unclear, however, how well the union succeeded in punishing its enemies. Of the seven guilty council members, two (a Democrat and a Whig) did not run the following year. Five did run, and of these three won (two Democrats, one Whig) and two (both Democrats) lost. On the other hand, the most prominent of the guilty aldermen was beaten up in January 1836. For names of aldermen, see ibid., 5:270. Election records from Aldermanic List. For the assault on Alderman Purdy, see New York City Board of Aldermen, *Documents*, vol. 2, doc. 79, pp. 391–403.

26 *TU*, 8 June 1836, p. 2.

27 *TU*, 20 May 1836, p. 3. *The Union* more generally objected to political interference in the fire department. See 16 May 1836, p. 2.

28 For progress on ten hours, see the National Trades' Union Report for 1835, in Commons, *Documentary History*, 6:253–4. Mechanics of New York and Brooklyn memorialized the secretary of the Navy to reduce hours on public works (in New York, the Brooklyn Navy Yard). The NTU supported this demand: "As the object of government should be the happiness and comfort of its citizens, it is in duty bound, when any of them are oppressed, to remove all just cause of complaint, as far as in its power lies; and those governments have crumbled to the earth that have studied the accumulation of wealth, instead of the comfort and happiness of its producers; we therefore believe that, as we constitute the bone and sinew of the nation, our complaints should be attended to; and that we should be allowed time to attend to the duties of our families, and the cultivation of our minds; as experience has proved that, to be virtuous, man must be intelligent, and that vice is always found to exist in proportion to the ignorance that pervades society ... We do not conceive that we demand anything from the government but our rights ..." (Ibid., 6:232–3, 247–8.) On education, see ibid., 6:255, on prison labor, see Hugins, *Jacksonian Democracy*, pp. 157ff. Van Buren's executive order is cited in Foner, *History of Labor*, p. 163.

29 The standard account is Byrdsall, *Loco-Foco Party*.

30 The Locofocos did best in two of the wards that had been Workingmen's strongholds six years earlier, eight and ten. In the fifth, ninth, and fifteenth, however, they were not strong, though the Workingmen had been. Whig dominance in the fifth and fifteenth wards was unaffected by the Locofocos; in the ninth ward, Whigs polled 2 percent less of the vote in 1837 than they had in 1834, while the Democrats lost 7.5 percent of their support. Similarly, in the eighth and tenth wards, Tammany took heavier losses than the Whigs. Only in the eighth ward did the Locofocos possibly obtain support from Whig voters. Despite the fact that prominent GTU members were also on the Democratic Workingmen's General Committee, Locofoco leadership was considerably more middle class than the leadership of the Workingmen's Party, another indication that this was as much a movement of party politicians as of workingmen. See Hugins, *Jacksonian Democracy*, p. 117.

31 Hugins assesses Moore as an ambitious politician who "used" the labor movement, much as Levi Slamm did. There seems to be an implicit equivalent here between selling out and winning an election. Moore was successful, but he was also an advocate of labor interests in his term in Congress. Even Slamm,

universally derided, edited the *Democrat*, a journal that helped to keep radical democratic thought alive and lively.

32 Hugins, *Jacksonian Democracy*, p. 48.

33 *TU*, 28 April 1836, p. 2; and 29 April 1836, p. 2.

34 This account is based on Robert Ernst, "The One and Only Mike Walsh," *New-York Historical Society Quarterly*, 36 (January 1952):43–65; and Frank C. Rogers, Jr., "Mike Walsh, A Voice of Protest," M.A. thesis, Columbia University, 1950.

35 Ernst, "Mike Walsh," p. 47.

36 Rogers, "Mike Walsh," p. 37.

37 Ibid., p. 78.

38 Ernst, "Mike Walsh," pp. 50–1. In judging the radicals as too farsighted, Walsh was offering the judgment historians would make as well. Philip Foner's assessment is characteristic of the literature. Foner pointed out that Associationists, Owenites, and Land Reformers were divisive, invading labor's organizations much as the dominant parties did. Moreover, spokesmen for these reform movements opposed or denigrated efforts that were central in workingmen's own point of view, unionization and the struggle for the ten-hour day. As a result, to the extent that radicals of various sorts were successful in recruiting adherents from the working class, Foner argues, they diverted working-class energies from addressing their immediate needs, and "by ignoring political action they took from the worker his key to freedom" (Foner, *History of Labor*, p. 190). My own sense is that the radicals were considerably more practical than this. For that reason, I have used the term "radicals" rather than the usual "utopians." Many of those prominent in various kinds of radical reform – whatever their initial outlooks – worked not only for a reorganization of society but more practically for the amelioration of current conditions.

39 Zahler, *Eastern Workingmen*, p. 82, n. 2.

40 Ibid., p. 55, n. 41.

41 Ibid., p. 82.

42 Commons, *Documentary History*, 8:285–309, for the New York City Industrial Congress and the tailors' support meeting.

43 Ibid., 8:305.

44 Degler, "Labor," p. 258.

45 Ibid., p. 266.

46 Stevens, *Typographical Union*, pp. 23–4.

47 Degler, "Labor," p. 260.

48 Ibid., p. 264.

49 Ibid., p. 262.

50 Ibid., p. 55.

51 Ibid., pp. 276–7. For the congress's platform, see Commons, *Documentary History*, 8:285–309.

52 Commons, *History of Labour*, 1:558–62.

53 Zahler, *Eastern Workingmen*, p. 83.

54 *NYTr*, 5 November 1850, p. 4.

55 *NYH*, 1 November 1852, p. 5.

56 *NYH*, 4 November 1850.

57 *NYTr*, 22 August 1850, in Degler, "Labor," p. 297.

58 Ibid., p. 181.

59 There are a number of accounts of these meetings. Degler, "Labor," provides an extensive description, pp. 161ff. Samuel Rezneck, "The Influence of Depression Upon American Opinion, 1857–1859," *Journal of Economic History* 2

(May 1942):1–23, briefly described the meetings and points out that other cities also witnessed "Bread or Work" meetings; p. 19. For contemporary coverage and commentary, see *NYH*, 25 November 1857, p. 1; 12 November 1857, p. 1; 13 November 1857, p. 1; 26 November 1857, p. 8; 28 November 1857, p. 8.

60 *NYH*, 3 November 1854, p. 7; 27 August 1855, p. 4.

61 *NYH*, 21 July 1855, p. 8; 20 August 1855, p. 3; 27 August 1855, p. 1; 5 October 1855, p. 1.

62 Degler, "Labor," pp. 161ff., and the newspaper coverage cited in note 61 above.

63 Rowe, politicians list, *NYH*, 21 August 1855; Commons, *Documentary History*, 8:288; George Adam, politicians list, ibid., 8:27, 287; *NYH*, 5 September 1855.

64 On Baker, see Commons, *Documentary History*, 8:301, *NYH*, 5 September 1855. On Henderson, see Commons, *Documentary History*, 8:287, *NYH*, 21 August 1855, 5 September 1855, 26 October 1855. On Morgan, see *NYH*, 5 September 1855; Commons, *Documentary History*, 8:337. On Price, see Commons, *Documentary History*, 8:288, 301, 316, 337, *NYH*, 5 September 1855. On Smith, see Commons, *Documentary History*, 8:287, *NYH*, 5 September 1855.

65 Degler, "Labor," p. 167; New York City Board of Aldermen, *Documents*, vol. 22, doc. 1, pp. 4–5.

66 New York City Board of Aldermen, *Proceedings*, 68:156–61.

67 *NYH*, 30 October 1857, p. 1.

68 *NYH*, 2 November 1855, p. 5; 30 October 1854, p. 4.

69 *NYH*, 3 November 1854, p. 1.

70 10 November 1857; quoted in Degler, "Labor," p. 192.

71 23 October 1857; cited in ibid., p. 185.

72 10 October 1857; cited in ibid., p. 192.

73 14 January 1856; cited in ibid., p. 168.

74 Ibid., p. 193.

75 Rezneck, "Influence of Depression," pp. 18–20.

76 *NYH*, 26 November 1859, p. 1.

77 The meeting at the Merchants' Exchange included some prominent Democrats. *NYT*, 16 November 1857. Howard B. Furer, *William Frederick Havemeyer: A Political Biography* (New York: American Press Publications, 1965), p. 103, reports the merchants dinner praising Wood.

78 Myers, *Tammany Hall*, pp. 189–90.

79 Degler, "Labor," p. 168.

80 Ibid., p. 166.

81 Ibid., p. 169.

82 *Irish News*, 14 November 1857, p. 2.

83 *NYH*, 26 November 1857, p. 8.

84 *NYH*, 24 November 1857, p. 1.

85 *NYH*, 28 November 1857, p. 8.

86 *NYH*, 26 November 1857, p. 8.

87 *NYH*, 29 November 1857, p. 8.

88 *NYH*, 25 November 1857, p. 8.

89 Quoted in Chalmer, "Tammany Hall," p. 200, n. 38.

90 Ibid., pp. 202–3.

91 *NYH*, 14 October 1859, p. 5.

92 *NYH*, 22 November 1863, p. 3; 2 January 1859, p. 5.

93 The draft rioters of 1863 had argued that because an exemption fee of $300

(about a year's wages for a laborer) could be substituted for conscription, the draft in fact was only forced conscription of the poor. The mayor vetoed a city council appropriation to pay the exemption fee for those who could not afford it, but the County Board of Supervisors succeeded in appropriating the funds, the initial appropriation being $2 million. The state government and various banks provided loans to the city, which by the end of the war had spent $18 million raising regiments, paying bounties to those who enlisted, and paying exemption fees. Leo Hershkowitz estimated that the city paid so many exemption fees that in fact conscription did not exist there. For the riots and governmental response, see Adrian Cook, *The Armies of the Streets: The New York City Draft Riots of 1863* (Lexington: University Press of Kentucky, 1974), and Leo Hershkowitz, *Tweed's New York: Another Look* (Garden City, N.Y.: Doubleday, 1977), pp. 93–9.

94 Alan Dawley, *Class and Community: The Industrial Revolution in Lynn* (Cambridge, Mass.: Harvard University Press, 1976), p. 228.

95 Laurie, *Working People of Philadelphia*, p. 95.

96 Holt, *Forging*, chapter 6. Griffin argues that it was fear of bond repudiation that lay behind elite funding of evangelical efforts in the West; see "Religious Benevolence", pp. 94–5.

97 Holt, *Forging*, p. 69.

98 Foner, *History of Labor*, pp. 240–5.

99 Dawley, *Class and Community*, chapters 4, 8.

100 Browne, *Baltimore in the Nation*, p. 214.

101 Ibid.

102 Justin Winsor, ed., *Memorial History of Boston* (Boston: James R. Osgood, 1881), 3:259–60. *Boston Daily Advertiser*, 10 January 1855.

103 *Evening Bulletin* (Philadelphia), 30 October 1857.

104 Laurie, *Working People of Philadelphia*, p. 54.

105 *Evening Bulletin* (Philadelphia), 17 April 1858.

106 Gerth and Mills, eds., *From Max Weber*, p. 180. Emphasis added.

107 Tammany infiltrated the Congress; Foner, *History of Labor*, p. 235. "Workingmen's" insurgents in the mid-1850s complained of being disrupted by party toughs; *NYH*, 5 October 1855.

108 The Democrats, of course, were a party of slaveholders, farmers, and merchants as well as workers (just as the Republicans were a party of railroad men, farmers, and industrialists as well as workers). I have argued at length elsewhere that widespread suffrage and minority status made partisans (Republicans and Democrats) of American workers, and that these partisan identities rather than "ethnic" identity or some peculiarly American sense of class was what made workers in the United States distinctively "American" before the Civil War. "Becoming American: The American Working Classes Before the Civil War," in Aristide Zolberg and Ira Katznelson, eds., *Working Class Formation: Patterns in Nineteenth Century Europe and the United States*, forthcoming.

7. A house of power in town

1 *NYTr*, 16 October 1860, p. 4.

2 *NYT*, 11 November 1857, p. 4; *NYH*, 1 October 1850, p. 4.

3 Warner, *Private City*, for example, argued that "professional politics" produced "weak, corrupt, unimaginative municipal government" because without business leadership in office "voters ... would not trust their government with large sums of money, big projects, or major innovations"; p. 98.

4 Robert A. Dahl, *Who Governs? Democracy and Power in an American City* (New Haven, Conn.: Yale University Press, 1961), chapter 1.

5 Warner, *Private City*, p. 86.

6 Gabriel Almond, "Plutocracy and Politics in New York City," Ph.D. dissertation, University of Chicago, 1938, p. 52.

7 Ibid., p. 48.

8 Pessen, *Riches*, pp. 283–7.

9 Gatell, "Money and Party," p. 263.

10 Edward Pessen's *Riches* provides a list of New York's 200 wealthiest citizens in 1828 and 300 wealthiest citizens in 1845. In addition, I constructed a list of New York's wealthiest 200 citizens from William H. Boyd, *Boyd's New York City Tax Book 1856 and 1857* (New York: William H. Boyd, 1857), which lists assessor's valuations of personal and real property for those who paid taxes in 1856. The three lists, totaling 700 names, reduce by redundancy and the elimination of a few widows to 470 men. I compared this list to a list of politicians compiled from newspaper accounts of partisan meetings, the party histories, and other secondary sources. These sources generated a Politicians' List of 1,067 names. In addition, lists as complete as sources allowed were constructed of men who ran for alderman and state assemblyman, and these generated an additional 916 names.

11 Gatell, "Money and Party," p. 257.

12 Nevins and Thomas, *George Templeton Strong*, 2:19 (5 October 1860).

13 Foner, *Business and Slavery*, pp. 82-3.

14 Ibid., pp. 81–2, n. 82; 152; 153.

15 Ibid., p. 132.

16 Ibid., pp. 100ff.

17 *NYH*, 2 November 1854.

18 *NYH*, 26 October 1855, p. 1.

19 Whitney, *NYTr*, 19 February 1845, p. 2; Lawrence, *NYTr*, 6 April 1842, p. 2, and 19 March 1845, p. 2; Allaire and Rohr, *JC*, 7 February 1838, p. 2.

20 On Alley, see *EP*, 28 March 1834, and Myers, *Tammany Hall*, p. 106. On Graham, see *EP*, 28 March 1834, p. 2; Graham was also the second-ward aldermanic candidate for the party in 1835. Henry Brevoort ran for alderman of the twelfth ward on the Democratic ticket in 1842 and 1843. Isaac Lawrence was a Mozart Hall activist; see *NYH*, 17 November 1859, p. 1. George Law was a member of the Democratic Vigilant Association in 1860; see *NYH*, 27 November 1857, p. 8; and *NYTr*, 1 December 1859, p. 4.

21 On Green, see Foner, *Business and Slavery*, p. 248. On Folsom, see *NYTr*, 2 December 1859, p. 5.

22 On Temperance, see *NYH*, 5 November 1854, p. 5. On Phelps as a Know-Nothing, see *NYH*, 8 October 1855, p. 5.

23 On Law as a Know-Nothing, see Scisco, *Political Nativism*, p. 219. On Prime, see ARP *Address*. On Woodruff, see ARP *Address* and Leonard, "Nativism and Reform," p. 382. On Post, see Politicians' List (fifteenth ward). On Schieffelin, see *NYTr*, 19 March 1845, p. 2. Schieffelin won, Post lost.

24 *NYTr*, 6 April 1842, p. 2.

25 Mushkat, *Tammany*, pp. 115, 215, 225.

26 *NYH*, 2 November 1854.

27 New York money was important in maintaining Whig, Republican, and Democratic parties in the West. Weed, *Autobiography*, p. 476; De Alva S. Alexander, *A Political History of the State of New York*, 4 vols. (New York: Holt, 1906), 2:282ff. Both authors felt that Seward lost the Republican nomination in 1860

in part because Republicans feared a dominance of New York in their party since New York money had given New York a dominant role in the Whig Party. New York played a similar financial role in the Democratic Party, particularly at the approach of the elections of 1856 and 1860. See Irving Katz, *August Belmont, A Political Biography* (New York: Columbia University Press, 1968), pp. 18-22, 74–83.

28 Weed, *Autobiography*, p. 476.

29 D. R. Fox, *The Decline of the Aristocracy in the Politics of New York, 1801– 1840* (New York: Harper Torchbooks, 1965 [orig. pub. 1917]), p. 417, n. 3.

30 Weed, *Autobiography*, p. 124.

31 Trimble, "Diverging Tendencies," p. 404.

32 Gatell, "Money and Party," p. 265; *JC*, 4 January 1838, and the week following; *NYH*, 3 January 1838, p. 1.

33 Sidney Pomerantz, *New York, An American City, 1783–1803* (New York: Columbia University Press, 1938), pp. 37, 51, 63. Staughton Lynd and Alfred Young, "After Carl Becker: The Mechanics and New York City Politics, 1774– 1801," *Labor History* 5 (1964):221.

34 Leo Hershkowitz estimated the patronage available to the city council in 1838 as 1,200 positions, and Ira Leonard estimated the official patronage available in the early 1840's as 2,000. Hershkowitz, "Local Politics," p. 318. Leonard, "The Politics of Charter Revision in New York City, 1845–1847," *New-York Historical Society Quarterly* 62 (1978):51.

35 Leonard, "New York City Politics," pp. 243–4.

36 *NYH*, 25 October 1850, p. 2.

37 Alexander, *Political History*, p. 38.

38 William Hartman, "The New York Custom House: Seat of Spoils Politics," *New York History* 34 (April 1953): 156.

39 Mushkat, *Tammany*, p. 116.

40 Chalmers, "Tammany Hall," pp. 48–9. As each new president assumed office, delegates and petitions demanding that particular individuals be rewarded with these posts left New York for Washington. After 1845, the factiousness of both parties put presidents in positions that had to be handled with great skill. For example, when New York's Democrats turned against Fernando Wood, part of their effort to isolate him involved convincing Buchanan not to give Wood any patronage. As a result, federal patronage in the city was divided between Hard Shells and the New York Hotel Committee. Ibid., p. 167.

41 Edward Dana Durand, *The Finances of New York City* (New York: Macmillan, 1898), gives an annual listing of the tax rate, pp. 372–3.

42 There was concern about this almost immediately. See Leonard, "Charter Revision," p. 66. New York City Board of Aldermen, *Documents*, vol. 12, doc. 1 (1845), p. 8.

43 In 1852, an additional kind of revenue-anticipation bond was created, the "assessment bond." Residents were required to contribute a portion of the costs for grading their streets, and these charges were special assessments. Contractors refused to wait to be paid until the special assessments were collected. Revenue from special assessments was pledged against the assessment bonds and revenue from bond sales was used to pay the contractors. Durand, *Finances*, p. 168.

44 Computed for 1844 from New York City Board of Aldermen, *Documents*, vol. 12, doc. 1 (1845), p. 8.

45 Computed for 1853 from Valentine, *Manual . . . 1854*, pp. 198–9, and for 1856 from Valentine, *Manual . . . 1857*, pp. 180–1.

46 The amount of bond revenue is in Valentine, *Manual . . . 1844–5*, p. 167, and the total budget is in Valentine, *Manual . . . 1854*, pp. 198–9 and Valentine, *Manual . . . 1857*, pp.180–1.

47 Ibid.

48 James R. Whiting claimed the city could not sell its bonds when he ran as the reform candidate for mayor. *NYH*, 30 October 1856, p. 1.

49 James C. Scott, *Comparative Political Corruption* (Englewood Cliffs, N.J.: Prentice-Hall, 1972), pp. 33, 99.

50 The Sixth- and Eighth-Avenue railroad contract, the contract investigated by the grand jury, was originally awarded to John Pettigrew and his associates, on payment of a bribe. When Kipp et al. were awarded the contract, the bribe was not returned to Pettigrew and his business partners. Carman, *Street Surface Railway*, p. 47.

51 This was an objection to Fernando Wood's candidacy. Wood had been sued by a former business partner.

52 Carman, *Street Surface Railway*, pp. 59–60.

53 Leonard, "Charter Revision," passim.

54 *NYTr*, 7 April 1849, p. 3.

55 *NYTr*, 9 April 1849, p. 3.

56 Chalmers, "Tammany Hall," p. 77.

57 Richardson, "Fernando Wood," p. 6.

58 "How New York is Going to be Punished," *Harpers Weekly*, 28 March 1857, p. 194; Chalmers, "Tammany Hall," pp. 146–8; Durand, *Finances*, pp. 80–8.

59 Myers, *Tammany Hall*, p. 179.

60 Mushkat, *Tammany*, pp. 252, 309.

61 Ibid., pp. 336–7.

62 *NYH*, 12 November 1857, p. 1.

63 Chalmers, "Tammany Hall," p. 162.

64 Mushkat, *Tammany*, p. 369.

65 *NYTr*, 7 March 1853.

66 *NYTr*, 8 June 1853, p. 3; New York State Assembly, *Documents*, vol. 3, no. 82 (1853). Both this ratification election and the one of 1849 had very low turnouts.

67 *NYH*, 28 October 1854, p. 8.

68 *NYH*, 18 October 1854; 2 November 1853.

69 *NYH*, 30 October 1854, p. 6.

70 *NYH*, 16 October 1855, p. 1.

71 *NYH*, 18 October 1854.

72 *NYH*, 28 November 1854, p. 8. Phelps declined graciously; Vanderpoel was angry.

73 Politicians' List.

74 Nevins and Thomas, *George Templeton Strong*, 2:369.

75 Degler, "Labor," p. 98.

76 Ibid., p. 177.

77 New York City Board of Aldermen, *Proceedings*, 68 (1857):156–61.

78 *NYT*, 16 November 1857.

79 *NYT*, 3 September 1857, p. 1; and Richardson, "Fernando Wood," pp. 10, 19.

80 *NYT*, 16 November 1857.

81 Chalmers, "Tammany Hall," p. 157.

82 Mushkat, *Tammany*, p. 309.

83 For the formation of the Fifth Avenue Democrats, see *NYT*, 10 November 1859, p. 4. For fuller coverage and lists of supporters, see *NYH*, 1 October 1859, p. 4; and 14 October 1859, p. 5. Later, this group changed its name to the New York Democratic Vigilance Association; *NYH*, 19 October 1859, p. 1. For Hoxie's remark, see *NYH*, 2 December 1859, p. 4.

84 *NYH*, 1 October 1859, p. 4.

85 Including George Folsom, Hamilton Fish, Moses Grinnell, Simeon Draper, John H. Griscom, R. M. Blatchford, and Frederick Law Olmsted. See *NYTr*, 2 December 1859, p. 5.

86 Chalmers, "Tammany Hall," p. 222; Myers, *Tammany Hall*, p. 201.

87 *NYTr*, 28 November 1863, pp. 1, 2; 30 November 1863, p. 8; Myers, *Tammany Hall*, p. 205.

88 *NYTr*, 1 December 1859, p. 4. Also see George Folsom in *EP*, 2 December 1859, p. 2.

89 *NYH*, 2 December 1859, p. 4.

90 *NYH*, 1 October 1859, p. 4.

91 *NYH*, 14 October 1859, p. 5.

92 *NYH*, 23 November 1861, p. 6.

93 *NYH*, 1 October 1859, p. 4.

94 Named for John McKeon, who had been a Democrat at least since the mid-1840s and was a one-time almshouse commissioner who, in 1863, struck out on his own.

95 Michael H. Frisch, "The Community Elite and the Emergence of Urban Politics: Springfield, Massachusetts, 1840–1880," in Stephan Thernstrom and Richard Sennett, eds., *Nineteenth Century Cities, Essays in the New Urban History* (New Haven, Conn.: Yale University Press, 1969), p. 289.

96 Ibid., p. 290.

97 *NYH*, 4 November 1854, p. 4.

98 Seymour J. Mandelbaum, *Boss Tweed's New York* (New York: Wiley, 1965), pp. 82–3.

99 Leo Hershkowitz, *Tweed's New York: Another Look* (Garden City, N.Y.: Doubleday, 1977), pp. 92–3.

100 *NYH*, 24 November 1861, p. 5; *EP*, 27 November 1861, p. 5.

101 Joseph Bucklin Bishop, *A Chronicle of 150 Years, The Chamber of Commerce of the State of New York, 1768–1918* (New York: Scribner, 1918), pp. 63, 59–60.

102 *NYTr*, 25 January 1944, p. 2.

103 Gilge, "Mobocracy," p. 129.

104 Quoted in Gusfield, *Symbolic Crusade*, p. 43.

105 Holt, *Forging*, p. 110.

106 Irving F. Flack, "Who Governed Cincinnati? A Comparative Analysis of Government and Social Structure in a Nineteenth Century River City, 1819–1860," Ph.D. dissertation, University of Pittsburgh, 1978.

107 Browne, *Baltimore in the Nation*, pp. 213–34; Laurence F. Schmeckbier, "History of the Know-Nothing Party in Maryland," *Johns Hopkins University Studies in Historical and Political Science* XVII:4–5 (April–May 1899), describes popular hostility to reformers in Baltimore. The couplet, he reported, "which probably most correctly represented the feeling of the majority of the meeting ... read: 'Reform movement – reform man, if you can vote, I'll be d____d.' " (p. 101).

108 Boston *Atlas*, quoted in the Boston *Advertiser*, 2 December 1856. Reformers

characterized previous administrations as "reckless and extravagant." *Advertiser*, 6 December 1856.

109 Herbert Gutman, "Class, Status, and Community Power in Nineteenth Century American Industrial Cities. Paterson, New Jersey: A Case Study," in Gutman, *Work, Culture, and Society*, pp. 234–60.
110 Gramsci, *Prison Notebooks*, pp. 181–2.

8. The Democracy

1 *EP*, 6 April 1844, quoted in Leonard, "Nativism and Reform," p. 437.
2 *NYH*, 28 November 1857, p. 1.
3 *NYH*, 3 November 1854, p. 1.
4 *NYH*, 24 November 1857, p. 1.
5 Though Tweed's association with the fire company was brief. Hershkowitz, *Tweed's New York*, pp. 11–13.
6 Ibid., pp. 66–8.
7 Ibid., p. 97.
8 Ira Katznelson, *City Trenches* (New York: Pantheon, 1981), chapter 5.
9 John W. Pratt, "Boss Tweed's Public Welfare Program," *New-York Historical Society Quarterly* 45 (1961):409.
10 Hershkowitz, *Tweed's New York*, pp. 95–6.
11 Myers, *Tammany Hall*, p. 217.
12 Ibid., p. 256.
13 Martin Shefter, "Trade Unions and Political Machines: The Organization and Disorganization of the American Working Class After the Civil War," paper presented at the Conference on Working Class Formation, Council for European Studies, Paris, 30 October–1 November 1980, pp. 42–3.
14 Ibid., p. 46.
15 Martin Shefter, "The Emergence of the Political Machine: An Alternative View," in Willis D. Hawley and Michael Lipsky, eds., *Theoretical Perspectives on Urban Politics* (Englewood Cliffs, N.J.: Prentice-Hall, 1976), p. 23.
16 Shefter, "Trade Unions," p. 27.
17 Mandelbaum, *Tweed's New York*, chapter 8.
18 Ibid.; Hershkowitz, *Tweed's New York*, chapter 30; Edward C. Mack, *Peter Cooper, Citizen of New York* (New York: Duell, Sloan and Pearce, 1949), chapter 19.
19 Hershkowitz, *Tweed's New York*, p. 140, for opposition to the assistance to Catholics; Mandelbaum, *Boss Tweed's New York*, pp. 77–80, for the bonds.
20 Mandelbaum, *Boss Tweed's New York*, p. 76.
21 Martin Shefter, "New York City's Fiscal Crisis: The Politics of Inflation and Retrenchment," *Public Interest*, no. 48 (1977), pp. 98–127.
22 Hershkowitz, *Tweed's New York*, p. 148 (workingmen's insurgency), p. 145 (German insurgency).
23 Dawley, *Class and Community*, passim; Foner, *History of Labor*, 240–5.
24 Howard Kemble Stokes, *The Finances and Administration of Providence* (Baltimore: Johns Hopkins University Press, 1903), p. 167.
25 *NYH*, 1 October 1859, p. 4.
26 *Providence Daily Journal*, 12 January 1854.
27 Hirsch, *Roots of the American Working Class*, p. 123, and chapter 6, passim.
28 Holt, *Forging*, chapters 7 and 8.
29 Hartz, *Liberal Tradition*, p. 17.

Selected bibliography

Books and articles

Abbott, Edith, ed. *Historical Aspects of the Immigration Problem, Select Documents*. Chicago: University of Chicago Press, 1926.

Abbott, Jacob. *The Harper Establishment, or, How the Story Books are Made*. Hamden, Conn.: Shoe String Press, 1956 [orig. pub. 1855].

Albion, Robert G., and Pope, Jennie Barnes, *The Rise of the New York Port, 1815–1860*. New York: Scribner, 1970 [orig. pub. 1939].

Alexander, De Alva S. *A Political History of the State of New York*. 4 vols. New York: Holt, 1906.

Almond, Gabriel. "Plutocracy and Politics in New York City." Ph.D. dissertation, University of Chicago, 1938.

Asbury, Herbert. *The Gangs of New York*. New York: Capricorn Books, 1970 [orig. pub. 1927].

Banner, Lois W. "The Protestant Crusade: Religious Missions, Benevolence and Reform in the U.S., 1790–1840." Ph.D. dissertation, Columbia University, 1970.

Barkan, Elliot R. "The Emergence of a Whig Persuasion: Conservatism, Democratism, and the New York State Whigs." *New York History* 52 (1971):367–95.

Bendix, Reinhard. *Nation Building and Citizenship: Studies of Our Changing Social Order*. New York: Wiley, 1964.

Work and Authority in Industry. Berkeley: University of California Press, 1956.

Bensman, David Harlan. "Artisan Culture, Business Unionism: American Hat Finishers in the 19th Century." Ph.D. dissertation, Columbia University, 1977.

Benson, Lee. *The Concept of Jacksonian Democracy: New York as a Test Case*. New York: Atheneum, 1969.

Billington, Ray Allen. *The Protestant Crusade: 1800–1860*. Chicago: Quadrangle Books, 1964 [orig. pub. 1938].

Bishop, Joseph Bucklen. *A Chronicle of 150 Years: The Chamber of Commerce of the State of New York 1768–1918*. New York: Scribner, 1918.

Bonomi, Patricia U. *A Factious People: Politics and Society in Colonial New York*. New York: Columbia University Press, 1971.

Bourne, William Oland. *History of the Public School Society of the City of New York*. New York: William Wood, 1870.

Boyd, William H. *Boyd's New York City Tax-Book, 1856 and 1857*. New York: William H. Boyd, 1857.

Bristed, Charles Astor. *The Upper Ten Thousand*. New York: Stringer and Townsend, 1852.

Browne, Gary Lawson. *Baltimore in the Nation, 1789–1861*. Chapel Hill: University of North Carolina Press, 1980.

Burnham, Walter Dean. *Critical Elections and the Mainsprings of American Politics*. New York: Norton, 1970.

Byrdsall, Fitzwilliam. *The History of the Loco-Foco or Equal Rights Party*. New York: Burt Franklin, 1967 [orig. pub. 1842].

Callow, Alexander B., Jr. *The Tweed Ring*. New York: Oxford University Press, 1965.

Carman, Harry James. *The Street Surface Railway Franchises of New York City*. Studies in History, Economics, and Public Law, no. 88. New York: Columbia University Press, 1919.

Chalmers, Leonard. "Tammany Hall and New York City Politics, 1853–1861." Ph.D. dissertation, New York University, 1967.

Commons, John R., et al. *A Documentary History of American Industrial Society*. 10 vols. Cleveland: Arthur H. Clark, 1910.

History of Labour in the United States. 4 vols. New York: Macmillan, 1926.

Conzen, Kathleen Neils. *Immigrant Milwaukee, 1836–1860: Accommodation and Community in a Frontier City*. Cambridge, Mass.: Harvard University Press, 1976.

Cook, Adrian. *The Armies of the Streets: The New York City Draft Riots of 1863*. Lexington: University Press of Kentucky, 1974.

Curran, Thomas J. "Seward and the Know-Nothings." *New-York Historical Society Quarterly* 52 (1967):141–60.

Darling, Arthur B. "Jacksonian Democracy in Massachusetts, 1824–1848." *American Historical Review* 29 (1924):271–87.

Davis, David Brion, ed. *Ante-Bellum Reform*. New York: Harper & Row, 1967.

Dawley, Alan. *Class and Community: The Industrial Revolution in Lynn*. Cambridge, Mass.: Harvard University Press, 1976.

Degler, Carl N. "Labor in the Economy and Politics of New York City, 1850–1860: A Study of the Impact of Early Industrialism." Ph.D. dissertation, Columbia University, 1952.

Donovan, Herbert D. A. *The Barnburners*. New York: New York University Press, 1925.

Dorfman, Joseph. "The Jackson Wage-Earner Thesis." *American Historical Review* 54 (1949):396–406.

Durand, Edward Dana. *The Finances of New York City*. New York: Macmillan, 1898.

Dwyer, Ellen. "The Rhetoric of Reform." Ph.D. dissertation, Yale University, 1977.

Edwards, George William. *New York as an Eighteenth Century Municipality, 1731–1776*. Studies in History, Economics, and Public Law, no. 178. New York: Columbia University Press, 1935.

"New York City Politics Before the American Revolution." *Political Science Quarterly* 36 (1921):586–602.

Ernst, Robert. "Economic Nativism in New York City in the 1840s." *New York History* 29 (1943):170–86.

Immigrant Life in New York City, 1825–1863. New York: King's Crown Press of Columbia University Press, 1949.

"The One and Only Mike Walsh." *New York State Historical Society Quarterly* 36 (1952):43–65.

Exman, Robert. *The Brothers Harper*. New York: Harper & Row, 1965.

Faler, Paul. "Cultural Aspects of the Industrial Revolution: Lynn, Massachusetts,

Shoemakers and Industrial Morality, 1826–1860." *Labor History* 15 (1974):367–94.

Feldberg, Michael. "The Crowd in Philadelphia History: A Comparative Perspective." *Labor History* 15 (1974):323–6.

Foner, Eric. *Free Soil, Free Labor, Free Men: The Ideology of the Republican Party Before the Civil War.* New York: Oxford University Press, 1970.

Tom Paine and Revolutionary America. New York: Oxford University Press, 1976.

Foner, Philip. *Business and Slavery, the New York Merchants and the Irrepressible Conflict.* New York: Russell and Russell, 1968.

History of the Labor Movement in the United States. 2 vols. New York: International Publishers, 1975.

Formisano, Ronald P. "Deferential-Participant Politics: The Early Republic's Political Culture, 1789–1840." *American Political Science Review* 68(2) (June 1974): 473–87.

Foster, Charles I. *An Errand of Mercy: The Evangelical United Front, 1790–1837.* Chapel Hill: University of North Carolina Press, 1960.

Fox, D. R. *The Decline of the Aristocracy in the Politics of New York, 1801–1840.* New York: Harper Torchbooks, 1965 [orig. pub. 1917].

Frisch, Michael H. "The Community Elite and the Emergence of Urban Politics: Springfield, Massachusetts, 1840–1880." In *Nineteenth Century Cities, Essays in the New Urban History,* pp. 277–96. Ed. Stephan Thernstrom and Richard Sennett. New Haven: Yale University Press, 1969.

Furer, Howard B. *William Frederick Havemeyer: A Political Biography.* New York: American Press Publications, 1965.

Gerth, H. H., and Mills, C. Wright, eds. and trans. *From Max Weber: Essays in Sociology.* New York: Oxford University Press, 1958.

Gilge, Paul. "Mobocracy: Popular Disturbances in Post-Revolutionary New York City, 1783–1829." Ph.D. dissertation, Brown University, 1980.

"The Baltimore Riots of 1812 and the Breakdown of the Anglo-American Mob Tradition." *Journal of Social History* 13(4) (Summer 1980):547–64.

Ginsberg, Stephen F. "Above the Law: Volunteer Firemen in New York City, 1836–1837." *New York History* 50 (1969): 165–86.

"The Police and Fire Protection in New York City, 1800–1850." *New York History* 52 (1971):133–50.

Gold, August B. "A History of Manufacturing in New York City, 1825–1840." M.A. thesis, Columbia University, 1932.

Greeley, Horace, and McElrath, Thomas. *The Tribune Almanac for the Years 1838 to 1868, being a Bound Edition of the Whig Almanac, The Politicians' Register, etc.* New York: New York Tribune, 1868.

Griffin, Clifford. *The Ferment of Reform, 1830–1860.* New York: Crowell, 1967.

Their Brothers' Keepers: Moral Stewardship in the United States, 1800–1865. New Brunswick, N.J.: Rutgers University Press, 1960.

"Occupational Mobility in Nineteenth Century America: Problems and Possibilities." *Journal of Social History* 5 (1972):310–30.

Gusfield, Joseph R. *Symbolic Crusade: Status Politics and the American Temperance Movement.* Urbana: University of Illinois Press, 1963.

Gutman, Herbert G. *Work, Culture, and Society in Industrializing America, 1815–1919.* New York: Vintage Books, 1977.

Hammond, Bray. *Banks and Politics in America from the Revolution to the Civil War.* Princeton, N.J.: Princeton University Press, 1957.

Hammond, Jabez D. *The History of Political Parties in the State of New York from* the Ratification of the Federal Constitution to December 1840. 2 vols. Albany: Van Benthuysen, 1842.

Political History of the State of New York from January 1, 1841, to January 1, 1847. Vol. 3: Including the Life of Silas Wright. Syracuse, N.Y.: L. W. Hall, 1852.

Handlin, Oscar, and Handlin, Mary Flug. *Commonwealth: A Study of the Role of Government in the American Economy: Massachusetts, 1774–1861.* Rev. ed. Cambridge, Mass.: Belknap Press of Harvard University Press, 1969.

Harlow, Alvin. *Old Bowery Days.* New York: Appleton, 1931.

Harper, J. Henry. *The House of Harper: A Century of Publishing in Franklin Square.* New York: Harper and Brothers, 1912.

Harrington, Virginia D. *The New York Merchant on the Eve of the Revolution.* Studies in History, Economic, and Public Law, no. 404. New York: Columbia University Press, 1935.

Hartman, William. "The New York Customs House: Seat of Spoils Politics." *New York History* 34 (1953):149–63.

Hartz, Louis. *Economic Policy and Democratic Thought: Pennsylvania, 1776–1860.* Chicago: Quadrangle Books, 1968.

The Liberal Tradition in America. New York: Harcourt, Brace, and World, 1955.

Hassard, John R. G. *Life of John Hughes, First Archbishop of New York.* New York: Arno Press and the New York Times, 1969 [orig. pub. 1866].

Hershkowitz, Leo. *Tweed's New York: Another Look.* Garden City, N.Y.: Doubleday, 1977.

"The LocoFoco Party of New York: Its Origins and Career, 1835–1837." *New-York Historical Society Quarterly* 46 (1962):305–29.

"The Native American Democratic Association in New York City, 1835–1836." *New-York Historical Society Quarterly* 46 (1962):41–60.

"New York City, 1834–1840: A Study in Local Politics." Ph.D. dissertation, New York University, 1960.

Hirsch, Susan E. *Roots of the American Working Class: The Industrialization of Crafts in Newark, 1800–1860.* Philadelphia: University of Pennsylvania Press, 1978.

Hobsbawm, Eric J. *The Age of Revolution.* New York: New American Library, 1962.

Primitive Rebels. New York: Norton, 1959.

Holt, Michael. *Forging a Majority: The Formation of the Republican Party in Pittsburgh, 1848–1860.* New Haven, Conn.: Yale University Press, 1969.

Hone, Philip. *The Diary of Philip Hone, 1828–1851.* Ed. Alan Nevins. New York: Dodd, Mead, 1936.

Horwitz, Morton J. *The Transformation of American Law, 1780–1860.* Cambridge, Mass.: Harvard University Press, 1977.

Hugins, Walter. *Jacksonian Democracy and the Working Class.* Stanford, Calif.: Stanford University Press, 1960.

Huntington, Samuel P. *Political Order in Changing Societies.* New Haven, Conn.: Yale University Press, 1968.

Hutcheson, Austin E. "Philadelphia and the Panic of 1857." *Pennsylvania History* 3 (1936):182–94.

Hutchinson, E. *A Model Mayor: Early Life, Capsule Career, and Triumphant Municipal Administration of Hon. Fernando Wood, Mayor of the City of New York.* New York: American Family Publication Establishment, 1855.

Jentz, John Barkley. "Artisans, Evangelicals, and the City: A Social History of

Abolition and Labor Reform in Jacksonian New York." Ph.D. dissertation, City University of New York, 1977.

July, Robert W. *The Essential New Yorker: Gulian Crommelin Verplanck*. Durham, N.C.: Duke University Press, 1951.

Katz, Irving. *August Belmont: A Political Biography*. New York: Columbia University Press, 1968.

Katznelson, Ira. *City Trenches*. New York: Pantheon, 1981.

Kerber, Linda K. "Abolitionists and Amalgamators: The New York City Race Riots of July 1834." *New York History* 48 (1967):28–40.

Kleppner, Paul. *The Cross of Culture: A Social Analysis of Midwestern Politics, 1850–1900*. New York: Free Press, 1970.

Krout, John A. "The Maine Law and New York Politics." *New York History* 17 (1936):262–72.

Laurie, Bruce, "Fire Companies and Gangs in Southwark: the 1840s." In *The People of Philadelphia, A History of Ethnic Groups and Lower Class Life, 1790–1940*. Ed. Allen F. Davis and Mark H. Haller. Philadelphia: Temple University Press, 1973.

"'Nothing on Compulsion': Life Style of Philadelphia Artisans, 1820–1850." *Labor History* 15 (1974):337–66.

Working People of Philadelphia 1800–1850. Philadelphia: Temple University Press, 1980.

Leach, Richard H. "The Impact of Immigration on New York, 1840–1860." *New York History* 31 (1950):15–30.

Leonard, Ira M. "New York City Politics, 1841–1844: Nativism and Reform." Ph.D. dissertation, New York University, 1965.

"The Politics of Charter Revision in New York City, 1845–1847." *New-York Historical Society Quarterly* 62 (1978):43–70.

"The Rise and Fall of the American Republican Party in New York City, 1843–1845." *New-York Historical Society Quarterly* 50 (1966):151–92.

Limpus, Lowell M. *History of the New York Fire Department*. New York: Dutton, 1940.

Livingston, William, et al. *The Independent Reflector or Weekly Essays on Sundry Important Subjects More Particularly Adapted to the Province of New York*. Ed. Milton M. Klein. Cambridge, Mass.: Harvard University Press, 1963.

Lubove, Roy. "The New York Association for Improving the Condition of the Poor: The Formative Years." *New-York Historical Society Quarterly* 43 (1959):307–27.

Review of *Their Brothers' Keepers: Moral Stewardship in the United States, 1800–1865*, by Clifford S. Griffin. *New-York Historical Society Quarterly* 45 (1961):90–1.

Lynd, Staughton. "The Mechanics in New York Politics, 1774–1788." *Labor History* 5 (1964):225–46.

Lynd, Staughton, and Young, Alfred. "After Carl Becker: The Mechanics and New York City Politics, 1774–1801." *Labor History* 5 (1964):221.

Mack, Edward C. *Peter Cooper, Citizen of New York*. New York: Duell, Sloan and Pearce, 1949.

Mandelbaum, Seymour J. *Boss Tweed's New York*. New York: Wiley, 1965.

Mangold, George Benjamin. "The Labor Argument in the American Protective Tariff Discussion." Economics and Political Science Series, no. 5. *Bulletin of the University of Wisconsin* 246 (1908):179–294.

Meyers, Marvin. *The Jacksonian Persuasion: Politics and Belief*. Stanford, Calif.: Stanford University Press, 1960.

Miller, Douglas T. "Immigration and Social Stratification in Pre-Civil War New York." *New York History* 49 (1968):157–68.

Jacksonian Aristocracy: Class and Democracy in New York, 1830–1860. New York: Oxford University Press, 1967.

Mohl, Raymond. "Education as Social Control in New York City, 1784–1825." *New York History* 51 (1970):219–37.

Montgomery, David. "The Shuttle and the Cross: Weavers and Artisans in the Kensington Riots of 1844." *Journal of Social History* 5 (1972):411–46.

"The Working Classes of the Pre-Industrial American City, 1780–1830." *Labor History* 9 (1968):3–22.

Mushkat, Jerome. *Tammany: The Evolution of a Political Machine, 1789–1865.* Syracuse, N.Y.: Syracuse University Press, 1971.

Myers, Gustavus. *History of the Great American Fortunes.* New York: Modern Library, Random House, 1937.

The History of Tammany Hall. New York: Dover Publications, 1971 [orig. pub. 1917].

Nash, Gary C. *The Urban Crucible: Social Change, Political Consciousness, and the Origins of the American Revolution.* Cambridge, Mass.: Harvard University Press, 1979.

Nevins, Alan, ed. *The Diary of Philip Hone, 1828–1851.* New York: Dodd, Mead, 1936.

Nevins, Alan, and Thomas, Milton Halsey, eds. *The Diary of George Templeton Strong.* 3 vols. New York: Macmillan, 1952.

New York Association for the Improvement of the Condition of the Poor. *First Report of the Committee on the Sanitary Condition of the Laboring Classes in the City of New York, with Remedial Suggestions.* New York: John F. Trow, 1853.

Nichols, Roy Franklin. "The Democratic Machine, 1850–1854." Ph.D. dissertation, Columbia University, 1923.

The Disruption of American Democracy. New York: Macmillan, 1948.

Ormsby, R. McKinley. *A History of the Whig Party.* Boston: Crosby, Nichols, 1859.

Pernicone, Carol Groneman. "The 'Bloody Ould Sixth': A Social Analysis of a New York City Working Class Community in the Mid-Nineteenth Century." Ph.D. dissertation, University of Rochester, 1973.

Pessen, Edward. *Jacksonian America: Society, Personality and Politics.* Homewood, Ill.: Dorsey Press, 1969.

Most Uncommon Jacksonians: The Radical Leaders of the Early Labor Movement. Albany: State University of New York Press, 1967.

Riches, Class, and Power Before the Civil War. Lexington, Mass.: Heath, 1973.

"The Workingmen's Party Revisited." *Labor History* 3 (1963):203–26.

Peterson, Arthur. *New York as Eighteenth Century Municipality Prior to 1731.* New York: Columbia University Press, 1917.

Pleasants, Samuel A. *Fernando Wood of New York.* New York: Columbia University Press, 1948.

Pomerantz, Sidney. *New York, An American City, 1783–1803.* New York: Columbia University Press, 1938.

Pope, Jesse Epiphalet. *The Clothing Industry in New York.* Columbia, Mo.: University of Missouri Press, 1905.

Pratt, John W. "Boss Tweed's Public Welfare Program." *New-York Historical Society Quarterly* 45 (1961):396–411.

Przeworski, Adam, and Sprague, John. "A History of Western European Socialism."

Paper presented at the Annual Meeting of the American Political Science Association. Washington, D.C. September 1977.

Remini, Robert V. *Martin Van Buren and the Making of the Democratic Party.* New York: Columbia University Press, 1959.

Rezneck, Samuel. "The Influence of Depression Upon American Opinion, 1857–1859." *Journal of Economic History* 2 (1942):1–23.

"The Social History of the American Depression, 1837–1843." *American Historical Reivew* 40 (1935):662–87.

Richards, Leonard L. *"Gentlemen of Property and Standing": Anti-Abolition Mobs in Jacksonian America.* New York: Oxford Unviersity Press, 1971.

Richardson, James F. "Mayor Fernando Wood and the New York Police Force, 1855–1857." *New-York Historical Society Quarterly* 50 (1966):5–40.

Rogers, Frank C., Jr. "Mike Walsh, A Voice of Protest." M.A. thesis, Columbia University, 1950.

Rozwenc, Edwin C., ed. *Ideology and Power in the Age of Jackson.* Garden City, N.Y.: Doubleday, 1964.

Savetsky, Seymour. "The New York Workingmen's Party." M.A. thesis, Columbia University, 1948.

Schlesinger, Arthur, Jr. *The Age of Jackson.* Boston: Little, Brown, 1945.

Scisco, Louis Dow. *Political Nativism in New York State.* New York: Columbia University Press, 1901.

Shefter, Martin. "The Emergence of the Political Machine: An Alternative View." In *Theoretical Perspectives on Urban Politics*, pp. 14–43. Ed. Willis D. Hawley and Michael Lipsky. Englewood Cliffs, N.J.: Prentice-Hall, 1976.

"New York City's Fiscal Crisis: The Politics of Inflation and Retrenchment." *Public Interest* 48 (1977):98–127.

"Trade Unions and Political Machines: The Organization and Disorganization of the American Working Class After the Civil War." Paper presented for delivery at the Conference on Working Class Formation, Council for European Studies. Paris, 30 October–1 November 1980.

Sheldon, George W. *The Story of the Volunteer Fire Department of the City of New York.* New York: Harper and Brothers, 1882.

Stevens, George A. *New York Typographical Union No. 6.* Albany: J. B. Lyon, 1913.

Thompson, E. P. "The Moral Economy of the English Crowd in the Eighteenth Century." *Past and Present* 50 (1971): 76–136.

Tilly, Charles, Tilly, Louise and Tilly, Richard. *The Rebellious Century: 1830–1930.* Cambridge, Mass.: Harvard University Press, 1975.

Trimble, William. "Diverging Tendencies in New York Democracy in the Period of the Locofocos." *American Historical Review* 24 (1919):396–421.

Tyler, Alice Felt. *Freedom's Ferment.* New York: Harper & Row, 1940.

Van Vleek, George W. *The Panic of 1857: An Analytical Study.* New York: AMS Press, 1967.

Wallace, Michael. "Changing Concepts of Party in the United States: New York, 1815–1825." *American Historical Review* 74:2 (December 1968):453–91.

Warner, Sam Bass, Jr. *The Private City: Philadelphia in Three Periods of Its Growth.* Philadelphia: University of Pennsylvania Press, 1968.

Weed, Thurlow. *Autobiography of Thurlow Weed.* ed. Harriet A. Weed. Boston: Houghton, Mifflin, 1884.

Weinbaum, Paul O. "Mobs and Demagogues." Ph.D. dissertation, University of Rochester, 1974.

"Temperance, Politics, and the New York City Riots of 1857." *New-York Historical Society Quarterly* 59 (1975):246–70.

Wilentz, Robert Sean. "Ritual, Republicanism, and the Artisans of Jacksonian New York." Paper presented at the Annual Meeting of the Organization of American Historians. New York, April 1978.

Wilkenfeld, Bruce. "The New York City Common Council, 1689–1800." *New York History* 33 (1952):249–73.

Wittke, Carl. *The Irish in America.* Baton Rouge: Louisiana State University Press, 1956.

Young, Alfred. "The Mechanics and the Jeffersonians: New York 1789–1801." *Labor History* 5 (1964):247–69.

Zahler, Helene Sara. *Eastern Workingmen and National Land Policy, 1829–1862.* Studies in the History of American Agriculture, no. 7. New York: Columbia University Press, 1941.

Pamphlets

Address of the General Executive Committee of the American Republican Party of the City and County of New York to their Fellow Citizens. New York: n.p., 1843.

Annual Report of the Executive Committee of the American Temperance Union. Philadelphia: L. Johnson, 1838.

The Crisis! An Appeal to Our Countrymen on the Subject of Foreign Influence in the United States [Issued under the sanction of the American Republican Party of the City and County of New York.] New York: 201 Broadway, 1844.

Hale, William H. *Useful Knowledge for the Producers of Wealth, Being an Inquiry into the Nature of Trade, the Currency, the Protective and Internal Improvement Systems, and into the Origin and Effects of Banking and Paper Money.* New York: George H. Evans, 1833.

[Kennedy, Jan P.] *Defence of the Whigs.* New York: Harper and Brothers, 1844.

The Know Nothings. An Expose of the Secret Order of Know Nothings. The Most Ludicrous and Startling Yankee "Notion" Ever Conceived. By a Know Something, Late of the Grand Council. New York: Stearns, 1854.

Moore, Ely. *Address on Civil Government, Delivered Before the New York Typographical Society, February 25, 1847.* New York: B. R. Barlow, 1847.

  Speech of the Honorable Ely Moore, in Reply to the Honorable Waddy Thompson and Others. Washington, D.C.: Blair and Rules, 1836.

[Morse, Samuel F. B.] *The Present Attempt to Dissolve the American Union, A British Aristocratic Plot.* New York: John F. Trow, 1862.

Roosevelt, Clinton. *The Mode of Protecting Domestic Industries.* New York: Benjamin H. Tyrrel, 1889 [orig. pub. 1831].

Sketches of the Speeches and Writings of Michael Walsh: Including His Poems and Correspondence Complied by a Committee of the Spartan Association. New York: Thomas McSpedon, General Agent, 1843.

Startling Facts for Native Americans Called "Know-Nothings," or a Vivid Presentation of the Dangers to American Liberty, to be Apprehended from Foreign Influence. New York: 128 Nassau Street, 1855.

Whitney, Thomas R. *A Defense of the American Policy as Opposed to the Encroachments of Foreign Influence, and Especially to the Interference of the Papacy in the Political Interests and Affairs of the United States.* New York: Dewitt and Davenport, 1856.

Selected bibliography

New York City newspapers

Champion of American Labor, 1847.
Evening Post, 1828–35.
Journal of Commerce, 1835–8.
New York Herald, 1837–63.
New York Times, 1851–63.
New York Tribune, 1841–63.
The Union, 1836.

Government documents

New York City Board of Aldermen, *Documents*, 1838–63.
New York City Board of Aldermen, *Proceedings*, 1831–63.
New York State, Secretary of State. *Census of the State of New York, for 1835.* Albany: Crosswell, Van Benthuysen, and Burt, 1836.
Census of the State of New York, for 1845. Albany: Carroll and Cook, 1846.
Census of the State of New York, for 1855. Albany: Van Benthuysen, 1857.
U.S. Bureau of the Census. *Sixth Census of the United States [1840].* Washington, D.C.: Thomas Allen, 1841.
Statistical View of the United States . . . Compendium of the Seventh Census [1850]. Washington, D.C.: Beverly Tucker, Senate Printer, 1854.
Eighth Census of the United States [1860]. Washington, D.C.: Government Printing Office, 1865.

Index

Adam, George, 117
Adams, John Quincy, 20
Adams, William, 76
Allaire, James P., 48, 53, 72, 73, 127, 129
Allen, Stephen, 47, 127
Alley, Saul, 47, 79, 127, 129
Almond, Gabriel, 126
Althusser, Louis, 7
Alvord, Alonzo, 76, 127
American Republicans, 62, 81, 87–8, 90, 92, 93, 96, 97, 98, 129, 156
  nativism of, 24, 29–30, 31
  Whig alliance with, 32, 64, 83, 84, 91, 154
Anderson, John, 129
apprentice system, 50, 53
Arbuthnot, William, 117
artisans (mechanics), 25, 45, 49–54, 71, 83, 91, 94–5, 98, 102, 103, 104, 106, 109
Aspinwall, William H., 47, 127, 139
Astor, John J., 127
Astor, William B., 127, 130, 139

Bailey, K. Arthur, 113, 114
Baker, Thomas, 117
Baldwin, Simeon, 138
Bancker, Evert A., 48
Banfield, Edward, 4
Bangs, Nathan, 86, 88
banks
  Whigs' views on, 28
  Workingmen's views on, 23, 58, 96
Barker, Joel, 102, 123, 155
Barnburners, 2, 33, 96
Barr, William V., 113
Beach, Moses, 139
Beatty, Robert, 68

Belmont, August, 126, 127, 129, 130, 140
Bennett, James Gordon, 116, 120, 126, 140, 142
Benson, Lee, 62, 63, 65, 70
Bergh, Christian, 50
Blunt, Joseph, 135
Boorman, James, 47, 130, 138
bosses, 3, 123, 153–4
Bowen, James, 130
Bowie, John H., 69, 109
Brevoort, Henry, 48, 129
Brodes, James, 115
Buchanan, James, 34, 129
Business and Slavery (Foner), 128
Butler, George, 138

Calhoun, John C., 111
Cambreleng, C. C., 133, 137
Cameron, Gilbert, 68
capitalists, 45, 55
career politicians, 74–5, 131, 146–7
Carman, Richard F., 72, 129
Catholics
  nativist opposition to, 31, 83, 97
  public education and, 85–6
Chandler, Adoniram, 62
Chittenden, Simeon, 37, 139
City Politics (Banfield and Wilson), 4
City Reform movement, 16, 83, 129, 137–8, 142–3
Clannon, Simon, 62
Clark, George, 68, 93
Clark, Myron, 96
Clay, Henry, 24, 62
Cochrane, John, 121, 141
Coddington, Jonathan I., 129
Colgate, William, 48, 127, 138

Index

women, in labor force, 57
Wood, Fernando, 101, 111, 118–20,
    121, 127, 136, 140, 141, 147,
    150, 152
  demagoguery of, 111, 118, 122, 153
  working classes and, 36, 117, 122,
    123, 134, 139, 144, 148, 149, 153
Woodruff, Thomas, 129
Wooly Headed Whigs, 2, 33
working classes, 6, 11, 57, 67, 92, 93
Working Man's Advocate, 90
workingman's advocates, 110–11, 123
Workingmen's Parties, 1, 15, 16, 18,
    26, 50–1, 123
  constituency of, 4, 103–4, 106, 110

ideology of, 22–4, 27, 58–9, 94–5,
    96, 108
Jackson backed by, 21
successors of, 62–3, 113, 114
Tammany's denunciation of, 25
Workingmen's Provisional Committee,
    117
Worral, Henry, 53

Yates, Douglas, 14
Young, J. D., 95
Young Men's General Committee, 63,
    78, 82

Zabriskie, Martin, 138